"Stephen Clark's work on the Eucharist is an important attempt to recover the scriptural understanding of the rite. It is respectful of Catholic traditions, while suggesting ways of enabling the biblical meaning to become more central. It is one of the most important liturgical works of recent years."

JAMES HITCHCOCK
Author of *The Recovery of the Sacred*

"Steve Clark provides a basic introduction to the Catholic understanding of the Eucharist."

ALAN SCHRECK, Ph.D.
Professor of Theology, Franciscan University of Steubenville

"Well-written introductions to the meaning of the Eucharist for ordinary churchgoers are rare, and one that relates the rite closely to its biblical roots is even more of a rarity. I am sure that many Catholics will find their participation in the liturgy greatly illuminated and enriched by this book."

PAUL BRADSHAW
Professor of Liturgy, University of Notre Dame

D1016010

Catholics and the Eucharist

A SCRIPTURAL INTRODUCTION

STEPHEN B. CLARK

CHARIS
SERVANT PUBLICATIONS
ANN ARBOR, MICHIGAN

Charis Books is an imprint of Servant Publications especially designed to serve Roman Catholics.

All Scripture quotations, unless indicated, are taken from the Revised Standard Version of the Bible, © 1946, 1952, 1971 by the Division of Christian Education of the National Council of Churches of Christ in the USA. Used by permission. All rights reserved.

Excerpts from the English translation of *The Roman Missal* © 1973, International Committee on English in the Liturgy, Inc. All rights reserved.

Excerpts from the English translation of the *Catechism of the Catholic Church* for the United States of America. © 1994, United States Catholic Conference, Inc.-Libreria Editrice Vaticana. Used with permission.

Servant Publications
P.O. Box 8617
Ann Arbor, MI 48107

Nihil obstat: Monsignor Robert D. Lunsford
                Chancellor
Imprimatur: Most Reverend Carl F. Mengeling
                Bishop of Lansing
                September 14, 1999

Cover illustration: The Ghent Altarpiece by Jan Van Eyck / Superstock. Used by permission.

00 01 02 03 10 9 8 7 6 5 4 3 2 1

Printed in the United States of America
ISBN 1-56955-133-2

LIBRARY OF CONGRESS CATALOGING-IN-PUBLICATION DATA

Clark, Stephen B.
    Catholics and the Eucharist : a scriptural introduction / Stephen B. Clark.
        p.   cm.
    Includes bibliographical references and indexes.
    ISBN 1-56955-133-2 (alk. paper)
    1. Lord's Supper—Catholic Church.   I. Title

BX2215.2.C53 2000
234'.163'08822—dc21

00-021469

Contents

Preface

T he prophet Haggai was sent by God to address the people of Israel who had returned from exile to rebuild their nation in the Promised Land. Their recent experience had not been pleasant. They had planted a great deal but harvested little. They never had enough to eat or drink. They did not have enough clothing to keep warm. Their experience was like bringing home their pay each week but always finding that by the time they got to their house hardly anything was left in their wallet (Hag 1:6).

There was a reason for their experience. They had been working with wrong priorities. They had begun by doing the humanly sensible thing—providing first for their own immediate material needs so that they could then get on to take care of other important things. Perhaps that would have been acceptable to God for a while, but not for very long. They could not prosper without the blessing of God. And God sent Haggai to tell them why they did not have that blessing:

> You have looked for much, and, lo, it came to little; and when you brought it home, I blew it away. Why? says the Lord of hosts. Because of my house that lies in ruins, while you busy yourselves each with his own house.
>
> HAGGAI 1:9

They had neglected the work of rebuilding the temple, the house of God. They had neglected the first priority—their relationship with God and their worship of him. Had they thought less with a wisdom focused on the realities of this world and more with a wisdom that reckons with the supreme importance of heavenly realities and divine blessing, they would have done better, even in purely earthly terms.

The documents of the Second Vatican Council use a similar line of thought. The opening paragraph of the first document issued, the Constitution on the Sacred Liturgy, begins by explaining the purpose of the Council—renewal. But after speaking of the goals the Council would try to accomplish, the document ends by saying, "Accordingly [the Council] sees particularly cogent reasons for undertaking the reform and promotion of the liturgy."[1] Further on, it states the reason why that should be foundational:

> The liturgy is the summit toward which the activity of the church is directed; it is also the source from which all her power flows.[2]

Most Catholics would easily give assent to such a statement about the liturgy. It is exalted theological language that somehow says that "the Mass" is very important. All Catholics know that is the case. But most of them probably could not say what it might mean to describe the liturgy as the summit, the high point, of what the Church does, although they probably would intuitively see it as the source of her power. Nor would they understand why the Council would speak about the liturgy rather than the sacraments. Still another question is, for how many full members of the Church would such a statement be true?

The book that follows, *Catholics and the Eucharist*, concerns the Eucharist, but the Eucharist seen in the context of the whole liturgy, including the Liturgy of the Hours, and as liturgical worship. The word *Eucharist* comes from a Greek word meaning "thanksgiving." The title of the book refers to **the Eucharist** in the sense of the whole Eucharistic celebration, the great Christian thanksgiving, what is still commonly called "the Mass," including the Liturgy of the Word. "The Eucharist" seems to be the most universally accepted term for the topic being covered[3] and is the term used in *The Catechism of the Catholic Church* (CCC).[4] "The Divine Liturgy" has many advantages as a term, but it is only used by the Eastern churches.

Catholics and the Eucharist is designed to be an introduction to the subject, and consequently it is restricted in scope. Catholic theology has traditionally been divided into "treatises," topics of teaching that are limited in extent. This book only treats the traditional topics of the Eucharist as sacrifice and sacrament and does not treat grace, conversion and Baptism, the ministerial priesthood, or many of the other topics of Catholic theology that would give a more comprehensive picture. Moreover, it does not treat all aspects of the Eucharist as sacrament, but primarily focuses on the Eucharistic celebration.

As an introduction, the book seeks to give an understanding of what we are doing at each stage of the Eucharist and why. However, it does not attempt to comment on the ceremony of the Eucharist in detail, treat the ways the Eucharist could be celebrated better, or cover all issues of sacramental or liturgical teaching. As an introduction, it is more of an introduction to liturgical theology than to liturgical practice, although the two should not be separated.

The goal is to provide the understanding that makes possible a "full, conscious and active participation" (SC 14) in Catholic Eucharistic celebrations. The goal also is to provide a basis for further study of the Eucharist. Both goals can only be reached by a spiritual reception of the truths of God's revelation.

Catholics and the Eucharist is designed to be accessible to all those who have a basic understanding of catechism teaching on the Eucharist. At the same time, it is intended to provide an orientation to current Catholic theology on the Eucharist as well as to the scriptures from which that theology is drawn. The text tries not to use technical language without explaining it or presuppose background that is not given in the text itself. The endnotes and bibliography provide an introduction to the resources by which the topic can be further pursued and special questions connected to what is said in the text can be followed up. They also provide support for positions taken by the text in areas where there is no consensus among orthodox Catholic theologians.

As the subtitle indicates, the book is designed to be a "*scriptural* introduction" to the Eucharist. Once instruction on the Eucharist would have relied on simple reference to the authoritative teachings of the Catholic Church (the decrees of Councils, mainly Trent, the encyclicals of popes, and approved catechisms and manuals of theology). The Second Vatican Council has instructed us that such an approach should change. Catholic teaching should be founded in the Scripture, because the Scripture is "the soul of theology."[5]

Many modern orthodox Catholic teachers do not seem to be able to teach about the Eucharist from Scripture. Yet the Catholic doctrine of the Eucharist is in the Scripture. To present it without presenting the scriptural basis is to do a disservice to people who need to know that this is what Christ taught, however much his teaching may have been developed or ordered by those who have come afterwards.

Catholics and the Eucharist is a Catholic book. It is primarily written for Catholics to help them participate in and teach about the Catholic liturgy. It also is Catholic in the sense that it presents doctrinal positions that the Catholic Church holds but not all Christians do. While both Eastern Orthodox and Oriental Orthodox, as well as some Protestants, will be able to accept the doctrine behind all sections of this book, some Protestants will not.

Because it is a Catholic book, *Catholics and the Eucharist* concerns not only the liturgy of the Roman rite but those of other rites as well. A **rite**, in this sense, is a form of liturgical celebration that has developed over the centuries in a particular community of Christians. To approach the liturgy as if there were only one version, the Roman rite, is provincialism.[6] Considering the other liturgies, especially those of the Eastern churches, whose liturgical traditions stem from the earliest centuries, can be very enriching to those who only know the Roman rite. Moreover, even though the contemporary Roman rite preserves the essential shape of the liturgy and even though the liturgical texts we now use are good in their theology and spirituality, it is difficult to understand what liturgy should be by the experience of most contemporary Roman-rite services. Eastern liturgical services, however, still normally present a fuller liturgical experience.

At the same time, *Catholics and the Eucharist* is intended to be a book that fosters ecumenical convergence, as all Catholic books should be now. It accepts the fact that there are many who are not Catholics but who are in real though imperfect communion with Catholics because they are Christians. It attempts to present Catholic faith in such a way that they can see that the Catholic understanding of the Eucharist has a good claim to be scriptural, traditional Christian faith. This book is also ecumenical in the sense that it is intended to be a book that can be given to Christians who are not Catholic to explain to them how Catholics approach the Eucharist and why they do so the way they do, without speaking polemically and without giving offense.

It is easier to take an ecumenically convergent approach in this area than it has been in the past because of the ecumenical dialogues. Many of them have centered on the Eucharist, and a great deal of unity has been reached, even on the difficult points of the Eucharist as a sacrifice and the nature of the presence of Christ in the eucharistic elements. As Pope John Paul II has emphasized, it is important for the whole church, the lay faithful as well, to "receive the results already achieved" by these dialogues and make them "a common heritage."[7] We should no longer present points of Catholic doctrine without having the presentation shaped by the results the dialogues have obtained. There is a brief guide to the most relevant dialogues in Appendix 2 (see pp. 235-237).

The Eucharist is "a means of grace." Since faith in Christ, union with Christ, makes us Christians, and since what Christ did in his death and resurrection allows us to receive grace, the Eucharist can only be understood by understanding what Christ did for us and how he did it. I have written an earlier book, *Redeemer*, that treats the death and resurrection of Christ (the "paschal mystery") and what that did for us.[8]

Those who find this book helpful will find *Redeemer* providing the foundational understanding of the "Christian mystery" which is the object of the Eucharist (CCC 1066-1068).

In the apostolic Letter on Preparing for the Third Millennium (TMA), Pope John Paul II directed that the year of the millennial celebrations should be one with a major Eucharistic orientation.[9] Moreover, in his instructions on preparing for the millennium, he gave an examination of conscience.[10] His first two questions regarding the reception of the teaching of the Second Vatican Council were:

1. To what extent has the Word of God become more fully the soul of theology and the inspiration of the whole of Christian living, as *Dei Verbum (DV)* sought?

2. Is the liturgy lived as the "source and summit" of ecclesial life, in accordance with the teaching of *Sacrosanctum Concilium (SC)*?

These questions summarize the two main concerns of this book. The liturgy, especially the Eucharistic celebration, is the Christian event that is the fullest expression of the purpose of the Christian life (the summit) and which should be the primary or necessary means for equipping us to live as Christians (the source). Within the liturgy, the Word of God is read and also forms the prayers, so that it may be the formative influence of Christian teaching (theology) and the inspiration for Christian living.

The Eucharist as a whole should be the "travelers' meal" that will allow the Christian people to thrive for as much of this next millennium as the Lord gives us and to live joyfully with him through all eternity.

Helps for the Reader

The Text

The text is designed to be an introduction to the Eucharist, or more precisely, a scriptural introduction to Catholic liturgical theology of the Eucharist. The text is intended to be self-explanatory.

In the text certain words are marked in bold italics, like *the Eucharist* on p. 8 above. They indicate that a word or concept is explained at that point in the text. Usually it will be a term that has a technical meaning in theology or liturgical practice, or it will be a word that is used in the Scripture in a way that may be unfamiliar. There is an index of these words at the back of the book (p. 273).

Many sections of the text contain presentations of scriptural passages. They are intended to interpret the passage for understanding and teaching about the Eucharist. Technical details that are not relevant for that purpose are normally omitted, but there are references in the notes to more detailed exegesis of the passages.

Meditations

The end of every chapter contains a meditation on one or more passages of Scripture. It is designed to help the reader appropriate the significance of the chapter. The meditation will be more helpful if readers read the Scripture passage on their own beforehand and then read the meditation.

Notes and Appendices

There is an essay in Appendix 1 for further Scripture study on the Eucharist. There is a select bibliography in Appendix 2 for further scholarly study. The endnotes are intended to cite the scholarly opinions on various subjects that either justify the position in the text or allow the subject to be pursued further. They refer to the main scholarly works currently accessible to English speakers but make no attempt to give exhaustive surveys of the bibliography for each point. Those can be found in the works referred to.

The Version of Scripture

The quotations from the Bible are drawn from the Revised Standard Version (RSV) unless otherwise indicated and use standard citations in the English-speaking world. I have chosen the RSV because it is the most widely accepted text that is ecumenically approved, and because it seems to be the most commonly used text at the moment in Christian theological discussions. Like most people who study the Scriptures in much depth on a subject, I have my own preferences for how the relevant texts should be translated, and they sometimes differ from the RSV. At times I include a retranslation or expansion in brackets. At other times I have retranslated the RSV at the points where I judged it to be especially helpful to do so.

Introduction

Jesus said to them, "I am the bread of life; he who comes to me shall not hunger, and he who believes in me shall never thirst."

JOHN 6:35

The liturgy, to most appearances, is something human beings do in order to reach or respond to God. From the perspective of Christian faith, at least in its traditional form, such a view is inadequate. For that reason the term "mystery" has been more commonly used in recent years to describe liturgy, thereby indicating that the liturgy is something that cannot be comprehended solely by its appearances. Behind it is God, and what God does in the liturgy transcends human actions which belong to this world.

We cannot, in short, understand the liturgy without understanding that God is behind it and present in it and without grasping something of how God acts in our space-time world. To do that we will begin by considering two principles of God's action, "the incarnational principle" and "the sacramental principle," which is based on the incarnational principle. The first of these is illustrated in a passage in the Scripture that provides a foundation of all that comes later—God's initial revelation of himself to Moses as described in the third chapter of Exodus.

The Book of Exodus gives us an account of Moses' background. He was born in the land of Egypt to a Hebrew family, descendants of Abraham, Isaac, and Jacob. At the time, the Pharaoh, the ruler of all Egypt and the most powerful human being in the world, was seeking to destroy the Israelites. He had chosen a policy of slow extermination, mainly by seeing that no males were raised to continue Israelite families.

By a chance, or, better put, providential set of circumstances, Moses was raised by a daughter of Pharaoh, a princess of Egypt. This made him a member of the ruling class of the greatest empire in the world. He was, however, put to a test when he came across a conflict between an Egyptian and a Hebrew. He sympathized with the Hebrew and killed the Egyptian. His actions showed that interiorly he had chosen to be a Hebrew. His crime was discovered, and he now was "wanted" as the dangerous murderer of an Egyptian and as a potential traitor.

Moses made his way to the tribe of Midian and there lived for many years as the son-in-law of the chief of the tribe, Jethro. While overseeing the care of Jethro's flock, the mainstay of Jethro's wealth, something extraordinary happened to Moses. It is described in the Book of Exodus as follows:

> Now Moses was keeping the flock of his father-in-law Jethro, the priest of Midian; and he led his flock to the west side of the wilderness, and came to Horeb [Sinai], the mountain of God. And the angel of the Lord appeared to him in a flame of fire out of the midst of a bush; and he looked, and lo, the bush was burning, yet it was not consumed.
>
> EXODUS 3:1-2

Moses seemed to be fulfilling normal responsibilities, seeing that his father-in-law's flock was cared for properly by the workers. They all, perhaps unwittingly, had followed the valleys to the foot of a special mountain, Sinai. Sinai was *the* mountain of God, the mountain where God himself "dwelled," that is, the mountain where the all-powerful Lord of the universe, the one who had created everything out of nothing, was especially present.

Moses was leading the herdsmen and the flock through the valley, keeping an eye out for anything dangerous. Then he saw something unusual. Near the bottom of the cliff, the spot where the mountain begins to rise steeply from the valley floor, he saw a bush on fire.

There might be any number of reasons why a bush might be on fire—most of them worth investigating by someone concerned for a vulnerable flock. But as Moses looked, the matter seemed specially significant. The bush was burning, but it was not turning black. It was the same color and shape as any other bush of that type.

Moses then walked over to the bush. As he did, something else, still more striking, happened. Exodus puts it this way:

> And Moses said,
>   "I will turn aside and see this great sight, why the bush is not burnt."
> When the Lord saw that he turned aside to see, God called to him out of the bush,
>   "Moses, Moses!"
> And he said,
>   "Here am I."
>
> EXODUS 3:3-4

In other words, Moses heard the bush, or something in the bush, speaking to him, and, even more, addressing him by name. Moses' response was to answer like a subordinate replying to his supervisor or commanding officer or king. He knew he was not dealing with a bush. He knew he was dealing with some Being that was greater than all bushes and greater than himself. He knew he could only "stand at attention" and see what this Being wanted from him.

The Being responded with what we might think was "a protocol matter." He said to Moses:

Do not come near; put off your shoes from your feet, for the place on which you are standing is holy ground.

This may not have made much sense to us if we were in Moses' place, but Moses understood what was being said to him. He had learned at an early age how to relate to temples and sacred precincts in Egypt, and likely in Midian as well. He understood that it was a god who had spoken to him, that he was in a place that belonged to the god, and that he now had to approach the situation very carefully.

Holy is a word used to speak about God and the things of God. Sometimes it is translated "divine." God is himself the one who is truly holy. His *holiness* or, to use a synonym, his *sanctity* is his divinity—his supreme greatness and power. Things connected to him are also called "holy." Books that come from God are described as holy writings; a man sent by God to speak for him is described as a holy prophet. Things given to God or taken by God to be his own are also described as holy. When a building is dedicated to God to be a temple, it becomes a holy building. When God chooses to be especially present in a place like a mountain, it becomes a holy mountain. Moses had strayed into such a holy place.

Moses at this point probably suspected he was in danger. It would be as if we had accidentally walked into the room where the Queen was present. If a guard came over to tell us to bow or curtsey to the Queen, especially if the tone of voice he used was a very serious one, we would likely think we were in some trouble.

But there was probably still more involved. According to all scriptural revelation, God's holy presence can be dangerous. The bush before Moses was on fire, and that fact itself showed that someone who came too close might be destroyed. Moses might have died, even died instantly.

If someone walked up to a high-tension wire and touched it, that person would die with no further discussion. The power company would not have to have something against the person or even set up a system for eliminating trespassers. The person would be just in the wrong place at the wrong time, and there would be nothing anyone could do about it. Nor would the power company acknowledge liability if that person had ignored a warning sign.

We may be reasonably certain that Moses complied. At this point he kept his distance. And he surely took his shoes off as a sign of respect.

Then the Being spoke to him again.

I am the God of your father, the God of Abraham, the God of Isaac, and the God of Jacob.

The Being, in other words, explained who he was. He told Moses that he was Moses' own God.

The world was filled with many gods, and Moses was used to them. There was a set of gods in Egypt that he dealt with: Amon, Ra, Seti, Horus, Isis. There would have been others he had to deal with when he settled in Midian, whose names we do not know. But none of those appeared to Moses at this point. The Being who spoke to him said he was the God of the people who gave birth to Moses, the Hebrews who were the cause of Moses' needing to leave the palaces and emporia of the greatest nation on earth and live in the desert with a relatively insignificant nomadic tribe of Bedouins. This god was somehow present in the bush and looked at Moses as someone who belonged to him, since Moses' father Amram was the descendant of Abraham, Isaac, and Jacob. Exodus then says:

And Moses hid his face for he was afraid to look at God.

The text does not tell us whether at this point Moses thought he was the recipient of good or bad fortune. But he knew he was dealing with a god, his own tribal god. And he knew that it could be dangerous to get too close to a god.

Then the Lord spoke to him, and Moses found out that at least his people in Egypt were to benefit from very good fortune. God said:

I have seen the affliction of my people who are in Egypt, and have heard their cry because of their taskmasters; I know their sufferings, and I have come down to deliver them out of the land of the Egyptians, and to bring them up out of that land to a good and broad land, a land flowing with milk and honey, to the place of the Canaanites, the Hittites, the Amorites, the Perizzites, the Hivites, and the Jebusites. And now, behold, the cry of the people of Israel has come to me, and I have seen the oppression with which the Egyptians oppress them. Come, I will send you to Pharaoh that you may bring forth my people, the sons of Israel, out of Egypt.

In other words, the reason God was revealing himself was so that he could deliver his people from their difficulties and, even more, establish them securely and prosperously in a land of their own.

Moses did not, however, think what he heard was good fortune for himself. He had no desire to confront Pharaoh, the high king or overlord of the known world. This Pharaoh probably knew him because they had been brought up together, and he was no longer favorably disposed to Moses. So Moses asked God how he could begin, how he could persuade Pharaoh that he had in fact been sent by someone Pharaoh should pay attention to and be respectful of.

Moses also wanted to know how he should begin with his own people, because they had not seen him for many years and would be very wary of some troublemaker who would get them into still worse difficulties with Pharaoh:

Then Moses said to God, "If I come to the people of Israel and say to them, 'The God of your fathers has sent me to you,' and they ask me, 'What is his name?' What shall I say to them?"

God said to Moses, "I AM WHO AM." And he said, "Say this to the people of Israel, 'The Lord, the God of your fathers, the God of Abraham, the God of Isaac, and the God of Jacob, has sent me to you'; this is my name for ever, and thus I am to be remembered [i.e., worshiped] throughout all generations."

God's name may have been surprising to Moses. The Hebrew word, translated above as "I AM WHO AM," indicated that he was no minor god, no spirit who simply protected a clan. His name indicated that he had power over the universe. And he was prepared to back up the claim implicit in his name by delivering his people from the hand of the most powerful nation and king on the face of the earth.

In other words, in an act that showed great favor, the God who spoke to him as his own family god revealed to Moses his name. He also told Moses that from now on he was to be worshiped by his people under his own proper name. He instructed Moses how he was to be worshiped with the implication that worshiping him by name would open the way to a better relationship. He had, in other words, given Moses the tremendously great privilege of knowing the name of the most powerful being of the universe, of being, as we might say, "on a first-name basis" with him, and therefore knowing the first step in coming into a direct relationship with him.

The Incarnational Principle [11]

The narrative of Moses' encounter with God in the burning bush begins the history of the people who belonged to the one true God as the bearers of his truth to the world. We are not interested in that history at the moment. We are here interested in how Moses came to understand what he was involved in and the principle behind the way God related to him.

To begin with, Moses made contact with God through a bush, a burning bush. We can easily lose sight of the significance of the bush, but we might say that the bush made possible the people of Israel. We might go even farther and say that the bush made possible all of Jewish and Christian history. And it was likely just an ordinary desert bush.

To see the reason for the importance of the bush, we have to begin at the other end of the relationship and attempt to see what was happening from God's point of view. We know a great deal more about God than Moses probably did at the time when he came across the bush. We know that God has created everything. Therefore, he is, in principle, "outside" space and time, outside the world of everything material, outside the world of everything created. To use the modern technical term, he transcends everything. If we look around and imagine that everything around us, everything we think of and know about, were taken away, God would still be there.

We might imagine some person we know and try to think of him as the only being in the whole universe. We will find that we cannot do so convincingly. If, for instance, the earth's atmosphere did not exist, he could not exist, because he needs it to breathe. If the earth itself did not exist, he could not exist, because he needs a place to exist in. It is not possible to imagine away very much and still think of him as functioning in a normal way or surviving at all. But with God it is different. We could imagine away everything we can think of and God would still exist and be capable of doing everything he did before.

Now let us think about God when he wants to communicate to a human being he has created. He cannot take his lips, tongue, and vocal cords and speak to that person. He does not have such things. He existed before he made them. He cannot appear in some shape or size or color so this person could at least see he is there. He existed before anything that had shape or size or color. He even existed "before" there was space and time, within which shaped, sized, and colored things exist.

God, however, has a "strategy of communication," and we can see it illustrated in the story of Moses and the bush. First, he picked something in Moses' world and made it behave in an unusual way, unusual enough that Moses would be convinced he was dealing with some being or at least some cause that was bringing about the unusual behavior. Because an ordinary bush began to burn without being burned up, Moses was convinced that there was something, some Being, behind what was happening—an unusual Being.

To use scriptural language, the bush functioned as a *manifestation* (or *epiphany*) of the presence of God. To use a word that later became very commonly used by Christian teachers, it functioned as a *sign* that God was in some sense there and about to do something. To use computer language, which is probably ultimately borrowed from Greek Christian language, it functioned as an icon that indicated some communication was about to begin.[12] Such terms indicate that something appears to us that calls our attention to the fact that God, or something else, is present or is ready to communicate with us.

But a manifestation, sign, or icon that is intended to communicate something does not effectively do so if it is just something unusual, a random striking event. If we just see an unusual blip on our computer screen, we are likely to ignore it as an accident. If, however, what we see on the computer screen is shaped in a certain way so that it looks like something we have been looking for, then we pay attention. The resemblance between the sign and what we might be looking for is important. It changes an unusual event into something that may be a significant communication. A burning bush that was not burnt up likely would lead Moses, or us, to think of some divine presence.

Yet to have a bush that was burning in an unusual way was not enough for communication. Moses could have stood (or prostrated himself) for hours before the burning bush, and he would not have known why such a thing was happening. He could have made some guesses. He could have guessed that he was seeing the manifestation of some powerful Being. He could have guessed that this Being was impressing on him its existence. He might have guessed even more than that. But it is unlikely that he could have guessed that this Being was the God of his people and wanted him to take a leading role in bringing his people out of Egypt.

For that he needed the bush to speak. Or, more correctly, he needed the

Being who caused an ordinary bush of the wilderness to burst into flames and yet not be burnt up to speak to him. That is what happened.

It may have been an audible voice that he heard. It may have been something in his mind that came to him with a conviction that he was not hearing his own subconscious but hearing a being who was speaking to him "mind to mind" or "spirit to spirit." But he was hearing HE WHO IS, the Lord, the Lord of heaven and earth, speaking to him. And he probably heard the Lord speaking the language of Moses' own family, not Egyptian, the most cultured language of the day.

This Lord, this God, told Moses, "I have come down" (v. 8). He came, in other words, from the place where God "dwells"—from heaven itself—to earth, our world. He came to speak to Moses directly, to help him and his people. The God of Abraham, Isaac, and Jacob, the God of what seemingly was just an insignificant desert tribe that ended up in Egypt and stayed there, that God had "come down" and was speaking to him.

Moses, of course, is one of our fathers in the faith. He is a father of the Israelites, a father of the Jews, and a father of Christians. He is not the ancestor of us all like Abraham was. He was, however, a prophet, a man who could go to God, hear his voice, and pass on what he heard reliably. But he was not just an ordinary prophet. He was the prophet who was able to receive the communications from God that constituted the foundation of what we would call old covenant religion. He also led a people to respond to that word so that they became the old covenant people of God. In that sense he was a father in the faith, our faith.

The bush, however, is also important. Moses would not likely have known that he was dealing with God if it were not for the bush. The bush was a manifestation or a sign of God's presence. What God spoke made clear why he was present, but the bush made clear that Something, Someone More-Than-Natural, was trying to interact with Moses. It was like an icon on our computer screen flashing as an indicator that we have a message.

The bush is so important because of what could be called "the incarnational principle." A bush is something in our world that is material (and alive), of little significance in itself. But the burning bush was the means of contact between Moses and God and therefore between us and God.

When God "comes down," when he begins to act within our world, the principle he normally follows is *the incarnational principle*. He chooses as an instrument of communication and interaction something that can exist as we do within a space-time world. He uses that to make contact with us so that we know he is there and know that we need to direct our attention to him.

The word "incarnational" comes from the fact that in the course of human history God chose a human being, Jesus of Nazareth, to be the one "in" whom he would be and "through" whom he would communicate so he might put us into relationship with himself. To speak in a theologically more adequate way, at one point in time God, in the person of his eternal Son, "came down" and became a human being. Equipped with a human nature, he could act and speak within our space-time world in such a way that he could effectively interact with us.

This event we refer to as his "incarnation," his "becoming flesh." We speak of the incarnational principle, then, to refer to the way God uses things in our space-time world to relate to human beings because the incarnation is the fullest example we have. Other instances of his interaction with us follow the principle behind his incarnation, albeit in a lesser way. We might call them successive approximations to what he was working towards in the Incarnation, if they occur earlier in time, or "prolongations" of it if they occur later, because they happen in a similar way.

Such an understanding has an unexpected consequence. When we are reading the Old Testament, we are actually reading about the beginnings of God's acting on the incarnational principle. We therefore, in a certain sense, are reading about Christ, because we are reading about events that led to the Incarnation of Christ, the fullest example of God's attempt to establish a good relationship with us and show us something about the principles of the way he works whenever he seeks to establish that relationship.

According to the New Testament (for example, 1 Cor 10:4) and the Fathers, we are also reading about Christ for a still more important reason. The Son of God who was to become incarnate was present and at work in the old covenant and was present and at work in the burning bush. For both reasons the old covenant realities *prefigured* or *foreshadowed* what would happen in the new covenant as a result of the Incarnation. They showed, in other words, in a sketchy way or in outline what was to come.

If we realize that the Old Testament concerns a foreshadowing of Christ and his work, we are better prepared to understand what the Scriptures teach about the Eucharist. Much of the teaching of the New Testament and of Christian tradition about the Eucharist can only be understood through what was revealed in the Old Testament. Because Christ was at work there and was preparing human beings to be able to understand the fuller revelation that was to come, he was beginning to lay the foundations for the Christian liturgical celebrations. Moreover, New Testament authors normally refer back to, or allude to, Old Testament texts when they speak about the Eucharist. Consequently, when we read the New Testament texts about Christian worship and the Eucharist against the background of the Old Testament, we understand them much better.

The Sacramental Principle

God first used the incarnational principle long before the Christian Eucharist and long before the burning bush—at the beginning of the creation of the human race. Once Adam had been created, he was put by God into a garden, the Garden of Eden, the Garden of Delight (Gn 2:8-9). But God had also put in that garden two trees, the Tree of the Knowledge of Good and Evil and the Tree of Life.

When we first read the account, the trees are somewhat mysterious to us. God put the Tree of the Knowledge of Good and Evil "off limits," at least for a while (2:17). Adam and Eve did not eat of the Tree of Life for reasons that are not explicitly stated. Only by seeing the consequences that come from eating the one and not eating the other can we understand their significance.

Many Christians have understood the Tree of the Knowledge of Good and Evil to be something bad, or at least something never intended for human beings to eat, because when Adam and Eve ate of it, bad consequences followed. Probably, however, that interpretation is a misunderstanding.[13] An early Christian understanding of the two trees is given to us in the *Epistle of Diognetus*, probably written at least in part within a few decades before the last book of the New Testament. There (in section 12) it says,

> Indeed there is a deep meaning in the passage of Scripture which tells how God in the beginning planted a tree of knowledge and a tree of life in the midst of paradise, to show that life is attained through knowledge.... And so the two trees were planted together.

In other words, the two trees were planted together, because one was meant to lead to the other. The Tree of the Knowledge of Good and Evil, or as it is sometimes termed, the tree of wisdom (see Gn 3:6), was meant to lead to the Tree of Life. True wisdom or knowledge leads to life.

According to this interpretation, God did not put the first tree off limits because it was bad or unfit for human beings, but because he intended to instruct his newly created creatures himself until they were ready to eat from the tree of wisdom. When they reached for it out of disobedience, they suffered the bad consequences of doing something they were not yet ready for. They were like children who receive a near-fatal jolt when they play with the electric plug their parents put off limits until they grow up more. But they were intended to eventually receive wisdom from the Tree of Knowledge, which in turn would help them to receive life safely from the Tree of Life.

Since the first two human beings already had life of a certain sort, the trees must have been intended to give them a better life. There are many views of exactly what the improvement would have been. Immortality is the only stated result, and that is only mentioned after they were deprived of it. At least it seems safe to say that the trees would have conferred a better life than human beings had simply through their creation, because the life they had then left them liable to possible death.

The two trees, then, were to be means of God's bringing the human race to the full undying life he ultimately wanted it to have. The two trees are like the bush in Exodus in that they are material things that God acts through to relate to the human race. But they were not just means of communication. They were intended to have interior transforming effects, what might be called "spiritual" effects, on the human beings who ate of them. They were intended to change human beings and how they could function.

We might call the two trees the first "sacraments." The word *sacrament* in this context means something of a holy nature or character that makes human beings holy. The two trees were holy things, that is, things that came from or were established for a certain purpose by God. They were also given so that the human race might become holy by having holy or divine life, that is, a better life that comes from God, better than the life the first human beings were created with. Moreover, there is something about the nature of the fruits of a tree, which feed us, that makes them a good sign that these trees bring a better, divine life. In these ways the trees are "sacramental."

We normally reserve the word "sacraments" for things that have functioned since the death and resurrection of Jesus Christ to pass on the new life that he won for us.[14] Many Christian teachers, however, have used the term more broadly.[15] Certainly the two trees are portrayals of God operating on *the sacramental principle,* the principle that God uses material things not only to communicate to us but also to change us, to make us holy, to give us life. It is this principle that gave rise to the new covenant sacraments, but the two trees are an earlier example.

As the *Epistle of Diognetus* indicates, the two trees foreshadow something about Christian life because by looking at what is said about the two trees in Genesis we can come to understand something about Christianity. The tree of wisdom foreshadows the Scriptures. The tree of life foreshadows the Eucharistic sacrament. God intended to use two material things, two trees, to give the human race the life he intended it to have. He now does the same thing by giving the Bible and the Eucharistic sacrament. During the time of the new covenant, which we are now in, they give us the wisdom and the life we need to be what God made us to be and to end up at the place he wants us for all eternity.

If we do not understand "the sacramental principle," itself based on "the incarnational principle," we will not understand the Christian Eucharistic celebration. If we can understand why a bush and two trees can be so important, that will help us understand why a book and bread and wine can be so important. That, in turn, will help us to understand how to approach them.

The Lord said,
The words that I have spoken to you are spirit and life.

JOHN 6:63

He also said,

Truly, truly, I say to you, unless you eat the flesh of the Son of man and drink his blood, you have no life in you.... He who eats my flesh and drinks my blood abides in me, and I in him.

JOHN 6:53, 56

It is the truth of these sayings that we will seek to understand.

The Liturgy of the Word

The Opening Ceremonies

The Liturgy of the Word
[The Little Entrance]*

Holy God, Holy Mighty One, Holy Immortal One, Have mercy on us. (Byzantine)

The Readings

Wisdom! Be attentive! (Byzantine)

A Reading from the Old Testament (Roman)
The word of the Lord! (Roman)

A Reading from the Apostolic Writings
The word of the Lord! (Roman)

Wisdom! Stand up! (Byzantine)

A Reading from the Gospels
The gospel of the Lord! (Roman)

The Homily
The Creed
Intercessions

The Liturgy of the Eucharist

*The material in brackets is only in the Byzantine liturgy.

ONE

The Word of God

When you received the word of God which you heard from us,
you accepted it not as the word of men but as what it really is,
the word of God.

1 THESSALONIANS 2:13

In the Acts of the Apostles (Acts 17:1-4) there is a description of the evangelization of the city of Thessalonica in Greece by Paul and Silas:

Now when they had passed through Amphipolis and Apollonia, they came to Thessalonica, where there was a synagogue of the Jews. And Paul went in, as was his custom, and for three weeks he argued with them from the scriptures, explaining and proving that it was necessary for the Christ to suffer and to rise from the dead, and saying, "This Jesus, whom I proclaim to you, is the Christ."

And some of them were persuaded, and joined Paul and Silas; as did a great many of the devout Greeks and not a few of the leading women.

Paul, with the help of Silas, began by speaking to the Jews at the local synagogue. Over a period of three weeks he argued with the Jews about what we would now call Christianity. He insisted that Jesus had died and risen again and that he was the Christ. He spent much of that time giving arguments based on Old Testament texts to back up his assertions.

Paul's work resulted in the beginning of a Christian church. It also resulted in the rejection of Christianity by many Jews in that city, a rejection which led to persecution of the apostles and the new Christians. The accusation presented by the Jews, who charged the apostles with what we might term "sedition," was complimentary to the power of the message they brought. They said, "These men have turned the world upside down!"

There was more that happened during that time. Not only did Paul and his coworkers reach Jews and Gentiles who had become believers in the one true

God; they also reached those who still worshiped pagan gods. In his First Letter to the Thessalonians, Paul referred to his initial evangelization of Thessalonica by saying,

> You turned to God from idols, to serve a living and true God, and to wait for his Son from heaven, whom he raised from the dead, Jesus who delivers us from the wrath to come.
>
> 1 THESSALONIANS 1:9-10

After reminding them of his labors, he explained the source of his success in these words,

> We thank God constantly for this, that when you received the word of God which you heard from us, you accepted it not as the word of men but as what it really is, the word of God, which is at work in you believers.
>
> 1 THESSALONIANS 2:13

Paul, in other words, spent something under a month in Thessalonica and left behind a Christian church. During that time he argued with Jews about Scripture and explained to them what Christianity was. He also worked with Gentiles, proclaiming the message to groups of them "in power and in the Holy Spirit" (1 Thes 1:5) and sharing the gospel with individuals in some kind of follow-up (1 Thes 1:8). In the above summary of his and Silas' efforts, he held that the decisive occurrence in all this was that the Thessalonian Christians had accepted the word of God.

Despite how human the process may have looked to some, there was something else going on when Paul spoke. In his arguments with Jews about the Old Testament, and in his proclamation to the pagans, God's word was at work, producing a spiritual change so that people could come to know him and live a new life. As Paul said in his Letter to the Romans, the gospel is "the power of God for salvation to every one who has faith" (Rom 1:16).

We still have the Letter of Paul to the Thessalonians and the one to the Romans, as well as the rest of what we call the New Testament. We have them because the early Christians knew that Paul's understanding of these writings was true. The Christians were not a society for historical studies. They were not even a society for religious studies. They were a group of people who knew that they had received new life when they heard certain words, and so they kept some of the writings that preserved what they had heard so that they could continue to receive life from them.

The first copies of these writings that we now obtain and read so easily were written out by hand, the only way of duplicating texts at that time. They were owned by Christian communities, carefully guarded, and read at worship services. People memorized portions of them as they were chanted, the normal way of reading in a public situation. To use the phraseology of Deuteronomy, they "laid up" the words of Scripture "in their heart" or, as we would be more likely to put it, they stored them in their memories as they heard them read repeatedly.

When they gathered as a community, the early Christians had two important purposes in mind. They gathered to hear the words that they believed were the word of God, the writings that we would call the Old Testament and, as time went on, the ones we call the New Testament. And they gathered to partake of special food, the Body and Blood of the Lord. They did both so that they might obtain life, better life here and now, but even more, unending life. And they did both so that they could take home what they had received, bearing it inside of them, and draw life from it in the course of the week.

We can read about the gatherings of the first Christians in the New Testament. When Paul came to Troas during one of his later missionary journeys (Acts 20:7-12), he spent a week with the community of Christians there. He met with all of them together on Sunday, their normal day for gathering. He gave them a talk, undoubtedly based on Old Testament readings as his talks in Thessalonica had been. They then "broke bread," a phrase that here refers to the special meal they had together that we would describe as a Liturgy of the Eucharist.[1]

In doing this Paul carried on a practice that, in its essentials, was the same as that of the first Christians in Jerusalem after Pentecost. They had "devoted themselves to the apostles' teaching and fellowship, to the breaking of bread and the prayers" (Acts 2:42). What the first Christians did in the beginning was based in turn on what the Jews did before them, as we shall see further on, but changed in important ways because of Christ.

We do what Paul and the early Christians did. There are two parts to our main worship service. The first part is the Liturgy of the Word, and during that time the Scriptures are read, meditated on, and explained. They are the written record of what people like the apostle Paul spoke as well as the writings of the Old Testament, which Paul approached as the foundation of his message.

There is a temptation, an old temptation, to think that the reading of the Scripture during the liturgy is just a "warm-up." It is designed to put us into a devout frame of mind to engage with the really important event, the Eucharist. To be sure, it does help us approach the Lord more spiritually and participate in the Eucharist more effectively. To see it only as a preparation, however, is a major mistake.

The Second Vatican Council (DV 21) and the *Catechism of the Catholic Church* (CCC 103) tell us:

The Church has always venerated the Scriptures as she venerates the Lord's Body. She never ceases to present to the faithful the bread of life, taken from the one table of God's Word and Christ's Body. (See DV21.)

For many Catholics today it seems like an extraordinary—and perhaps not quite orthodox—statement to say the Scriptures are venerated "as the Lord's Body." And it seems at best paradoxical to say that we are fed the bread of life by both.

In saying this, however, the Council fathers restated a teaching of many of the Fathers of the Church. One of them, Caesarius of Arles (*Sermo* 78, 2), expressed it dramatically by saying:

I have a question for you, brothers and sisters. Which do you think more important—the word of God or the body of Christ? If you want to answer correctly, you must tell me that the word of God is not less important than the body of Christ! How careful we are, when the body of Christ is distributed to us, not to let any bit of it fall to the ground from our hand! But we should be just as careful not to let slip from our hearts the word of God.

We cannot, then, understand the Eucharistic celebration if we do not know that there are two parts of it, the Liturgy of the Word and the Liturgy of the Eucharist, and believe that they are both important. Therefore we cannot understand the Eucharistic celebration if we do not understand why the reading and receiving of the Scriptures is so important. We are hearing the Word of God, which feeds us with the Bread of Life.

We will consider the Liturgy of the Eucharist further on after considering the Liturgy of the Word. The outline just preceding this chapter shows us its main parts and will be referred to in the next two chapters. The outline presents elements from both the Roman rite, the rite of most "Western" Christians, and the Byzantine rite, now the main rite of the Greek-speaking Christians and those who were evangelized by them in the Slavic world. In the chapter after this we will consider how we can participate in the Liturgy of the Word so that we might receive the blessing and life it is intended to convey. In this chapter, we will consider the center or focus, the Scriptures, and why they are important enough to receive the repeated, reverent attention we give them in the liturgy and hopefully at home every day.

During the Liturgy of the Word the lector reads a book that was written two millennia or more ago and concludes by saying, "The word of the Lord!" To this the congregation replies, "Thanks be to God!" In responding with their lips that way, the members of the congregation should be agreeing in their hearts with what the lector said. They are affirming, "Yes, this is the word of the Lord." The question we will ask in this chapter is: what are they agreeing to?

The Scriptures

The Written Word of God[2]

The word *scriptures* means "writings." "The Scriptures" is short for "the *Sacred* Scriptures" or "the *Holy* Scriptures." Adding "sacred" or "holy" means they come from God. The Scriptures, then, are "the *holy* writings," the writings that come from God.

We sometimes refer to the Scriptures as *The Bible*, which translated literally from the Greek means "The Books" and in English means "*The* Book," or perhaps even "The Book of Books." The Scriptures, then, are the most important book ever written, the one book human beings cannot do without. It is the writings in this book that are the word of God.

The word of God is a literal translation of a Hebrew phrase. In the English language, we usually use "word" to mean a single word. The Hebrew equivalent could be used for a single word, a statement, or a lengthy discourse. If we are going to look for one word in English that would convey the range of meaning that "word" has in Hebrew, we might pick "message" or perhaps "communication."

In Christian theology, "the word of God" could refer to all that God wishes to reveal to us (his communication as a whole), or to Christ, the concrete embodiment or fulfilment of what God wishes to communicate to us, or to the

Scripture itself. It is the Scripture that is our concern here. If, then, we were going to retranslate, "The word of the Lord!" more idiomatically, we might translate it, "This is what the Lord is saying to you!" or, "This is the message that the Lord has for us!" The response "Thanks be to God," then, would mean, "We are very fortunate that God has been willing to say this to us"—or say anything at all to us for that matter. With full justice he could have ignored us.

However, the "message that the Lord has for us" that we read above was actually spoken in Greek by Paul close to two millennia ago. Perhaps we might hear a reading from the prophet Jeremiah. That would have been spoken about six hundred years earlier in Hebrew.

There is a famous story about an early president of Yale University who insisted that all Yale graduates needed to learn Hebrew, a requirement that has long since lapsed. When asked why, he explained that he wanted them to know the language when they got to heaven. But does God speak in Hebrew?

Perhaps Paul made mistakes in his Greek. Would that mean that God made mistakes in Greek? Some have said that Paul's Greek and his way of speaking and writing would not have been good enough for him to pass a modern writing class. If so, did God speak poor Greek?

While such criticisms of Paul are something of an exaggeration to make a point, especially since the people in his day would not have subscribed to many of the rules taught in modern writing courses, he himself tells us that others criticized him by saying that "his speech [is] of no account" (2 Cor 10:10). He also admitted that he did not try to use "lofty words" (1 Cor 2:1), perhaps what we might term "elegant speech" or "literary speech." For the sake of the example, let us grant that Paul made grammatical mistakes and wrote and spoke low-quality Greek, somewhat the way some foreign person who has recently immigrated to the United States or Britain from some country with a different language might speak English. Does that mean that God communicates poorly?

God does not speak Hebrew or Greek or even English, although he understands all the languages in the world and can communicate to every human being in a way that human beings can understand. Nor do mistakes or inelegancies in what we proclaim to be "the Word of God" mean that God makes mistakes when he speaks or speaks inelegantly. But to communicate to us he does use the words of human beings who speak Hebrew or Greek or English and who sometimes make grammatical mistakes or speak without literary ability. In an analogous way, when we speak to others through translators, the words our hearers receive have many of the characteristics of the translators, even if they translate accurately.

This brings us back to the incarnational principle. The Lord uses things that exist in the space-time world to make contact with us. When he wishes to communicate, he most commonly uses human speech. But he has no tongue, lips, or vocal cords, since he transcends space and time. Therefore he makes use of human beings who do have them to convey the message or communication he wants us to receive. Otherwise he would need to produce miraculous skywriting or something similar.

Just as the burning bush no doubt had the normal characteristics of a desert bush of its kind, so those human beings who spoke or wrote the words we have in the Scriptures probably had the normal characteristics of speakers or writers of their time. Because those words come through the communication medium of human speech, they must have many of the characteristics of the channel through which they come. But that is not all that can be said of them.

The writings in the Scriptures, then, are human words with human characteristics. But they are not "merely" human words. The word *merely* is used in this and similar contexts to acknowledge that we are dealing with something that is human, or at least truly part of this space-time world, but is not only that. It comes from God or is united or joined in some way to God so that it is not only human and created. In the case of the Scriptures, the message we receive is usually a human message. Nonetheless, it is not only human. It is, more importantly, God's message that comes to us.

The Importance of Scripture
Christian teaching over the centuries has made use of various terms to help us understand what it means to say that words like those of Jeremiah or Paul can be God's word. One of the most important is *revelation*. We say that the scriptures, and the words in them, "contain revelation," God's revelation.

Using an old distinction in Christian theology, theologians often contrast "revelation" with "reason." "Reason" in this sense is the natural human ability to know and understand things. Knowledge we have by reason, then, is knowledge we human beings have acquired by our own efforts. Knowledge we have by "revelation," in contrast, is knowledge that has been given to us by God.[3]

In principle, God might reveal to us things that we could come to understand by ourselves. According to Columbus in his *Book of Prophecies,* "With a hand that could be felt, the Lord opened my mind to the fact that it would be possible to sail from here to the Indies." If his account is accurate, because he believed he had the revelation of God that such a journey was possible, he was motivated to attempt it. He then discovered for himself that the Atlantic Ocean could be crossed and so discovered the existence of the American continent, landing initially in "the West Indies." The same fact, in short, can be learned by human effort ("reason") or by the revelation of God. We are mainly interested in those truths in the Scriptures that could only have been known by God's revelation.

God might have decided only to reveal facts about insects and reptiles that died millennia ago and left no records. Biologists then would be the ones mainly interested in the Scriptures. In fact, however, he revealed tremendously important truths about human life. He revealed who he himself was, how dependent human beings were upon him, how they could relate well to him, how they could achieve the purpose for which they were made, and how he himself would help them fulfill it.

God, in short, revealed truths that make it possible for the lives of human beings to go well, especially in the long run. Without this revelation, human beings are in serious trouble. Sometimes this is summed up by saying that God revealed truths "necessary for salvation." For that reason, we all should be interested in what the Scriptures say. The phrase "the Scriptures contain God's revelation," then, tells us why the Scriptures are so important.

Inspiration and Canonicity

Not everything in the Scriptures is there because it was revealed. Paul wrote a letter to the Philippians in which he explained that he was in prison and spoke about some of the things that resulted from his imprisonment. Those words are part of what we consider to be the Word of God. But Paul must have been able to figure out that he was in prison without getting special revelation from God! The Scriptures may be important to us because they contain revelation, but it is not true to say that everything in them is the word of God because it has all been revealed.

A passage in the Scriptures, 2 Timothy 3:16-17, contains the word that has come to be used to assert that the whole Scripture is the Word of God,

All scripture is inspired by God and profitable for teaching, for reproof, for correction, and for training in righteousness, that the man of God may be complete, equipped for every good work.

The important word here is "inspired." All of the Scriptures have come to us through *inspiration*.

The English word "inspired" in this text translates a Greek word that means "God-breathed." Scripture, then, is "God-breathed" or "breathed by God." Behind this word is a helpful image. When we speak, we make sounds, sounds that we have come to recognize as words. But we do so by breathing. When we stop breathing, when we "hold our breath," we cannot speak anymore. Only as we breathe out and form the resulting breath by our lips, tongues, and vocal cords do we make sounds that are words. To say that the Scriptures are inspired is to say that they are "breathed out" by God, spoken by him. What results is his word or message.

God "breathes his word out" through human beings. He does so through his own "Spirit." The Hebrew word that is translated "Spirit" could also be translated "breath." God's Spirit is God's breath, so God breathes into or through human beings by the Holy Spirit (the Divine Breath) to produce his message to us. In so doing, he "moves them" (2 Pt 1:21). Perhaps he moves them, as some of the Fathers thought, somewhat as if they were vocal cords, so that they speak what he wants spoken. Or, to use still other scriptural words, he "works" or "operates" in and through human beings by his Spirit to communicate to us (see 1 Cor 12:6). All these are New Testament ways to say that the Scriptures come to us "by the inspiration of the Holy Spirit."

Since we breathe through our vocal cords to produce words, it would be possible to say that our vocal cords speak. However, we rarely if ever feel it useful to say that we had a conversation with a set of vocal cords or that some vocal cords spoke to us. We rather say that another person spoke to us, because that person is the source of the speech. The same thing is true for God's word. To say that the Scriptures are inspired is to say that God is the source of them, the most important source of them. Therefore, he is the one speaking to us, not just the human being he is speaking through.

This does not mean that the human authors of the Scriptures are as passive or receptive in the process as vocal cords are when we speak. After all, God did not write to the Philippians. Paul did—in his own name. Nor did God have Paul write the letter as a mere secretary to tell them that God wanted them to know that Paul was in prison. Paul was writing the letter in the first person, and he was speaking to them about himself. Nor was he giving a prophecy. He was describing his own experience and thoughts to a group of people who knew him and whom he wanted to encourage and thank for sending him money.

To say, however, that the books of Scripture are inspired must at least mean that God is the ultimate source of what is said. It therefore must be true to say about everything in Scripture, however the content came to the human author, that God spoke it. The word "inspiration," then, tells us that the Scriptures originated in some action or work of God that means he is using them to speak to us.[4] As the Second Vatican Council (DV 24) put it,

> The sacred Scriptures contain the word of God and, since they are inspired, really are the word of God.

The concept or word "inspiration," however, is not enough by itself to explain the nature of the Scriptures, because there are other inspired human words that have come in the course of human history. The Scriptures themselves tell us about true prophecies that are not part of our Bible. For instance, Paul speaks about many prophetic messages in the Corinthian church that he seems to think were real prophecies, and hence from God, which were not recorded and kept (see 1 Cor 14).[5] He even says to the Thessalonians (1 Thes 5:20-21), "Do not despise prophesying, but test everything; hold fast what is good." This implies that when the early Christians gave "prophecies," some of what was said was given by God and completely faithful to imparting a message from God, although some was not.

We can read about Christian men and women in past centuries who got messages from God and spoke them to those who came to them—or perhaps to those who did not want to come to them. Nowadays, we can visit meetings of orthodox Catholics who are "charismatic" and can hear messages that purport to be prophecies. Solid charismatic teachers would say that the messages need testing. Some are, in fact, simply not from God. More significantly, some are only partly from God or have been distorted in their transmission. But some of them likely are from God, at least in part, because God still works in human beings to speak through them in a way that is more than just passing on human grace-filled meditation upon Christian teaching or the Scriptures.

We therefore need another word that allows us to describe the difference between the Scriptures and other inspired messages or writings. The word that has been most commonly used in theological writings is *canonical.* We also would speak about the *canon* of Scripture.

The word "canon" was originally a Greek word. It meant, at least in this context, ruler or yardstick or standard. The "canon" was the ruler or standard against which other things were measured. The United States National Bureau of Standards contains a yardstick of sorts that is the official "yard." If it were important to find out whether something were exactly an American yard, it could be compared to the "yardstick" that is in Washington, D.C. We might say, using theological language, that that is the canonical yard.

A yardstick measures the length of something. The Scripture "measures," or can be used to assess the truth of, writings or speech. If we want to know if something is true Christianity, the truth that God wanted to reveal to us so that we might know how to be saved, we can compare it to the canon of the Scriptures. If some statement or writing does not compare adequately, it is not Christianity. At the very least it cannot contradict what is in Scripture and be considered "orthodox" ("straight" or correct believing) Christianity.

Canonicity tells us something more about what it means to say that the Scripture is the inspired Word of God. First, it tells us that all of it is true or reliable for knowing how to assess what Christianity is. There cannot be anything in it that falsely presents what has been revealed. It is not like some Corinthian (or modern) prophecies, a mixture of inspired words and human fancy, or perhaps a highly distorted transmission of something that began with a genuine inspiration. If it were, it could not be an effective standard.

Second it tells us that the various writings in the scriptures have been recognized by the church as the standard for Christian truth, just as the "yardstick" in the U.S. Bureau of Standards has been recognized as the standard for yards. The early church handed down to us books that were accepted as the inspired word of God and to be used as such. In the course of the process, synods of bishops sorted through the various questions that came up about the status of the books that different churches had preserved and determined authoritatively which ones were to be considered canonical scriptures.

Some of the questions about the canonical status of certain writings came from the fact that there were different versions of the Old Testament that circulated among Jews. Some came from the fact that there were various collections of Christian writings that were attributed to the apostles or at least used for authoritative teaching. By the end of the patristic period there were authoritative decisions by councils of bishops about what books should be in the canonical scriptures, certainly about which books belonged to the New Testament. Catholic teaching would say that any remaining disputed questions about which books should be considered Scripture, mainly which books should be included in the Old Testament, were most authoritatively settled by the

Council of Trent, basing itself on synods and papal statements in patristic times. In making such decisions, however, the earlier councils and the Council of Trent did not understand themselves to be adding new books to the canon of Scripture. The canon was closed (completed) in the time of the apostles. The later decisions simply recognized which books that were claimed to belong to the canon of Scripture were to be accepted.

The result is that the Scriptures are, according to the Second Vatican Council, "the supreme rule of faith, since, as inspired by God and committed once and for all to writing, they impart the Word of God Himself without change, and make the voice of the Holy Spirit resound in the words of the prophets and Apostles" (DV 21).

If they are "the supreme rule of faith," the canon, nothing else can take precedence over them. Although the church authorities or scholars can interpret what they mean, no one can cancel them or override them. They are the supreme rule of faith because they have been reliably discerned to be the inspired Word of God.

Catholics speak of other things as canonical. There is, for instance, canon law. Canon law tells us, to simplify a bit, how to conduct a properly run church. If something contradicts canon law, it is "out of order" or worse. There are also canonical doctrinal definitions, usually made by ecumenical councils. These tell us what opinions in a theological dispute cannot be held without denying something that has been revealed to us. To say that they are canonical is to say that they are the recognized standard in some matter.

Canon law and canonical definitions from ecumenical councils, or any other kind of canonical writings, are not, however, Scripture. They cannot be entered into the collection of scriptural writings, nor may they be read in the liturgy in place of the Scriptures. They are not the canonical Word of God, however authoritative they might be. They do not, according to the above statement of the Second Vatican Council, by their very nature "impart the Word of God Himself."

Apostolicity

Understanding inspiration and canonicity still leaves us with the question of why some good, true, perhaps inspired, Christian writings are in Scripture and some not. Suppose that the Nicene Creed was actually inspired in all its parts. Suppose the Fathers of the Council of Nicaea had spent days prostrating themselves in prayer before the Lord, beseeching him to solve the problem they were wrestling with of how the human being Jesus of Nazareth could be said to be the eternal Son of God. Suppose at the end of the time each one wrote down what he believed he received from the Lord. Suppose all of them heard exactly the same thing and wrote down what we now call the Nicene Creed (the Nicene Fathers actually agreed to an earlier version). Since there were 318 of them, most of us would be suitably impressed if such a thing happened and, except for the most hardhearted, would probably be willing to agree that the creed was inspired.

Even such a manifestly supernatural act of inspiration, however, would not qualify the Nicene Creed to be included in the Holy Scriptures that we read in the liturgy. We may read it somewhere else in the liturgy and give it high honors, but not the highest honors. That tells us something else important about the Scripture.

The Nicene Creed could not be entered into the Scripture, no matter how inspired it might be, because it lacks *apostolicity*. This is a criterion for being Scripture that only concerns the "new covenant" or, to use the commonly employed translation, "New Testament" writings. Since the Nicene Creed concerns Christianity, it would have to be added to the New Testament. For that to happen, it would have to be apostolic.

The criterion of apostolicity means that a New Testament book either had to be written by an apostle (like the letters of Paul) or written under his authority (like the Gospel of Luke) or at least somehow accepted as authoritatively from the apostles by the early church. The New Testament, then, contains only "apostolic writings." The Nicene Creed, only written in A.D. 325, is not an apostolic writing, however true or even inspired it might be.

The canon of the New Testament has been closed since the death of the last apostle (probably in the nineties of the first century), because Christ chose the apostles to lay the foundations of the church and so to establish how Christianity was to be handed on. Most of the revelation they needed for this task they got from Christ when he was on earth, from the time they had been called to the time when he ascended to heaven (Acts 1:21-22). Some they got from subsequent revelation (Acts 15:6-22; Eph 3:4-6). But the task of sorting out the essentials of Christianity and of establishing the church was completed once they had completed their time on earth. It is for this reason that in the vision of the Church in heaven, the heavenly city, the Book of Revelation (Rv 21:14) says that the wall of the city had twelve [foundation stones], and on them the twelve names of the twelve apostles of the Lamb. The church is built on the foundation of the apostles (Eph 2:20).

The *Catechism of the Catholic Church* has an interesting section in which it treats the question of "private revelations," that is, revelations given to individuals who did not officially speak on behalf of the Church to pronounce on what God has revealed, but who simply reported what they believed God had said to them. It says:

> Throughout the ages, there have been so-called "private" revelations, some of which have been recognized by the authority of the Church. They do not belong, however, to the deposit of faith. It is not their role to improve or complete Christ's definitive Revelation, but to help live more fully by it in a certain period of history (CCC 67).

This statement is based on important truths about Scripture that explain to us the significance of the fact that the New Testament is only made up of apostolic writings. First of all, it speaks about "the deposit of faith." That phrase refers to what is said in 1 Timothy 6:20 (and 2 Timothy 2:14), where Paul, speaking of the teaching that had been passed on to Timothy by himself as a member of the college of apostles, says, "O Timothy, guard what has been entrusted to you."

"What has been entrusted to you" translates one Greek word that is also translated "deposit." We would use the word to describe what we put into a bank account, but also for what we put into a safe deposit box in a bank. The latter is probably closer to how Timothy would have understood it. He was supposed to act like a banker who kept safe something that was very valuable.

The phrase in the catechism tells us more. It tells us that "the deposit of faith" was made in the past and cannot be added to now. The names of the apostles were on the safe deposit box, so to speak, and now no one can be granted access to the box to add or take away anything from the deposit of faith. The box has been sealed, and not even a pope or ecumenical council can change its contents. It cannot be added to or subtracted from because it contains Christ's "definitive revelation."

Nothing more is needed than the deposit of faith (in a sense that we will consider farther on) because it contains a full understanding of what Christianity is and what we need to believe or do to be saved. That understanding is stated, at least implicitly, in the canonical Scriptures, the supreme rule of faith. As we will see later on, that same deposit is handed on in other ways, and more is needed for its sound interpretation than simply reading the Scriptures, but the deposit of faith is nonetheless contained in the Scriptures and they are the supreme rule, the supreme canon, for determining what Christianity is.

The deposit of faith concerns new covenant Christianity. It also, however, concerns old covenant truth. It concerns which books written by old covenant people are Scripture and how those books should be interpreted and used by new covenant people. The new covenant is a republishing of the old covenant in the light of God sending his Son to us, and so it is based on an understanding of the old covenant in the light of the new.

When we read the New Testament (or the Scriptures as a whole), we come across a variety of writings. Some are accounts of the preaching of the gospel, of healings and miracles. Some are pedestrian exhortations to live better or perhaps genealogies whose importance may elude us. Some are relatively trivial comments about where an apostle left his books or how a Christian worker's stomach is acting up. All, however, are the inspired, canonical word of God. We may not see the use of all of them. Each book, however, contains revelation, and together they contain the deposit of faith. We do not have to find something useful in every word or sentence, although many Christian teachers have thought that we should be able to. We do, however, need to hear the Scriptures as a whole in such a way that we learn from them how to be saved.

When we hear the Scriptures read in the liturgy, then, God is speaking to us. We can be distracted and not hear it. We can fail to understand it. We can misunderstand it. We can believe it is just a human historical document. But regardless of anything we do, it is the Word of God, and God speaks to us in it. Moreover, he is not just doing it to entertain us or to interest us or to satisfy our curiosity. He is doing it because our life depends upon it. He is doing it "for our salvation," so that we might be saved.

Interpreting the Scriptures

Interpretation

It is one thing for a message to be given, another thing for it to be understood. In Acts 8:26-40 there is a description of Philip sent by an angel to talk to an Ethiopian official. The eunuch was a Jew, or perhaps a Jewish proselyte, traveling through Palestine, and was reading the prophecy of the suffering servant in

Isaiah 53. Philip began by asking him, "Do you understand what you are reading?" The Ethiopian replied, "How can I understand unless someone guide me?" Like the eunuch, at times all of us need guidance to understand what is in the Scripture. According to Luke 24:45, one of the main things the risen Lord did for his disciples was "opened their minds to understand the scriptures."

In English, we would say that someone "interprets" for others when he or she makes it possible for them to understand a written or spoken word. *Interpretation*, then, is the process of helping someone else to understand. If God speaks to us using human words, those words may need to be interpreted. In this case, the interpretation is very important, because if we are mistaken in what we think that God is saying, we are likely to be seriously misled in a very important matter. We may, according to Catholic as well as Protestant and Orthodox teaching, miss our salvation.

The Book of Nehemiah describes how Ezra, a scribe who had returned to the reestablished province of Judah in the Persian Empire in the fifth century B.C., sought to bring the Jewish people to follow the "law of Moses which God had given to Israel" (Neh 8:1). In this he had the help of Nehemiah the governor. Together they held a special meeting so that everyone might hear the law of God and decide what to amend because of what they heard (Neh 7:5-10:39).

In this special meeting, Ezra presided. He held up the book of the law and he read it. Then Levites who were helping him "gave the sense, so the people understood the reading." In other words, they translated the Hebrew, the language of the reading, into Aramaic, the language the people now spoke.

Here we have the first meaning of "interpret." When something is in a language we do not know, we need an interpreter or translator. The interpreter takes the original words and puts them into the language we use so that we can understand them. In order to do that, the interpreter needs to "give the sense" or "give the meaning" reasonably accurately.

We also, as Ezra and his Levite assistants did, deal with other problems besides differences in language. Many of us have listened to the Bible read in the King James or the Douay-Rheims version. The language there is the same one we use, but it is so old that it is not the same variety we speak.[6] For instance, many people nowadays need to be told that "thee" and "thou" are outdated familiar forms of "you," not especially formal or reverential ones used to address only God. We often, then, need certain "interpretations," explanations of features of the language we do not understand anymore, in order to fully understand what is being said to us.

But there are other difficulties in our reading the Scriptures. Some words are used differently than we would use them. "Scribe" in the passage in Nehemiah above would be an example. We would likely understand a scribe to be a kind of stenographer, someone who simply wrote down the words (one function that, in fact, scribes might have performed in the time of Ezra). But a scribe normally functioned more like a theology professor or canon law professor. Ezra, as a scribe, was an expert in God's law, and we might miss that without an explanation.

Or the circumstances might be unknown to us. If we did not know that the people of Israel had spoken Hebrew before the exile (so that their books were all in Hebrew) but began to speak Aramaic in exile, because that was the international language—something like English is now—we would miss completely what the Levites were doing for Ezra. We also might find it helpful to know that their translation technique was probably somewhat free, even expansive, somewhat like our *Living Bible*. Scripture scholars refer to the result as a *targum*, and we might consider it a paraphrase.

The most important aspect of interpreting, however, is explaining what is actually being asserted by the words. It is one thing to translate the Hebrew text into the English words "Thou shalt not kill." It is another to say what the text means when it says "kill." If the text contains instructions for how to live or act, this process is sometimes described as applying the text to our circumstances or as the *application* of the text.

For this aspect of "interpretation" some things need little if any explanation. If one person just hates another person, decides to kill that person, figures out how to do it in order to not get caught, and then poisons that person's soup, we know that the commandment has been transgressed. But would that be true if that person shot the other person accidentally while hunting? Would it be true if someone had an abortion? Would it be true if someone used a sophisticated contraceptive device that actually aborted a fetus? And so on.

For the most part such questions do not come into play. We do not need to have every possibility covered in order to know how to follow what is commanded in most situations we deal with. But at times we would want to say that we do not understand what was said to us by God, because we do not know how to apply it in the situation that is most important to us.

Catholic Interpretation
How do good Catholics deal with the need to interpret Scripture?[7] For the most

part they deal with it the way anyone else would. They learn "how to read." They get translations that have been "interpreted" by competent translators. They use "recognized authorities," that is, dictionaries, history books, commentaries, and such as aids to interpretation. They hear the Scriptures explained in church or Bible studies or courses, hopefully by people who themselves understand the Scriptures and can explain them well.

As people who believe that the whole Scripture is the inspired Word of God, they, like Orthodox and Protestants, also go to the Scripture itself and let one part of the Scripture help them to understand another part. They read Scripture, they meditate on it, and they let it form their understanding.

This process is similar to learning another language. If we move to a foreign country, we may use language courses and books to help us begin. However, the main way we learn is by speaking the language, that is, listening to others speak it and interacting with them. We pick up a great deal just by using the language where it is natively spoken and by being familiar with what people are talking about. Likewise, unless we "live in" the Scriptures, we will not understand what God is saying to us through them.

But there is something else involved in good interpretation of the Scriptures. When there are special questions about what the meaning really is, disputed questions, especially ones that bear upon our salvation, we can go to the "recognized Christian authorities" to find out if there are solid answers, or at least to find out if some answers are not compatible with Christian truth. In this the Catholic approach to interpretation is similar to the Orthodox one, but is also shared in large part by Protestants who preserve the Reformation tradition.[8]

The first authorities for scriptural interpretation are the early Christian teachers, the Fathers.[9] They have handed on the teaching of Christ to us and with it the interpretation the early church followed. The Fathers had an advantage over us because they not only had the Scriptures but they also came from Christian communities that had been taught by apostles or by teachers who were close in time to the apostles. As a result they were more likely to have been taught the Scriptures the way the apostles interpreted them and so can witness to what was handed on by them. Many of the Fathers also represented the teaching authority of the church during the foundational centuries. According to Catholic teaching, if we can see that there is a "consensus of the Fathers" on what God is teaching through a passage or a set of passages in Scripture, that interpretation is a true one.[10]

Reading the Fathers is perhaps the main way Catholics who have had basic instruction ought to learn the traditional orientation to interpreting Scripture when they begin to seriously study the scriptural texts. For this reason, among others, the Catholic liturgy gives us the Office of Readings in the Liturgy of the Hours. It contains many patristic readings selected in relationship to scriptural texts. By meditating on the Scripture with the guidance of the Office of Readings, we can begin to learn how to read the Scriptures as the Fathers did.

In addition, we might read the great teachers throughout the centuries, many of whom are also represented in the Office of Readings. For Catholics, Thomas Aquinas is especially important, but Bernard of Clairvaux, Bonaventure, Ignatius Loyola, and John Cardinal Newman, to pick a few authors referred to in the *Catechism of the Catholic Church*, are also important. By reading them we learn how different teachers have grappled with the various teachings in Scripture and the various interpretations of the Scripture that are in the Fathers, and have put them together into a harmonious whole. Or we see how they have come up with a way to handle some area or question that is consistent with the Scriptures and tradition as a whole.

Finally, we have the official Catholic teachings of the ecumenical councils, the popes, and various synods and general councils.[11] These contain statements about disputed points that clarify what cannot be held if one is to believe or teach in accordance with the deposit of faith, the revelation of what Christianity truly is. Some of these statements, according to Catholic teaching, are certainly true and obligatory for us to hold. Others are not but are important guides.[12]

Christ and the apostles handed down their teaching verbally, by a process of instruction. They did so in the context of handing down the new life that Christ came to bring, the life of a new community, the church. In Catholic theology, based on Jewish usage, we speak of *tradition* when we refer to the reliable transmission from generation to generation of the revealed teaching that makes that life possible.

Tradition includes the handing on of the Scriptures themselves. It also includes the understanding of the Christian life, which involves the corporate life of the Christian people and the way to interpret the Scriptures, all of which was passed on verbally before being written in the Scriptures. In various ways, the writings of the Fathers and the great Christian teachers and the official decisions of the teaching authority of the Church bear witness to the handing on of the revelation of God and of the life that comes from it. In so doing they ·instruct us in how to understand the Scriptures, although reading them also can present us with a challenge in distinguishing merely human tradition or opinions from the handing on of the apostolic teaching.

We are looking for a Catholic understanding, a Catholic mind, when we seek to hear and believe the Word of God. Some Catholics describe that as "faithfulness to the magisterium." If "the magisterium" is understood as the authoritative teaching of the church, and is seen broadly enough as the great tradition of teaching throughout the centuries that has been passed on in faithfulness to Christ's own teaching, "faithfulness to the magisterium" could sum up the Catholic mind.

If, however, we understand "the magisterium" the way it most commonly seems to be understood, as referring to those who currently hold the teaching authority of the church, the competent hierarchical authorities (usually ecumenical councils and the pope and his doctrinal commissions), or if we understand "faithfulness to the magisterium" as referring to acceptance of its decisions in controversial matters or even of other authoritative instructions throughout the centuries, then it is too restrictive.[13] Such decisions perform an important role in ruling certain things in or out of bounds. The Catholic hierarchy throughout the world under the presidency of the pope are the only ones who have the authority to definitively interpret the Scripture and tradition[14] when there is a dispute or a danger of someone distorting or denying Christian revelation. Their authoritative instructions also give important pastoral directions for how Catholic teaching should be shaped and taught today. But their statements do not give us the breadth and depth of Catholic tradition, much less the full spiritual life we are seeking, nor are they intended to do so.

Some Catholics, when they speak about Christian truth, put their major emphasis on "the Church's teaching." They speak about it as what we need to know and defend. By that phrase they usually mean hierarchical pronouncements of the highest authority, not just authoritative decisions in controversial matters but also instructions like the *Catechism of the Catholic Church.*

If that is the meaning, then the Church's teaching is the most authoritative contemporary interpreter of what has been revealed to us in the deposit of faith. It is, however, primarily meant to function as the interpreter of Scripture as understood in the tradition of the Church, not as a replacement for the scriptures (or the earlier teachings from the tradition of the Church).[15] It is no accident that in the liturgy we are not permitted to read papal encyclicals, conciliar decrees, or the catechism instead of the Scriptures, nor that we rarely read such documents in the Office of Readings.[16] If by "the Church's teaching" we mean all of the Church's teaching, the main book of the Church's teaching is Scripture itself.

There are times when we want to use the phrase "the Church's teaching" to specifically indicate that we mean Scripture as interpreted in the light of tradition as handed on in the church and by the church's magisterium throughout history, as distinguished from Scripture alone. However, when we do so, we should not take the emphasis off divine revelation handed on to us through Scripture and tradition and so inadvertently fall into ecclesiocentrism,[17] an exaggerated centering on the Church. We should be centered on God ("theocentrism") and on Christ ("christocentrism").

Most Catholic doctrine is not true because the Church teaches it. The Church teaches it because it is true. Catholics believe that the official Catholic teaching authority has preserved faithfully and handed on what Christ taught. But the teaching it has preserved is important because it was taught by Christ, revealed by God, not by the Church.[18]

To be sure, there are elements of Catholic doctrine that we hold on the Church's authority because the Scriptures and tradition were not clear enough for us all in a united way to answer certain important questions. These have usually been taught because of new situations or opinions that arose since the apostolic Church. It is, however, misleading to normally proclaim Christ's teaching as the Church's teaching instead of as his own. We are mainly interested in the word of God, what God is saying to us that we might be saved.

For most people, including most priests, the goal is not to be a Scripture scholar or a theologian. The goal is to hear what God is saying to us in the Scriptures, to respond to it in faith and obedience, and to help others to do the same. We do need guidance to understand it well. Some of that guidance comes from the tradition of the Church, some from the teaching of the Church today, some from sound scholarship. Such guidance, however, should not substitute for Scripture itself, but should equip us to actually listen to or read the Scriptures and hear what God wishes to communicate to us.

Meditation: The Word of Life
John 11:1-54

The Word of God is not simply a source of Christian information or cognitive truth. It is also a source of life. Psalm 33 proclaims to the whole human race,

By the word of the Lord the heavens were made,
and all their host by the breath of his mouth....
Let all the earth fear the Lord,
let all the inhabitants of the world stand
in awe of him!
For he spoke and it came to be;
he commanded, and it stood forth.

PSALM 33:6-9

The Lord made everything there is. He did not need to figure out what he wanted, make a plan, find consultants, assemble the materials and tools, and work on developing a good universe. He just needed to decide what he wanted, to speak the word, and it came into being. By the word of the Lord, everything that exists or has existed came to be.

Speaking a word can make changes, even on the human level, often surprising changes. We learn many things by hearing people speak—acquire information and understanding. But sometimes merely to be spoken to can change us for the better—when we are spoken to by the right person in the right way.

Toward the end of her life when she was close to ninety, my mother had a bladder problem and had to go into the hospital for treatment. At that age, even when something is treated, the body often declines in overall strength and ability. When she got back to her room, she seemed less functional.

I came for a visit along with a Christian sister who was helping me care for her. The nurse from the hospital had told me that I should make sure my mother walked soon. If she did not, the nurse warned, she might not walk again.

After I talked with my mother a bit, I encouraged her to get up and walk. She said she could not walk. I coaxed her to get up and hold on to her walker. When she did, her legs started trembling and she said again, "I can't walk. I can't."

That would have been the end of it. I had reached the end of my ability to get my mother to walk. But the sister who was with me, who knew my mother and was a physical therapist, walked up to my mother, looked her in the eye, and said, "You can too. Now walk!" And my mother did walk. And she walked from then on.

Human words often have power, but they are nothing compared to the word of the Lord. The Gospel of John, chapter 11, narrates an instance of this close to the end of Jesus' earthly life. Jesus was in Galilee, when he heard that a friend and disciple of his, Lazarus, was very ill. He was ill enough for his sisters, Mary and Martha, to ask Jesus to come, no doubt because they had seen his miraculous power.

Jesus did not leave for Lazarus' house in Bethany right away. He apparently deliberately delayed until Lazarus died. He then went to Bethany to "wake" Lazarus.

By the time Jesus arrived in Bethany, Lazarus had been buried and in the tomb for four days, long enough to have started to decompose. When Martha heard of Jesus' arrival, she went to meet him, and said,

Lord, if you had been here, my brother would not have died. And even now I know that whatever you ask from God, God will give you.

To this Jesus replied,

Your brother will rise again.
Then Martha said,
I know that he will rise again in the resurrection at the last day.

Martha responded, in other words, with the faith of devout Jews of her time. God would raise her brother at the last day of this world. That she too believed.

But she had misunderstood Jesus. He then made clearer to her what he had meant.

I am the resurrection and the life; he who believes in me, though he die, yet shall he live, and whoever lives and believes in me shall never die.

Jesus' language here is unusual. What does it mean for a person to say he *is* the resurrection and life? Jesus seemed to mean that he *gives* resurrection and life. But by the way he put it, he also seemed to be indicating that the power to raise people from the dead and give them life was in him because of who he is. As the First Letter of John puts it, he himself is "the word of life" (1 J n 1:1).

Jesus then asked Martha, "Do you believe this?" Her response was quietly affirmative. "Yes, Lord," she said, "I believe that you are the Christ, the Son of God, he who is coming into the world."

The Lord then called Mary to come as well and with the two sisters, followed by the Jewish leaders who were there for the mourning, went to the tomb. Jesus had some of those present take away the stone that closed the entrance to the tomb. He then blessed God his Father and spoke a simple word of command, "Lazarus, come out!" And come out he did, still wrapped in the grave clothes so that he could hardly move and probably could not see.

The word of God was spoken, and Lazarus was raised from the dead. Jesus did not explain to Lazarus how to rise from the dead or give him an instruction about how to apply his own faith to God's promises and rise up. None of those things would have helped. He simply spoke to Lazarus and life entered him. Lazarus then stood up and began to walk.

The word of God teaches us and encourages us and reproves us and consoles us. But there is something more to it. When God speaks his word, it communicates life to us, spiritual life. As we listen to it and as we have it interpreted to us, our minds and hearts come to understand more of God's truth. But over and above that, when God's word is spoken to us, by the power of the Holy Spirit, it communicates life directly. And at the same time it lets us come to know the one who is speaking to us and giving us new life.[19]

TWO

Hearing God's Word

The words that I have spoken to you are spirit and life.

JOHN 6:63

Twice every day, Jews pray what is called the *Shema* ("Hear"), so called from the first word of the first passage of Scripture which is recited during it:

Hear, O Israel: The Lord our God is one Lord; and you shall love the Lord your God with all your heart, and with all your soul, and with all your might. And these words which I command you this day shall be upon your heart; and you shall teach them diligently to your children, and shall talk of them when you sit in your house, and when you walk by the way, and when you lie down, and when you rise.

DEUTERONOMY 6:4-7

We call the *Shema* a prayer because it is surrounded by prayers of blessing, but the heart of it is the above passage from Deuteronomy. Moses spoke these words right after describing the giving of the Ten Commandments on Sinai, and they summarize the response to the covenant God offered. They are perhaps the chief scriptural exhortation addressed to those who have listened to the word of God.

Our Bibles sometimes translate the Hebrew word *shema* as "hear." At other times the word is translated "obey" or, in older English, "hearken to." When we hear someone speak, we can just take in the words. If, however, we "really hear them," we understand what is said, accept it, and, where appropriate, carry it out.

Fathers will at times give their children a lecture for misconduct and at the end will say, "Now, did you hear me?" By that they mean, have you accepted what I said and will you do it (or at least, do you realize that there will be consequences if you do not)? The above passage from Deuteronomy is preceded by the exhortation "Hear therefore, O Israel, and be careful to do [what has been spoken to you]" (6:3). Jesus uses the word *hear* the same way, and pronounces a blessing on those who "hear the word of God and keep it" (Lk 11:28; see Lk 8:21).

There is nothing more important than to have God speak to us. We belong to a relatively self-confident human race. We live after centuries of technological development. We can handle more and more of the uncertainties of life, acquire more and more knowledge, power, and comfort. Those of us who are adults with an adequate education, job, financial standing, and home often feel that we can get our lives to go much the way we want them to.

Yet, we also know that tragedy may happen to us or those close to us. We know we are not doing well with our responsibilities in various respects, and the consequences may be bad for us and others. Accidents also may happen at any time. Moreover, even though we resist the thought, we know that a destructive global war that might destroy all we hold dear is still possible. And we all know we will die one day and perhaps become helplessly incapacitated before that. Our lives are still in God's hands and not in our own. We need to hear him.

In the last chapter we considered what it means to say that the Scripture is the Word of God. There are many ways God may "speak" to us: through the words of someone else, through an interior inspiration, even, in a certain sense, through events. Scripture, however, is the normal way God speaks to us as Christians. Properly interpreted, it is the most accessible way that we come to understand who he is, who we are, and what we must do to fulfil the purpose for which he made us.

Scripture is the Word of God in an objective sense. Because it is inspired, because what God wanted to communicate to human beings for their salvation is in it, it is the Word of God. We may not believe it or we may ignore it, but it is still the Word of God. It is like a letter that is unread in our mailbox. Whether we read that letter, understand it, or respond to it, it is objectively a communication to us. And it is there waiting for us.

Cardinal Newman among others spoke of the Scripture as a sacrament. He said:

The Word of God ... cannot be put on the level of other books, as it is now the fashion to do, but has the nature of a Sacrament, which is outward and inward, and a channel of supernatural grace.[1]

In other words, like a sacrament, the Scripture is objectively something given by God, a means of grace. It has an outward material form. In this case, it is seemingly a mere book, perhaps badly printed, even shabby. But it contains the words of the Bible, and those printed words are "a means of grace." They are a means God is prepared to use to convey something very important to us—what he wants to say to us.

In the Gospel of John, at the end of a passage we will discuss further on (Jn 6:63), the Lord speaks to his disciples and teaches something similar. He says,

> It is the spirit that gives life,
> the flesh is of no avail;
> the words that I have spoken to you
> are spirit and life.

In this passage Jesus seems to be speaking about his own words.[2] He is the one sent by God to reveal to us God's plan, the way of salvation. His words are "spirit and life."

Here again we see a manner of speech often found in the Gospel of John. When Jesus says, my words *are* spirit and life, he probably means, my words *give* spirit and life. But by saying "are" he is likely emphasizing that spirit and life are contained in them. Spirit and life come to us with Jesus' words, not just because of what we decide to do with those words, not just because we put faith in those words, but because they are the Word of God in the fullest way. They are the new covenant words of God spoken by the Word of God himself. Spirit and life belong to those words, are in them, regardless of how we receive them or how they affect us.

The Gospel does not use the word ***contained***. Nonetheless, "contained" is commonly used by traditional Christian writers to speak about created realities that are stably joined or connected to God in such a way that his presence or action is always available through them, at least if the necessary conditions are met. It does not mean that God's presence or action is restricted to these things, much less limited by them, or inseparably (exclusively) joined to them. It does, however, mean that his presence or action can be relied upon to be there when these realities are there. Consequently, it is an equivalent of the Johannine use of "is," "are," or "am" in passages like the above.

By "spirit and life" Jesus may mean "spiritual life" and so be saying that his words convey spiritual life. He may also mean "the Spirit of life," the life-giving Spirit, the one we would refer to as the Holy Spirit, and so be saying that his words "contain" the Holy Spirit. He may mean both at the same time, because it is the Spirit who gives life (2 Cor 3:6), and the life he gives is the life of the new covenant, eternal life, true spiritual life. He gives us that life by enlightening our minds when the Word of God is spoken so that we can understand spiritually. As a result when we read or listen to the Scriptures we receive a communication directly from God, one that can bring us to life just as the word of Jesus raised Lazarus from the dead.[3]

Yet, as we know, we do not automatically receive anything when we hear God's Word. When we read the Bible or listen to it, we sometimes "hear" nothing, perhaps because we are distracted, perhaps because we do not understand, perhaps because we do not want to hear. We do not experience grace coming to us, nor do we seem to receive spiritual life. Nothing much happens. The question is, how can we hear the Scriptures so that God speaks to us, so that we hear what he wants us to hear, so that we receive light and life from him?

In this chapter, we will be considering the Liturgy of the Word. The Liturgy of the Word is a ceremony. A *ceremony* (or **rite**) is a complex of words and actions that expresses the importance of something. Some ceremonies are secular. We speak, for instance, of a graduation ceremony. We are here concerned with ceremonies that are intended to honor God or the things of God. A Liturgy of the Word is one of them.[4]

Certainly we can find many people who endure the Liturgy of the Word and hear little or nothing of God's word during it. On certain days, all of us find ourselves in that category. There are even some for whom the services they attend are normally an obstacle. Yet, if we learn the meaning of a Liturgy of the Word and the principles behind it, it can be a help to us.

In this chapter we will first look at some of the spiritual truths that allow us to listen to God's Word well. We will then consider how the Liturgy of the Word is put together on principles drawn from those truths. Our primary purpose is to look at the Liturgy of the Word in the Eucharistic celebration. We can also, however, find Liturgies of the Word in the Liturgy of the Hours and in other services for prayer. We can even "hold our own" Liturgy of the Word in our private prayer. Whenever we listen to the Scripture read or read it ourselves, if we "hear" the Word, it will be a means of grace for us, a source of true spiritual life.

Assembled in Reverence

Word and Covenant

In the last chapter, we considered how God spoke to Moses. In that event, he began the process of delivering his people Israel from the power of Pharaoh "with signs and wonders" and brought them to Sinai (Horeb), "the mountain of God." In Exodus 19–20, we can read the main description of what happened when the children of Israel arrived at Mount Sinai, and that passage illustrates some important truths about how God speaks to human beings.

God began by speaking to Moses to give him a message for his people, an explanation of why he had instructed them to come to this mountain:

> And Moses went up to God, and the Lord called to him out of the mountain, saying,
> > Thus you shall say to the house of Jacob,
> > and tell the people of Israel:
> > You have seen what I did to the Egyptians,
> > and how I bore you on eagles' wings and brought you to myself.
> > Now therefore, if you will obey my voice and keep my covenant,
> > you shall be my own possession among all peoples;
> > for all the earth is mine,
> > and you shall be to me a kingdom of priests and a holy nation.
> > These are the words which you shall speak to the children of Israel.
> So Moses came and called the elders of the people, and set before them all these words which the Lord had commanded him. And all the people answered together and said,
> > All that the Lord has spoken we will do.
> And Moses reported the words of the people to the Lord.

God, in other words, had brought the people of Israel "to himself" by bringing them to Mount Sinai, the place of his special presence on earth. He did so in order to make them into a kingdom and a nation. But they were not to be just any people or nation, like the Egyptians or Canaanites or Assyrians. They were to be a holy nation, that is, a nation that belongs to God himself. And they were to be a kingdom of priests, that is, a nation who worship him in a unified way.

When we think about relationship to God and about the worship of God, we often tend to think in an individualistic manner. The focus is on ourselves and what we personally will receive. The main question is how I can find something good or helpful—grace or salvation from God—or perhaps find a good experience—peace or joy that God might give me. Less often, but still often in an individualistic way, the focus is on how we can relate to God and glorify him. God does relate to us individually, but we can see in the Scriptures that more fundamentally he relates to a people, a corporate body. He even relates to the individuals in that body primarily because they belong to the people.

God briefly stated in the above passage the condition for being his people. The people of Israel had to "hear" his voice and keep his covenant. These are two synonymous phrases that indicate the need to obey what he said. If Israel would be willing to do that, he would explain to them what they would need to do to be his people. The people responded that they were willing.

The Lord then instructed them how he would speak and how they needed to prepare themselves:

And the Lord said to Moses,

Lo, I am coming to you in a thick cloud, that the people may hear when I speak with you, and may also believe you forever.

Go to the people and consecrate them today and tomorrow, and let them wash their garments, and be ready by the third day; for on the third day the Lord will come down upon Mount Sinai in the sight of all the people.

And you shall set bounds for the people round about, saying to them,

Take heed that you do not go up into the mountain or touch the border of it; whoever touches the mountain shall be put to death; no hand shall touch him, but he shall be stoned or shot; whether beast or man, he shall not live.

When the trumpet sounds a long blast, they shall come up to the mountain.

The Lord, in other words, was going to do something similar to what he did when he appeared to Moses in the burning bush. He was going to show his presence to his people so that they would know that he was speaking to them. But they would have to be ready. Just as Moses had to keep his distance and take his shoes off, they would have to stay away from the mountain and would have to purify themselves so that they would be in the right condition.

Then God manifested himself to the people:

On the morning of the third day there were thunders and lightnings, and a thick cloud upon the mountain, and a very loud trumpet blast, so that all the people who were in the camp trembled. Then Moses brought the people out of the camp to meet God; and they took their stand at the foot of the mountain. And Mount Sinai was wrapped in smoke, because the Lord descended upon it in fire; and the smoke of it went up like the smoke of a kiln, and the whole mountain quaked greatly. And as the sound of the trumpet grew louder and louder, Moses spoke, and God answered him in thunder. And the Lord came down upon Mount Sinai, to the top of the mountain; and the Lord called Moses to the top of the mountain, and Moses went up.

According to this description, God's manifestation on the mountain must have been spectacular. Sinai, although not a volcano, looked something like one erupting. There was a tremendously loud noise, a kind of prolonged trumpet blast, and a pillar of cloud and fire came down upon the mountain. The mountain seemed like it was burning up, with cloud and flames heading to the sky. At the same time there was an earthquake that shook the whole mountain.

At that point the people of Israel must have been very glad that God had told them to keep their distance. They would not have survived coming closer into his presence. They may even have preferred it had he told them to stand in a different valley.

Then God spoke to them. According to Exodus, they actually heard a voice speak out of the mountain. There are very few places in the Scriptures where people hear the Word of God except by means of a human intermediary. At Sinai his word apparently came directly:[5]

I am the Lord your God, who brought you out of the land of Egypt, out of the house of bondage.
You shall have no other gods before me.
You shall not make for yourself a graven image, or any likeness of anything that is in heaven above, or that is in the earth beneath, or that is in the water under the earth; you shall not bow down to them or serve them....
You shall not take the name of the Lord your God in vain....
Remember the sabbath day, to keep it holy.

We know the rest. These are what we would call the Ten Commandments, summarized by Jesus in the two great commandments of love of God and love of neighbor.

The later account of this same event in the Book of Deuteronomy (Dt 4:11-14) gives another description of what happened:

You came near and stood at the foot of the mountain, while the mountain burned with fire to the heart of heaven, wrapped in darkness, cloud, and gloom. Then the Lord spoke to you out of the midst of the fire; you heard the sound of words, but saw no form; there was only a voice. And he declared to you his covenant, which he commanded you to perform, that is, the ten commandments; and he wrote them upon two tables of stone. And the Lord commanded me at that time to teach you statutes and ordinances, that you might do them in the land which you are going over to possess.

This second description makes even clearer that in giving them the "Ten Commandments" God was giving his people a covenant. He promised to be their God and told them what they would have to do to be his people. They would have to keep the Ten Commandments. They would have to follow the way of life that can be summarized by "love of God and love of neighbor." God gave them the covenant, in short, by telling them what they would have to do to be in relationship with him.

God's offer of the covenant with the subsequent response of the people was similar to what we would call "the exchange of vows" during a marriage ceremony, the time when a marriage covenant is finally established. Both parties commit themselves to a faithful relationship of a certain sort. In this case, however, we are not looking at a mutual contract, a negotiated agreement among equals. God offers the covenant and establishes the content of it. The people simply accept the offer by committing themselves to be faithful to it. The result, however, to use a phrase repeated often in the Scriptures is, "I will be your God and you will be my people" (Jer 31:33; Ez 36:28).

God's word made the covenant relationship possible. If the people of Israel had not heard his word, they would not have understood what was going on. They would have been impressed with "the fireworks." But they could not have entered into a committed, covenantal relationship with him and become his people.

God spoke to his people when they were assembled together. He did not speak to them individually, so that when they came together they discovered that they all had heard the same thing. The account of "the assembly at Sinai" makes that very clear. The rest of the Scriptures illustrate the same principle:

God normally does not give his revelation to individuals for themselves but for a people assembled together as a whole or by subgroups. Although he speaks through individual prophets or preachers, his message is usually delivered to bodies of people gathered together. This is true not only for the old covenant but for the new as well.

Reverence for God

There are conditions for entering into a relationship with God. Those conditions make clear that we are not looking at an equal partnership. The relationship is not symmetrical, to use a technical term. God has to be honored and respected as God. The first commandment (or two commandments by the reckoning of the Reformed and most Eastern Churches) makes that clear. We need to "worship and serve" God as God—and no one else and nothing else. Only the one true God, the God of Abraham, Isaac, and Jacob, only he is to be related to as God.

"Worship" and "serve" are two words that are rough synonyms. They both can be used for honoring some being as a god, and therefore honoring the one true God as God. We will return to the meaning of "serving" God shortly. Here we will just consider "worshiping" him.

The Hebrew and Greek words for *worship*[6] mean to bow down to or prostrate oneself before. They refer to a physical action that is a way of acknowledging someone's position. An Israelite might bow down to or prostrate himself before a king, for instance, to show that he accepted that man as his king. To do so was to make a sign of submission and a pledge of obedience.

Of course, the first commandment(s) instructs us that we are not to submit to any being as God other than the one true God. This includes the most powerful of kings. Therefore when a given action is meant to express that we are accepting some other being as God, or could be interpreted that way, we are strictly to avoid it. We may show, for instance, by a bow or curtsey that we respect and submit to a king, but not if that sign of submission is taken to indicate that we are submitting to him as a god. In English now we would normally reserve "worship" for the sign of respect given to a god.

The word translated by many versions of the Scripture as "worship" is translated by others as "adore." Some use that term for a type of prayer, often a wordless prayer, in which we "contemplate" God. That usage, however, although helpful in certain contexts, loses much of the scriptural and traditional theological meaning and so is usually avoided now in translations of the Bible.

In the Scriptures, then, "worship" or "adoration" involves an outward expression of the fact that we recognize God as God and that we are submitting to him as our Lord, as the highest authority in our life. The physical or verbal expression of that fact in prayer expresses an inner reality. The inner reality is realized most fully when we "hear" his word, that is, when we hear it as God's word, and, because it is his word, we accept it fully—by believing it and obeying it.

The chief response to the one being we accept as God is to believe and obey him above all, to submit to him precisely as God, the sovereign creator of the universe. But a divorce between inner and outer worship is foreign to Scripture, as well as to most Jewish and Christian tradition. Because we are human beings, we should express our submission to God as God outwardly by some words and gestures when we are prepared to inwardly submit to him by truly hearing his word.

Worship of God is associated with hearing God's word with fear. The proclamation of the angel in the Book of Revelation is "Fear God and give him glory!" (Rv 14:7). By *fear* we would probably mainly understand "being afraid of" him, afraid that he will hurt us or punish us. Such fear, of course, is never completely out of place in relation to God. As the people of Israel must have realized when they watched Mount Sinai go up in cloud and flames and shake to its roots, God can be very dangerous, and we need to know that he is willing to receive us before getting too close. As he said in the Book of Jeremiah (Jer 30:21), "Who would dare of himself to approach me?" Moreover, from the beginning to the end of the Scripture he has assured us that punishment for disobedience will never be outdated.

But the English word "fear" does not communicate the whole meaning. The Hebrew word is sometimes translated **reverence**.[7] That too is a form of fear. When we appreciate the greatness of God, when we appreciate the fact that he has created us out of nothing, when we appreciate his holiness of character, his pure goodness, we should want to reverence him. We should "fear" to treat him as we would any other being. We should desire to interiorly regard him as the one worthy of fullest honor and respect, as God, next to whom we are nothing. The English word "reverence" normally conveys not only fear of bad consequences but, even more, inner recognition of the way God, or other beings, is greater than we are, and a readiness to respond out of such a recognition. From our inner reverence should come any outward worship.

Reverence, then, puts us into the condition that allows us to hear God. It is the interior attitude that orients us rightly in relationship to God's word. We cannot truly hear God's word without recognizing that it is the word of the creator of the universe and that we need to believe and obey whatever he says simply because he says it. Among all the many things that come our way in the flood of information and communication nowadays, we have to pick out those things that truly are words from God and give them reverent attention.[8]

Old Covenant and New Covenant Worship

There was a time not very long ago when Christians of all kinds—Catholic, Orthodox, and Protestant alike—understood their response to God the same way. They knew that the commandments were to be kept, God's word attended to with reverence, worship to be performed with solemnity and care. Now a casualness often enters into people's interactions with God. Obedience has been forgotten. God's approachability is stressed in an unqualified way.

Behind such attitudes is often a loss of respect for the Old Testament. According to some, the God of fear, the distant God, is the God of the Old Testament. Jesus has come and changed all that. For all practical purposes, he has canceled the Old Testament. Yet, according to a passage we have already looked at, "All scripture is inspired by God and profitable for teaching, for reproof, for correction, and for training in righteousness, that the man of God may be complete, equipped for every good work" (2 Tm 3:16-17). "Scripture" here must refer to the Old Testament writings, because the New Testament had not yet been completed and put into a book.

In Hebrews 12:18-29 we have a New Testament commentary on the Exodus passage about the Sinai assembly that we have looked at. The commentary gives us a summary of the relationship between the old covenant and the new covenant and helps us to see that reverence is appropriate to both:

For you have not come to what may be touched, a blazing fire, and darkness, and gloom, and a tempest, and the sound of a trumpet, and a voice whose words made the hearers entreat that no further messages be spoken to them. For they could not endure the order that was given, "If even a beast touches the mountain, it shall be stoned" [Ex 19:12-13]. Indeed, so terrifying was the sight that Moses said, "I tremble with fear." But you have come to Mount Zion and to the city of the living God, the heavenly Jerusalem, and to innumerable angels in festal gathering, and to the assembly of the first-born who are enrolled in heaven, and to a judge who is God of all, and to the spirits of just men made perfect, and to Jesus, the mediator of a new covenant, and to the sprinkled blood that speaks more graciously than the blood of Abel.

See that you do not refuse him who is speaking. For if they did not escape when they refused him who warned them on earth, much less shall we escape if we reject him who warns from heaven. His voice then shook the earth; but now he has promised, "Yet once more I will shake not only the earth but also the heaven" [Hag 2:6]. This phrase, "Yet once more," indicates the removal of what is shaken, as of what has been made, in order that what cannot be shaken may remain. Therefore let us be grateful for receiving a kingdom that cannot be shaken, and thus let us offer to God acceptable worship, with reverence and awe; for our God is a consuming fire [Dt 4:24].

Perhaps the most common word in the New Testament for the relationship between the old covenant and the new covenant is "fulfillment." The new covenant replaces the old covenant not by simply canceling it, much less rejecting it, but by fulfilling it. This seems to mean that the new covenant brings about the intended purpose of the old covenant, but in a fuller or more perfect way.

The Letter to the Hebrews speaks of the relationship in a different way. According to Hebrews, the new covenant takes old covenant realities and makes them better (Heb 8:6). The change does not involve destroying something bad, like idol worship, but taking something good and making it better, that is, spiritually more effective (Heb 7:19; Heb 10:1). That, of course, means that certain externals, like the temple sacrifices, are not retained, but what replaces them accomplishes the same fundamental purpose in a better way and could be seen as a continuation or development of the old.

The focus in the Book of Hebrews is on worship. The worship of the old covenant is replaced by a better worship, one that establishes a better relationship with God. The passage in Hebrews 12:18-29 begins with a contrast. It says Christians have not come to "what may be touched." Then follows a description of the appearance of God on Mount Sinai that we already looked at. It is clear that Hebrews sees that event as an instance of "what may be touched," because it was an appearance of God on earth, in a location in the Middle East.

In the new covenant, however, we come to the heavenly Jerusalem. It is heavenly and not earthly. That potentially could be understood in an unhelpful way. "Heaven" could be seen as something that is even farther away from us.

At least we can travel to the earthly Jerusalem in order to come close to God, even if we could only manage to do so once in our lives. But the Book of Hebrews is making the point that we have a better relationship with God because we can come to heaven itself every day of our lives. Paradoxical as it may seem, through the new covenant we have direct access to the place of God's presence in heaven and therefore can join with all the angels and saints in the worship of God at any time.

We can come to heaven because of what our Lord Jesus Christ has done. He has offered the true sacrifice which replaces all the old covenant ones. He has "sprinkled us with his blood" in a rite of purification that allows us to be received by God because it merits the grace of God. As a result we have a new covenant, a new atonement, and consequently a new access to God's presence.

The old covenant knew what faith was. When the New Testament teaches about faith in passages like Hebrews 11 or Romans 4, the teaching is based on Old Testament passages. But faith has a new importance in the new covenant because we come into a new relationship with God through what Christ has done for us. That we receive by accepting the gospel in faith. New covenant relationship to God and new covenant worship, then, are most fundamentally based upon faith, specifically faith in Christ and in what comes to us through his priestly mediation.

There is an interior change that goes along with our new relationship with God in Christ. Quoting the prophet Jeremiah (Jer 31:31-34), the Book of Hebrews tells us that the law of God will be put inside of us, in our minds and hearts (8:8-13; 10:15-18). Hebrews here is speaking about the same reality that other New Testament books describe as the outpouring of the Holy Spirit. As a result of this change we know God more directly (8:11) and can hear him when he speaks.

According to the passage we have been looking at (Hebrews 12:18-29), faith in Christ should produce in us not less but greater reverence for God and his word. Precisely because we have been spoken to by the Son of God himself who came from heaven and is now seated at the right hand of God the Father on the throne of God (Heb 1:1-4), we should listen with even greater reverence (12:25). Precisely because we have been given a more secure inheritance, a kingdom that will remain when all that is earthly, including the old covenant order, will be taken away, we should hear what has been said to us with greater earnestness (12:26-28) lest we lose that inheritance. Precisely because we have been brought into a closer relationship with God as his sons and daughters, we should approach our heavenly Father with even greater respect (12:9).

As a result, we should worship God with reverence and awe (12:28). Faith in Christ does not eliminate the need for reverence in worship; it increases it. We are now standing in the heavenly presence of the God who manifested himself as a fire on Mount Sinai because he *is* a consuming fire (Dt 4:24). We therefore have to offer worship to him in the way that is acceptable to him. The new covenant should bring greater conviction, greater thankfulness, but also greater obedience and greater reverence.

Liturgy of the Word

Liturgy and Word

The Lord told Pharaoh through Moses to let the Israelites leave Egypt "that they may serve me" (Ex 8:1). The commandment against idolatry, as we have seen, forbids worshiping and serving idols and therefore, by implication, commands worshiping and serving God. Jewish teaching speaks of idolatry as "the service of idols,"⁹ and when it wishes to refer to honoring the true God speaks about "the service of God." *Service*, then, is a word that can be a synonym of "worship" and that can be used for honoring a god as divine and therefore for honoring the one true God. It can refer to all the ceremonies that honor God as God, and especially to sacrifice.

Liturgy is a Greek word brought into English. The Greek word was used in the Greek Bible to translate the Hebrew word for service. It commonly referred to the ceremonies performed in the temple to honor God as God. The Book of Hebrews tells us that Christ "did liturgy" in his ministry as a priest (Heb 10:11-13). "Liturgy" then is service of God, a way of honoring God as God.¹⁰

In the Catholic Church, it is common to speak about the Liturgy of the Word to refer to the first part of the Eucharistic celebration (see the outline on p. 27). That phrase emphasizes that we take part in order to serve God, to worship him. We are present, in other words, to honor him as God, and central to that is hearing his Word reverently.¹¹

The clearest description of a "Liturgy of the Word" in the Scriptures occurs in the eighth chapter of the Book of Nehemiah (Neh 7:53–8:18). After the people of Israel returned from exile, they had a struggle to reestablish their life. Some of that struggle was physical and was partly overcome by rebuilding the walls of Jerusalem to avoid being at the mercy of hostile neighbors. The more important struggle was spiritual and was partly overcome by rebuilding the temple.

God could be worshiped in the rebuilt temple. External worship, however, would only be pleasing to God if it came out of a life of obedience and if it were done in the way God wanted, a way that was acceptable to him. By the time of Nehemiah 8, the people who had returned to the land of Israel had rebuilt the temple, but they apparently did not have much knowledge of God's commandments about worshiping him. Those who knew those things, those, as we might put it, educated in theology, were still living in Babylon.

One of them, perhaps the most important one, was Ezra, "a scribe skilled in the law of Moses which the Lord the God of Israel had given" (Ezr 7:6). Realizing the need in the land of Israel, he "went up" from Babylonia to Jerusalem with a party of priests and Levites. Some time after his arrival, he held an assembly of all the Israelites living in Palestine to read and explain the law to them, so that they might carry it out.

By the time of Ezra there was a written text of the Law of God. The exiles believed it had been "given by God" through Moses. In other words, during the assembly they listened to "Holy Scriptures." They were, therefore, attending a Liturgy of the Word, a worship service centering upon the reading of the written Word of God.

The beginning of the assembly is described this way:

And all the people gathered as one man into the square before the Water Gate; and they told Ezra the scribe to bring the book of the law of Moses which the Lord had given to Israel. And Ezra the priest brought the law before the assembly, both men and women and all who could hear with understanding, on the first day of the seventh month. And he read from it facing the square before the Water Gate from early morning until midday, in the presence of the men and the women and those who could understand; and the ears of all the people were attentive to the book of the law.

And Ezra the scribe stood on a wooden pulpit which they had made for the purpose; and beside him stood Mattithiah, Shema, [and others]. And Ezra opened the book in the sight of all the people, for he was above all the people; and when he opened it all the people stood. And Ezra blessed the Lord, the great God; and all the people answered, "Amen, Amen," lifting up their hands; and they bowed their heads and worshiped the Lord with their faces to the ground. Also Jeshua, Bani, [and others], the Levites, helped the people to understand the law, while the people remained in their places. And they read from the book, from the law of God, clearly; and they gave the sense, so that the people understood the reading.

NEHEMIAH 8:1-8

A group of God's people were here assembled or gathered for the purpose of hearing the Word of God. They were to respond in a united way in the assembly, but even more importantly that response was to change their life as a people thereafter. Since the people came together so that God could speak to them "as one," as a people, a corporate body, they were assembled before God solemnly, in a way that showed that they were one people ("one man"). They were therefore drawn up in order, with the priests and Levites, the ministers or religious officials of the body, on a raised platform and the people below.

They began with a time of praise and worship. The people stood. Ezra praised God on their behalf, blessing him for his goodness. A summary of the kind of prayer he prayed can be found later on in this section of the Book of Nehemiah (Neh 9:5):

Blessed be your glorious name which is exalted above all blessing and praise.

The people answered Ezra's prayer, "Amen, amen," while lifting their hands toward heaven. In this context *Amen*, the Hebrew word we still use, means, "It is so; it is true; we too make this prayer." Responding to the prayer with "Amen" indicates accepting what has been said as something we too pray.[12] They then bowed down and worshiped the Lord in humility, ready for what he would say through the reading of the Scriptures.

The text of the Scripture was then read. The text was read as the Word of God, something the people should obey as soon as they understood it. The people listened and after, as we saw in the last chapter, received an interpretation of what had been said, not only a translation of the words but also instruction in their meaning. Judging from what happened some days later, they then concluded with a petition for God's mercy and help and with a pledge to "keep the covenant" (Neh 9:38ff).

The outline of the meeting Ezra led has the same elements as our Liturgy of the Word. It includes an initial worship of God, a time of solemnly listening to his written Word, some kind of interpretation, and a response. In this case the response was a pledge of repentance, but often it could be simply a prayer that what was read about be fulfilled. These four elements have normally been present in Jewish and Christian worship services from that time until now.

The service described in Nehemiah is similar to what happened on Mount Sinai, although at Sinai there was no written text. Important for our topic, the service was also much the same as what the Jews did every Sabbath in their synagogue services at the time of Christ and the apostles. We find a description of such synagogue liturgies in the New Testament. We can read, for instance, in Luke 4:16-22 about Jesus attending synagogue at his hometown, reading a selection from the prophet Isaiah and then commenting upon it afterwards. We can also read in Acts 13:14-15 of Paul and his companions visiting a synagogue in Antioch of Pisidia, where the law and the prophets were read, and of how they were invited to give the "word of exhortation" (the homily) afterwards.

The early Christians, who were at first all Jews, continued to have such services. In the Letter of James we read of Christians, possibly Jewish Christians, having "synagogue services" (RSV: assemblies). We have already looked at one such service that occurred during Paul's visit to Troas in Acts 20:7-12. Later on we will look at the pattern the Christians followed right after Pentecost (Acts 2:42, 46). We will also look at Jesus' appearance to the disciples at Emmaus, which seems to take the pattern of a Christian worship service beginning with a Liturgy of the Word (Lk 24:13-35). As we shall also see, there is even some possibility that the opening vision of the unfolding of God's plan in Revelation describes a heavenly "liturgy of the word," with the scroll containing a "reading" from God (Rv 4–5). There are, in addition, many other references to the assembly of Christians that show the same elements (see Appendix 1).

Our phrase *Liturgy of the Word* refers to a service of this pattern. When we use it, we refer to a service centered upon hearing God's word through the reading of the Scriptures and the explanation of them. Such a service is, however, conducted as a liturgy, not as a lecture or a discussion or a "Bible study." It is conducted as an act of prayer and worship, usually with worship preceding the readings and prayer following. A liturgy of the word is done, in other words, in a manner that honors God and expresses the fact that those who are listening to his word are people who live for his glory and seek to express appropriate honor to him. It is also done as a corporate ceremony, a gathering of some body of God's people who are listening to his word together and honoring him in common as their God.

Our Liturgy of the Word

We now have to look more directly at our own worship services. In what follows, we will seek to focus on the "common principles" of liturgies of the word in all the rites of the Catholic Church. There are, however, distinctive features from rite to rite, and we will consider some of them where helpful.

The opening prayer and worship. As with the Jews and the early Christians, the services that we call liturgies of the word begin with a time of praise and worship. Western Catholics sometimes do not realize that, because the "opening ceremonies" of Roman rite Eucharistic celebrations (Masses) are very brief. Ideally, however, a Eucharistic celebration should be preceded by a longer prayer service from the Liturgy of the Hours. Moreover, in most Eastern liturgies, not only does a prayer service precede the Eucharistic celebration, but the opening ceremonies begin with lengthier prayers to praise God and ask for his mercy.

The initial time of worship includes various hymns and prayers. It includes prayers of repentance, like the *Confiteor* (I confess ...) in the Roman rite, because they are prayers that acknowledge our submission to God, express the fact that our failures in obedience do not indicate the state of our heart, and seek his forgiveness so that he will bless us with his grace during the service. It also includes hymns and prayers of praise, because Jewish and Christian worship normally begins by lifting our minds and hearts to heaven and praising God for his greatness and goodness. As Nicholas Cabasilas, the fourteenth-century Byzantine theologian, put it in his *Commentary on the Divine Liturgy,* 12,

> In doxology we lay aside ourselves and all our interests and glorify the Lord for his own sake, for his power and his glory. And so the very nature and the appropriateness of the act demand that the doxology should come first.

While we often approach these "set prayers" somewhat routinely, preparatory prayer is spiritually important. Where God is truly acknowledged and worshiped, he gives his blessing (Ex 20:24). Likewise, when we set our minds and hearts on God, we are opened spiritually to receive his presence and his word. Renewal in liturgical worship has to begin with preparation for the service.

Honor to the Scriptures. In the Byzantine liturgy, before the readings the book containing the Scriptures is brought to the center of the church in front of the altar in a procession and is "enthroned." This is called "the Little Entrance" (see the outline on p. 27), as distinguished from another ceremonial "entrance" later on in the ceremony. During the procession a hymn is chanted, most commonly,

Come let us worship and bow down to Christ. O son of God, who rose from the dead, save us who chant to you: Alleluia.

These ceremonies express the fact that the Scriptures contain the Word of God, and therefore the coming of the Scriptures is a coming of Christ.

In this ceremony and others like it, the Eastern liturgies have preserved the customs of the early Christians, at least in the patristic period. Such ceremonies are also being revived in the Western Church. The early Christians expressed honor for the physical presence of the Scriptures. They did so in the liturgy, but also whenever the Scriptures were present. It was a book containing the Scriptures that was placed on the altar to represent the presence of Christ in the Church throughout the day. For the same reason the Scriptures were also often enthroned in homes wealthy enough to have a copy.

Starting about 1150 in the West (late in Christian tradition), people began to pay honor to the Eucharistic elements the way they previously had honored the Scriptures: carrying them in procession, exposing them for veneration, putting them in a central place in the church (often on the altar), and showing outward signs of reverence to them by genuflecting and bowing. This practice gradually almost completely displaced the earlier honor given to the book of Scriptures in the Western Church. Traditionally, however, honoring the actual Bible has been the most common way of honoring the presence of Christ in our midst.

The main honor that should be paid the Scriptures is to hear them and obey them as the Word of God. The external expression of honor to the book, however, is important, because it forces us as human beings to realize what we think of the Scriptures inside. Nowadays we may even find Bibles propping up something on a desk or sitting in the bathroom "for convenience." When we treat the external book in such ways, we are less likely to be conscious that the written words inside actually contain, actually are, the Word of God.

The reading. Next, the Word of God, the Scriptures, is read. It is read solemnly, that is, reverently and carefully, because in the Scriptures God is objectively present through his Word. The reading of the Scriptures is "sacramental" and should be approached in a way similar to the distribution of Communion. In both, the Bread of Life is given out to feed God's people.[13]

In every service a selection of the Scriptures is read. It is impractical to read the whole Scripture at one sitting, but even if we could do so, we would not be able to receive what was read. The Scriptures are written for many readings and for many kinds of readings on different occasions. They are, however, telling us about one truth: the love of God which comes to us through Christ by the power of the Holy Spirit and which allows us to have true spiritual life and so fulfil the purpose for which we have been made by loving God and loving our neighbor.

Each reading of Scripture, from Genesis to Revelation, then, is meant to let us see an aspect of one truth, the truth that is sometimes called the "mystery of Christ" (Eph 3:4, 9):[14] the presence of God in the world in our Lord Jesus Christ by the Holy Spirit. We are to meditate on the Scripture section by section throughout the year to renew our understanding of the truth that has been shown us and to renew our faithfulness to what has been commanded us. But we should do so in a way that brings us back to the one truth and a deepening personal relationship with the one true God.

The order of readings emphasizes the selection that is taken from the Gospels. This is "the Good News," the Word of God that tells us the Good News about our Lord Jesus Christ. Even more, it contains the words of Christ, God made flesh. Therefore, we give the reading of the Gospel the highest honor because it is the Lord himself speaking to us, not through a messenger like an angel or a prophet or an apostle but in person.

God does not speak his word without giving his Spirit. The words of the Scriptures are objectively the inspired Word of God, but it is the Holy Spirit who works through the reading of the Word to give us light. "It is the God who said, 'Let light shine out of darkness,' who has shone in our hearts to give the light of the knowledge of the glory of God in the face of Christ" (2 Cor 4:6). Stored away on a shelf, the Bible still is the Word of God. Only, however, when it is spoken to human beings, either by a reader during the liturgy or by ourselves when we read it or recite it from memory, does God actually speak to us through it.

The homily. A homily follows the reading of the Scripture. It is now, among Western Catholics at least, common to distinguish between a sermon and a homily. A *sermon* is any Christian instruction or speech about an important occasion in the life of the church (perhaps the installation of the parish council or a national holiday). A *homily* is a talk that interprets the Scripture and helps us to hear it. As the instruction *Inaestimabile Donum* puts it, "The purpose of the homily is to explain to the faithful the Word of God proclaimed in the readings, and to apply its message to the present."[15]

The homily is supposed to be the most common kind of "talk" in a Liturgy of the Word, even though at times other things need to take precedence. It is liturgical worship and fosters the sacramental nature of the reading of the Word. The homilist is to be "a good minister of Christ Jesus" (1 Tm 4:6), someone who serves him in solemn worship.

The written Word is supposed to be interpreted for people who live many years after it was written. Nowadays it does not need to be translated right after it is read, as in the time of Ezra or the Jewish synagogues in the first century, because we read written translations. Its meaning, however, does need to be made clear, both the sense of the words and the things they refer to (1 Tm 1:6–7), and even more what God is saying to us in our times and circumstances.

To give a homily, then, is a spiritual activity. It is supposed to come out of study, especially study of the Fathers and the tradition of the church, so that the Scriptures may be understood by God's people as they have been understood by the Church throughout the centuries. The homily should be born of a spiritual investigation. The homilist should seek to have God work in his own understanding and then help him direct and apply the light he has received to those who will listen.

It has traditionally been said that the homilist (or preacher) should "seek an anointing" or should speak "with unction (anointing)." Too often that phrase has been understood in terms of his ability to speak with enough force and liveliness to stir a response in those listening. Useful as that is, in fact "unction" or "anointing" mainly refers to the ability to make a spiritual connection between the Word of God and those who listen. However much good speaking ability may be helpful, it does not automatically impart spiritual light and truth.

Still more fundamental, however, is submission to God in his Word. If the homilist does not have the conviction that he is explaining and applying the Word of God, he cannot give a true homily. The homilist is not supposed to be teaching "the theology of Paul" or "the mentality of the pre-exilic Israelites," unless considering these helps in receiving what God wishes to say through the text. To do such things, as the Danish philosopher Soren Kierkegaard once said in a famous example, is like standing before a mirror and looking at the surface of the glass rather than using the glass to see our face. Even less should the homilist use the text as an occasion to purvey popular philosophy or societal values. If he himself is not convinced that the most important thing in life is to believe and obey the Word of God, he will not be successful in giving a homily.

The whole. Many will be tempted to think that while the above describes what the liturgy should be, it is not a description of the actual liturgies we attend. Sometimes it is, often it is not. We will consider the question of how to respond to the actual liturgies we attend in a later chapter. Here it is enough to say that while the Scripture is read, and while we ourselves hear it in faith and obedience, God is present through his Word, even when what is going on around us is not much help, or even a distraction.

Because of attitudes our modern culture gives us, most of us are tempted to go off alone and worship God by ourselves. This is especially our tendency when we think of understanding God's Word. Many of us find solitary study, alone with our Bibles, concordances, and commentaries, the most fruitful way of acquiring knowledge of the Bible.

We are, however, intended to listen to God's Word together. We can and should listen to God's Word at home alone. To do only that would, however, not make us a Christian community, a people, a Church. Only when we listen to him together, with others, presided over by someone who leads us corporately, can we be united in the common understanding that allows us to be one people. We are not supposed to be a group of people who can simply engage in some common activities together, for whatever reason each of us individually decides he or she wants to do so. We are supposed to be "one in heart [mind, mentality] and soul" (Acts 4:32). We are supposed to be together because we believe the same truths about reality and want to keep the same commandments of God, understood in the same way. A Liturgy of the Word is designed to express such a response to God.

Ideally we should be part of parishes that are communities. Now, however, most Catholic parishes are oriented toward caring for all the people in their geographical limits to the extent that those people are ready to receive care. Such an approach to parish structure is perhaps the best way at the moment to help as many as possible to find life in Christ. However, especially in urban areas, it rarely produces communities of Christians who live as one in mind and in heart and experience together unity in the Spirit.

It is therefore no accident that throughout the world in the Catholic Church today there are growing Christian communities that are not simply parochial communities.[16] Such communities are most often united around the presence of Christ in their midst by a Liturgy of the Word. There God himself can be truly present even when there cannot be a Liturgy of the Eucharist, normally reserved for the whole parish. There subgroups of the broader people can be united in their response to God's Word, and so begin to renew the communal life of God's people.

If we come before the Lord in faith, in the name of the Father and of the Son and of the Holy Spirit, he is present with us, because he is with his people when they honor him. He is also present with us because it is his Word that we read, and it is truly his Word, independently of how we respond to him. He is, however, always and everywhere present to his people, because he is alive and desires to speak to us so that we might understand the mystery of Christ in which we have true life. If we respond to him in reverence, if we receive his Word in faith, he will act in us spiritually and give us light and life.

Meditation: *The Light of the World*
John 9:1-41

The Gospel of John tells us about a miracle Jesus performed when he was at Jerusalem for the Feast of Tabernacles. He was walking through the streets of the city when he saw a man who was blind from birth. His disciples called Jesus' attention to the blind man and took the occasion to ask him why the man was born blind.

Jesus' answer was surprising to them. He said that it was by God's special decision that this man was blind. God intended to use his blindness to show the world that he was working through Jesus, the Christ he sent into the world. "I am the light of the world," Jesus said, "and it was for this that the Father sent me."

Jesus spat on the ground and made clay out of the dirt. He then, the Gospel says, "anointed the man's eyes with the clay" and sent him off to wash in the pool of Siloam, which could be translated the pool called "Sent." When the man came back, he could see.

It was the neighbors, the ones who knew him from birth and who had seen him sitting at the edge of the street begging for so many years, who were the most surprised when they saw him come home. They knew him, yet he looked so different because he could see and walk like a normal person. Some of them could not even believe it was the same person. But he himself talked to them, assuring them that he was the one they knew. It must have been clear to them that he was, even though such a change seemed to be impossible. He explained to them that he had been healed by a man called Jesus, but he did not seem to know who Jesus was or how to find him.

They then brought him to scribes who were Pharisees, religious teachers who should have been able to explain how to approach the situation. They asked the man how he had received his sight, and he said, "He put clay on my eyes, and I washed, and I see." The Pharisees had, for the most part, rejected Jesus, and these Pharisees were skeptical once they heard the story and probably, along with it, the name of the healer. They objected, as they had before, to the fact that he had healed someone on the Sabbath rather than waiting to the next day when he would not be violating the commandment to rest on the Sabbath.

They could not, however, quite agree on what to think. They ended up in a discussion about the matter, much like discussions we sometimes observe among people who do not accept Christianity but cannot agree on what is wrong with it. Some of these Pharisaic scribes simply held that Jesus could not have been from God because he did not keep one of the Ten Commandments. Others could not accept that view, because the miracle seemed too impressive for God to allow if the person who performed it simply despised his commandments.

The discussion with the Pharisees seemed to bring greater understanding to the man born blind. As he listened, he came to a personal conviction. Jesus must be a prophet like Elijah. He must be someone who was sent by God.

The Jewish leaders then investigated further. They decided to see if there might be some fraud in the matter. Many beggars who seemingly were blind could actually see and only pretended to be blind. So they called in his parents as witnesses, probably trying to put them under oath. His parents, however, were wary. They knew that the Jewish authorities would take action against anyone who confessed that Jesus was the Messiah, the Christ. They dodged the question by saying, "He is of age. Let him speak for himself."

The Jewish leaders therefore had a second discussion with the man born blind. Using their authority as Jewish teachers, they insisted that Jesus was not from God. The man born blind, however, knew what had happened to him. He had been blind from birth; now he could see; and Jesus had been the one who gave him sight. He was convinced that Jesus was from God. His insistence, however, only had the result of provoking the scribes into excommunicating him.

Jesus heard what had happened. He then found the man and spoke to him. He asked him if he believed in the Son of Man, the heavenly figure spoken about in the Book of Daniel who was to come on the clouds to judge the world (Dn 7:13-14). The man seemed to comprehend that believing in the Son of

Man had something to do with the fact that he himself had been healed, and maybe with his hope of staying healed. He then responded, probably asking where he could find this Son of Man:

And who is he, sir, that I may believe in him?
Jesus answered:
You have seen him, and it is he who is now speaking to you.
The man then said,
Lord, I believe.
He then worshiped Jesus.

The miracle Jesus performed was not just a wonder, a demonstration of power. It was a sign, a sign of what Jesus was about. It was a sign that was performed within this material world and at the same time pointed to something spiritual, something about new covenant life in the Spirit. Certain details were included as part of the account so that we might understand the meaning of the sign.

The man's blindness points to the blindness of fallen human beings. Fallen human beings need revelation from God in order to understand what human life is about. But in order to even receive revelation when it is given to them, they need something spiritual to happen first.

The inborn human blindness needs to be healed by having Jesus put on an ointment that he himself makes as he made an ointment from ordinary dirt to heal the blind man. The ointment is an image of his word, a material sound that he makes by the breath of his mouth, but even more by the Holy Spirit. When Jesus speaks his word to human beings and they are touched by the Holy Spirit, they then can see spiritual truth, if they receive that word with faith in him.

The pool Jesus sent the man to was called "Sent." It too seems to be symbolic, in this case of Baptism, where people are immersed in water "into Christ," the one sent by God, and as a result are given light, a spiritual enlightening. He is the Light of the world. He is, in fact, the true Light that has come into the world, so that as he becomes present in us, he shines into our darkness and we receive the Light of God (Jn 1:4-9).

For those preparing for Baptism, as with the man born blind, this story has one meaning. Instruction in the Word of God brings people to faith in Jesus and makes it possible for Baptism to immerse them into Christ. It brings spiritual enlightenment (Heb 6:4), and with that a capacity to receive new life. The story, then, concerns the way becoming a Christian cures spiritual blindness.

For those of us who have been already baptized, however, the truths are similar but the application is different. Some of us who have sat year after year listening to the reading of the Word of God and discussion about it but who have only gotten as far as to say that we have a conviction that Jesus must be from God need more. We need something that will bring us to the point where we can say we have personally received light from God and an experiential knowledge of spiritual truth. We need to be helped to a spiritually more effective faith.

Some of us, however, have received spiritual knowledge of the truth which is in Jesus. We now need to be able to hear the Word of God each Sunday in the Eucharistic celebration and in our regular Scripture reading in such a way that it brings us light, spiritual knowledge of God and the things of God. We need to be able to receive the Word of God in a way that is effective in giving us more and more spiritual life. We need to read it spiritually and learn how to do so in an ongoing way, not just from time to time.

Further on, we will consider more fully how God leads us to fuller spiritual experience. For all of us, however, the truths that make the needed difference are basically the same. We need to hear God's Word, not just listen to it. Like the man born blind, we need to put faith in it and listen with the conviction that this is not just the word of men but the words of God himself. And we need to worship the Lord as he speaks to us. We need to submit ourselves to him and acknowledge him as God. We need, in short, to say with personal conviction, "This is the Word of God. Let us believe it and obey it."

During the Liturgy of St. John Chrysostom, the main Byzantine Eucharistic service, the priest prays the following prayer before the reading of the Gospel. It expresses well what God wants to do through our hearing his Word.

Shine within our hearts, loving Master, the pure light of Your divine knowledge and open the eyes of our minds that we may comprehend the message of your Gospel. Instill in us, also, reverence for Your blessed commandments, so that having conquered sinful desires, we may pursue a spiritual life, thinking and doing all those things that are pleasing to You. For You, Christ our God, are the light of our souls and bodies, and to You we give glory together with Your Father who is without beginning and with Your all holy, good, and life giving Spirit, now and forever and to the ages of ages. Amen.

The Liturgy of the Eucharist

The Great Entrance (Byzantine)
The Preparation of the Gifts (Roman)

The Eucharistic Prayer / The Consummation
He took ... and gave thanks.

    The Preface

    The Invocation (Roman)

    The Institution Narrative

    The Memorial Prayer

    The Invocation (Byzantine and Roman)

    The Intercessions

The Communion Service
He broke ... and distributed.

    The Preparation
    Our Father, who art in heaven,...

    The Fraction and Commingling

    The Reception of Communion
    Holy things for those who are holy! (Byzantine)
    Behold the Lamb of God, who takes away
    the sins of the world. (Roman)

The Concluding Ceremonies

THREE

Sacrifice and Christ

When Christ appeared as a high priest of the good things that
have come ... he entered once for all into the Holy Place, taking not the blood of goats and calves but his own blood, thus
securing an eternal redemption.

HEBREWS 9:11-12

P salms 42 to 43 are two parts of one psalm, and they have often been used
as a preparation for the Eucharistic celebration. They were originally prayed
by a Levite or priest in exile, deprived of the chance of going to Jerusalem for
the great feasts. Therefore they are psalms that we pray to express our desire to
come to God. They begin,

> As a deer longs for flowing streams,
>> so longs my soul for you, my God.

How do we come to God and fulfil our longing for him? The only way to
do that fully is to "go to heaven," that is, to pass to the heavenly land, the new
Jerusalem, which God has prepared for those who love him. But even now we
can come into God's presence and begin to experience satisfaction of our desire
for God.

The psalmist in exile is not completely deprived of God's presence, because
he can rely on God's steadfast love and, as he says, "[God's] song is with me"
(v. 8). In other words, he can count on God's being with him and worship God
in his heart with the words of Scripture wherever he is. But he remembers the
times when he most experienced the presence of God:

> These things I remember, as I pour out my soul:
>> how I went with the throng,
>> and led them in procession to the house of God,
> with glad shouts and songs of thanksgiving,
>> a multitude keeping festival.

The psalmist is remembering a feast as the high point of his relationship with God. The *feast* was the main worship event of the people of the old covenant. It was a time when they would "go up" to Jerusalem, to Mount Zion, the mountain of God, the place of his presence. There they would honor God with special ceremonies and in the course of that come the closest to him that they could.

The primary Latin word for keeping a feast has been taken into English as "celebrate," so we could also say that Israelites went up to Jerusalem to celebrate or to hold a *celebration*. They did this by calling to mind something God did for them and thanking him for it. At Passover, for example, they would celebrate the way God delivered them from bondage. A feast, then, is a celebration of something God has done for his people.

The word "celebration" is an unfortunate translation, because it now simply connotes something like a party, that is, something happy, pleasant, and usually informal. Although full of joy, the Israelite events we are talking about were marked by solemn worship services and were considered the most important regular events in life. We have, however, no other commonly used word to speak of the nature of feasts and similar events in which people honored and worshiped God in a special way.[1]

The feasts of Israel, the great pilgrim feasts of Passover, Pentecost, and Tabernacles, were characterized by solemn rejoicing. They centered on praising and thanking God for his goodness to his people. This is clearly expressed in Psalm 43:

Oh send out your light and your truth;
    let them lead me,
let them bring me to your holy hill
    and to your dwelling!
Then I will go to the altar of God,
    to God my exceeding joy;
and I will praise you with the lyre,
    O God, my God.

This passage also points to another aspect of feasts. They involved sacrifice. When God commanded Pharaoh to let his people go, he commanded him to let them hold "a feast to the Lord." He also commanded him to let his people sacrifice to him, and the way he spoke made clear that holding a feast involved sacrificing (Ex 5:1-3). The high point of the worship of God for old covenant people, then, was to go to the appropriate place of worship, the temple, and there at the altar offer sacrifices at a feast in ceremonies of praise and worship of God.

A feast always involved more than one sacrifice (Dt 12:5-7; 17-18). Each feast had its own set of offerings which expressed the nature of the feast (Lv 23; Nm 28-9; Dt 16:16-17). We tend to think of sacrifices in terms of one individual giving one sacrifice for a specific purpose. This seems to have come about partly because of the tendency to use individual sacrifices as the main Scripture source of instruction for teaching about sacrifice.[2] It seems to have also come about because the death of Christ is the chief Christian example of a sacrifice and has been taught about in recent centuries primarily in terms of its benefit to the individual. The main experience of sacrifice that most Israelites had, however, was the feast with many sacrifices, most of them expressive of the nature of the feast, not of individual needs. Sacrifice is primarily offered in the context of a feast.

The word "sacrifice" is used to describe what happens in the Eucharistic celebration during the Liturgy of the Eucharist. While, as has been emphasized in recent years, the Eucharist is a communion meal, while it makes Christ present in a special way among us, the Eucharist is first of all a sacrifice offered to God. Moreover, it is a sacrifice that is intended to be offered as part of a celebration.

"Sacrifice" comes from a Latin word that literally means "holy thing" or "something made holy," although it can also refer to the action of making something holy. Sacrifices are often referred to in the New Testament, but their nature is not explained there. To understand that, we have to go to the Old Testament and see how the Old Testament understood sacrifice, especially in the context of feasts.

In this chapter, then, we will look at the nature of sacrifice. We will begin by considering old covenant sacrifice. In that light we will look at the death and resurrection of Christ, the sacrifice of the new covenant. Then in the next chapters we will consider the Eucharist as a sacrifice.

Understanding the nature of sacrifice is helpful for understanding the meaning of the redemptive work of Christ and the Eucharist. There is, however, a further benefit that comes from understanding sacrifice better. It helps us to understand Christian worship and prayer more broadly.

Christian liturgy, Christian service of God, has what has been described as a "sacrificial pattern" or "a sacrificial nature." Those phrases indicate that there is a certain shape or structure to sacrifice, and that shape or structure gives an orientation to how we pray that makes our prayer truly scriptural, truly Christian. That pattern is based on God's nature and on how he has revealed we should relate to him, so that it is a fitting way to relate to the one true God who has indicated to us how he should be worshiped. Therefore, understanding sacrifice not only will help us to understand the nature of the Eucharist but it also will help us to understand the nature of Christian prayer better and how the Eucharist forms part of that. We will treat that topic more fully in the last chapter.

Offering Sacrifice

The Sacrificial Ceremony

We will begin with a description of sacrifice for old covenant people in the first century.[3] We will imagine a family in Nazareth: Eliezer, a reasonably prosperous farmer, his wife Sarah, and his sons and daughters and relatives. Using the sources available, we will look at old covenant sacrifice as Jesus and the apostles knew it, because the Eucharist began with new covenant people who had taken part in first-century old covenant worship services and understood sacrifice in terms of them.

Eliezer did not participate in a sacrifice every day of his life. Certain priests, like the high priest in Jerusalem, probably did, or at least did so on most days. Eliezer, an ordinary Israelite, lived too far away from Jerusalem and also had to make a living as a farmer. He attended synagogue regularly for prayers and for the Sabbath liturgy of the word, to use our term for what happened in the main weekly synagogue service. But he did not experience an actual sacrifice very often—normally only on great feast days when he "went up" to Jerusalem, the only place where according to the law animal sacrifice could be offered (Dt 12:2-14).

As we find Eliezer he is going up to Jerusalem for the Feast of Pentecost. We will look at his attendance at the festivities of Pentecost because they do not contain some of the complications of Passover, which will be discussed in the next chapter. Pentecost was a harvest feast, but at least by the first century it was also commonly understood to be the celebration of the giving of the law on Mount Sinai.[4] It was seen as the completion of Passover season, because it celebrated the completion of the grain harvest, which began at Passover, and also the completion of the work of God in the Exodus, his bringing of the people of Israel "to himself" on Mount Sinai and his establishing the covenant with them.

Eliezer had just completed the grain harvest. His barns were full, his flocks numerous, and his spirits high. On this occasion only the men of Eliezer's immediate family went up. His daughter had just given birth to his second grandchild, and his wife was needed to help her. Their other daughter, a young girl, stayed behind to be of assistance. According to the law, only the men were actually obligated to take part in the public responsibility of worship (Ex 23:17; 34:23-24; Dt 16:16-17), unless of course they were sick or had some other good reason they could not go. Women did not have the same obligation to fulfil the worship requirements of the Law, precisely because they had to care for the children and could not be sure they could get away from their primary (not sole) responsibility as women. They did, however, normally attend the feasts.[5]

Eliezer and his sons packed up the donkeys and headed off to Jerusalem. He took along the first fruits of the new harvest, as well as some lambs, kids, and flour for offerings (a burnt offering, a festal offering, as well as all his tithes and other obligatory contributions and his votive and freewill offerings). He also took considerable food and wine for the accompanying festivities.[6] The trip took a couple of days each way, and they stayed some time in Jerusalem for the feast, so that there was some effort and expense involved.

Eliezer went with a group made up of his brothers and their families, a sister and her family, and an unmarried cousin—those who were able to go up and belonged to the family grouping. They always looked forward to the trip, because there they would see relatives and friends they would not see otherwise. They also looked forward to the feast because they would take part in many festivities, some required by the feast, some "after hours." In addition, color and interest were added by the Jews who lived outside the land of Israel who took advantage of the better weather at sea to travel to Jerusalem in summer, the time when Pentecost fell.

Most of all they looked forward to the ceremonies in the temple. These were drama and pageantry of the highest order they knew and were solemn, as well as the most important, events of their lives. There they, as part of God's people, would interact with the Lord himself in the place on earth where he "dwelled." This was the time of the year they would be closest to their Lord and be most able to receive his blessings.

When they arrived, they encamped in "greater Jerusalem," that is, within the boundaries of Jerusalem as they had been extended by the authorities so that the area of the city could accommodate all the pilgrims for the feast. Eliezer's family was helped by relatives from the branch of the family that lived in Jerusalem. By now they were pretty well practiced in what to do, like a modern family that goes to the same trailer camp for vacation every year.

They went up early. Eliezer had made a vow as a prayer for the healing of his son, and now he had to fulfil it by offering a sacrifice, as Paul had intended to do when he came to Jerusalem for his last visit (Acts 21:15-26). Eliezer brought a lamb for his vow. It was an expensive offering, but he was glad to give it, much as a modern parent would be glad to pay an expensive doctor's fee for an operation that had saved his child. His nephew's wife also was ready for the purification ceremonies after the birth of her third child, like Mary after the birth of Jesus (Lk 2:22-24). There was a sacrifice involved in this as well. Moreover, those in the party needed some purification to be ready for the feast.

According to Deuteronomy 12:5-6, as interpreted by the rabbis in the first century, all the offerings designated for God should be brought on the first possible occasion.[7] For most Israelites, this meant the closest feast. If Eliezer had lived in or near Jerusalem, he would likely have "gone up" to pay his vow at some other time, but he could not take a long journey too often.

The feast itself began at the legally prescribed time. Pentecost was only a one-day feast, the feast to conclude Passover season. To attend the celebration, the whole extended family went up to the temple. The women went only as far as the Court of the Women. The men would be mainly there as well, but to offer sacrifice they would enter the Court of the Israelites inside the Nicanor Gate. There they would be in the court in which stood the altar and the temple building, the place that contained the Holy of Holies. For all the ceremonies they were crowded in, because in the first century the courts could not easily hold everyone who came.

Because this was the Feast of Pentecost, the main offerings were provided by the priests out of the temple treasury for the people of Israel as a whole. The public festal offerings for Pentecost included a first-fruits offering of the newly harvested grain, burnt offerings of animals to honor God, sin offerings in case anything was done wrong in the sacrifice, and peace offerings or communion offerings to express the nature of the feast as an occasion for communing with God. These were also accompanied by offerings of bread baked with oil, incense, and wine. Eliezer, like all Israelites present, also brought a burnt offering and two loaves of bread and a lamb for his family festal offering.

Meat, flour, oil, incense, and wine were a symbolic banquet for God, some of which, the peace offerings, God shared with the worshiper. Everyone knew that God did not really eat the offerings, but they also knew that making offerings was a way of expressing their relationship with him. They also knew that like the father of a family or the host at a banquet, he would share these gifts with them. All these were of the best quality, with no defects or blemishes (Lv 22:17-25), because God deserved the best.

Eliezer and his family went up to the temple mount during the night, the time when the sacrificial offerings were examined by the priests to see if they met the requirements. When dawn came, the trumpets were sounded to announce the beginning of the day and of that day's service of God. Then the offerings began. The official sacrifices were conducted in the Court of the Priests by the designated priests representing the nation as a whole. This day the high priest presided.

The first offering was the daily morning offering, the "continual offering," so called because it was one of the two offerings given to God on a regular daily basis. For the morning offering the lamb was killed by one priest, while another took the blood and splashed it on the altar. Meanwhile still another priest with two assistants offered incense at the altar of incense in the holy place before the throne of God. On this occasion it was the high priest. When he completed the incense offering with its accompanying prayers, the high priest mounted the steps of the altar and received the pieces of the body of the lamb. He put them on the altar so that they might be burned, sending up "a pleasing odor to the Lord." Then the cereal offering was burned on the altar, and the libations of wine were poured out at the base.

As the smoke of the burning sacrifice went up and the fragrance of the wine was added to it, the Levites blew the trumpets as a way of proclaiming the fact that the sacrifice was being offered and of calling God's attention to it, "a blast to resound mightily as a reminder before the Most High" (Sir 50:16). The people fell prostrate in worship before the Lord. The hymns continued as "over the throng sweet strains of praise would resound" (Sir 50:18). All the people shouted with joy to God and prayed for his blessing.[8]

At the end of the offerings, the high priest came down from the altar. He raised his hands in blessing over the people who lay prostrate. He blessed God for his goodness as a way of calling God's blessing down upon the people. Because they had offered sacrifice according to the Law, they were assured that God's acceptance and blessing were theirs.

Such would have been a normal morning offering. Since this was the day of

Pentecost, after the morning offering came the festal offering: first the sin offering, then the burnt offering. Then came the special offering for the Feast of Pentecost itself, the offering of the first fruits concluding the harvest season. This was also accompanied by burnt offerings, a sin offering, and peace offerings.[9]

The various individual sacrificial gifts were then brought forward. Private sacrifices were killed in the Court of the Israelites by the person who presented the offering. They were then given to the Levites and priests, along with bread and wine. The priests took all these and offered them at the altar. Eliezer brought his family's sacrifices and killed them, and then they were offered at the altar by the priests.

Not all the offerings were burnt up or poured out. The peace or communion offerings[10] in particular were not. For the peace offerings, a portion of the body and the bread were burned, "the memorial portion." The priests would take the remainder of the public peace offerings as well as a piece of the private offerings. The person who brought the offering for himself and his family would take most of his own offerings. It was something holy, because it had been given to God, although shared by God with the worshiper.

Then the people of Israel had a meal of which these offerings were a part. It was a meal taken "in companies."[11] The meal had to be eaten by the priests within the temple area and by the Israelites within the legal limits of Jerusalem. All had to be in a state of ceremonial purity to eat it. Eliezer and his family ate the meal together and distributed portions to those who could not afford the feast and were not part of their "company."

The meal was a fine meal, a festal meal, with the sacrificial offering the center. Because Pentecost celebrated the giving of the Law, the meal included milk and honey. These were the symbols of the blessing of new life in the Promised Land that would come through the observance of the Law. Eliezer, as father and oldest brother, presided over his family's meal. The main part of the meal began with a blessing of bread and wine, followed by the main course, in which the offering was eaten as the most honored part. Eliezer concluded with a final blessing, a solemn thanksgiving over a cup of wine, and hymns were sung to end with praise of God.

When we speak of "a feast," we usually just mean a fine meal. Our use of the word probably derives from the time the meal was an important part of an Israelite feast. The festal meal, however, was not something done after the important ceremony was over, as, for instance, a Sunday meal might be for us, but was integrally part of the feast or celebration and a way of deepening relationship with God.

In a similar way, when we speak of a holiday, we usually just mean a vacation or time off. Our usage here is also probably derived from the time when holy days were important parts of Israelite life. Then, however, they were not just time off but were days taken off from normal work to celebrate feasts. They were times to honor God (Rom 14:6) and to deepen relationship or communion with him. They were the most important times in life. The original meaning of many of the words we use are rooted in Israelite ceremony.

The Meaning of the Ceremony

The feasts of Israel, Pentecost included, were great events. It is not hard to understand the main ideas behind them. Many of us have been at Christian celebrations that are similar. At the same time certain features of Israelite worship seem strange to us. Some, to be sure, involved customs whose origins have been forgotten and were often unknown to Jews in the first century. But most of them, though culturally foreign to us, can be understood even now.

The Israelites offered their sacrifices together, at the communal feasts, because they related to God as a people. As we have seen, when we think of sacrifices, we usually think of one person offering one animal for a special purpose, usually to atone for a sin. There were such sacrifices. However, the main events when sacrifices occurred were communal events. There was a common ceremony that included offerings of the people as a whole, as well as offerings of individuals or families. The event also included common festal meals. Individuals might make offerings on their own at times, but their most important worship and offering of sacrifice was as part of a people.

The Israelites went to Jerusalem because the temple was there. The *temple* was the house of God, the place where God dwelled, the place of his special presence on earth. When we think of a temple, we often think of it as a Christian church. Churches, however, are assembly halls, places where the people gather. The temple building was God's place. There he had put his throne, or at least the footstool of his throne (1 Chr 28:2; Ps 99:5; 132:7), and the people gathered in front.

Jewish people knew that God was not simply to be found in a spatial location (see 1 Kings 8:27-30), but they did believe that God was specially present at certain holy places. These were places where they could have access to God and receive his help. After the temple was built, however, it was the sole location on earth of his special presence (Dt 12:5-14). The Holy of Holies within the temple building was the earthly throne room or audience hall of God and so was the holiest place on earth. It was the place where God made himself available so his people could make contact with him and receive blessings from him.

The temple building, then, was for God to be present in, to "dwell" in. On specified occasions certain of his ministers, priests, were allowed inside, but the people were never allowed to enter. They assembled in front of the building to worship him and present him with their sacrifices.

The *priests* and the Levites had access to the Court of the Israelites, where the altar was, and on special occasions to the Holy Place inside the building. Once a year on the Day of Atonement, the high priest could enter the Holy of Holies. We tend to think of the priest as the one who kills the sacrifice. As we have seen, however, that was only somewhat true. He was responsible, as the representative of the people, for killing the public sacrifice, but he did not kill the private sacrifices. His special responsibility was to be the one who offered the sacrifice to God, because he was the only one who had access to the places sacrifices could be given or presented to God.

The priests and Levites were *ministers* of God. Ministers are servants, but not menial servants. They are servants in the sense that the prime minister of many countries is the servant of the king or queen. They are officials who take a responsibility for the "governmental" service of the sovereign. Priests and Levites were appointed by God to represent the people to God and God to the people in the temple services. They made the interchange involved in that worship possible.

The Israelites gave *sacrifices* because sacrifices are gifts to God. In Scripture, sacrifices were commonly described as gifts (for example, in Mt 5:23-24). They were, however, a special kind of gift, a gift to show honor to God and to acknowledge him as God.[12] Sometimes the word is restricted to gifts of animals; other times it can be used to refer to gifts of grain (bread, cakes), oil, and incense.

In English the word "sacrifice" can refer to the thing which is sacrificed or to the action of sacrificing. The lamb, once it has been offered, is a sacrifice, a gift that has been given to God and therefore now belongs to God. The technical term for the sacrifice in this sense is *victim* or *host*, to use an older English word. The action of giving the lamb can also be described as a sacrifice. In this sense, "sacrifice" can be more narrowly understood to mean the ceremonial killing of an animal or more broadly understood to mean the whole action of making gifts over to God, so that giving bread, wine, or incense could also be described, in Greek at least, as sacrificing.

The more common scriptural way of describing what we would call a sacrifice is *offering*. Like "sacrifice," "offering" can refer to both what is offered and the act of offering. The Hebrew word for "offer" is literally "brought near" and indicates that to give the gift to God it had to be brought near to him, to the place where he was present.

The English word "offer" comes from Latin. It usually connotes a certain tentativeness. We cannot presume that God will be concerned with us or take our gifts. He could ignore us and our gifts, and he would not be unjust or even impolite to do so. He is God, and we are less significant in comparison to him than ants are to us. We can only offer our gifts to him. We fortunately know that he will accept gifts from us, because he is gracious to us by disposition.

There is another scriptural term for making an offering, and that is *consecration*. To consecrate something is to make it holy. When something is "holy" it belongs to God, so when a gift is made over to God, it is *made holy* or "consecrated." Things that had been offered to God, especially those that were to be eaten in a sacrificial meal, were called *holy things*.[13] Sacrifices, then, were consecrated, that is, put into God's possession, when they were offered to him and as a result were holy things.[14]

The sacrificial gifts that were given under the old covenant were domestic animals (sheep, goats, and cattle), bread, oil, and wine. These were the main things Israelites ate or lived on. To give some of these things to God was to give something personally valuable, something that sustained life. It was a way of expressing the value of the relationship with God.

The strangest part of the sacrifice to us, however, was the actual ritual, especially the burning of the bodies of the animals or the loaves or cakes of bread, the pouring out of the blood and of the wine. These were done as a way of making the gifts over to God. Once the animals, for instance, were killed and the bodies were burned and the blood poured out, they were by that fact taken out of human possession and given to God. The smoke and fragrance that went up were the giving of these to God, as was the pouring out of the blood or wine.

The offering was made on the *altar*. The altar was directly outside the throne room of God. It was "the table of the Lord" (Mal 1:7), where gifts could be put in order to give them to God, as we might place them on a table at a wedding ceremony in order to give them to the couple.

We tend to think that the death of the animal was given to God. As a consequence we identify sacrifice with death and with pain. But the purpose of the killing of the animal was not to offer the death of the animal, it was to offer the animal itself. The animal, in fact, was killed as painlessly as possible. In the offering, the animal was given to God, as were the bread and wine and oil is.[15]

The placing of the gifts on the altar also involved God's taking of these gifts, making them his own. We would see a sacrifice or offering as something we do for God, and that is certainly an aspect of it. But in the old covenant understanding, something could not really be a sacrifice until it was accepted by God. This was accomplished by putting it on the altar, either burning it on top or pouring it out at the side. Doing so in an acceptable way meant that God had taken it and it now was holy or sacred (Mt 23:17). The fire on top of the altar was especially significant. It seems to have been understood to be the fire of God's presence, which received the gift and brought it to heaven (see, for example, 2 Chr 7:1-3; 1 Kgs 18:38-9).[16]

Not all of the sacrificial offerings were completely burned. As we have seen, most of each peace offering was saved for a meal. These had been given to God but now were eaten by the priests who officiated at the offering or by those who had given the offering. Since the offerings the people ate were God's, they were something that God shared with his ministers and his people.[17]

The peace offerings seem to have been called peace or communion offerings because the meal was intended to strengthen the relationship between God and his people. Some of the peace offerings were called thanksgiving offerings or sacrifices of praise, because they were given especially to thank God for some way he had blessed his people. As a result, the meals were a special celebration of his goodness to them.

These meals were *holy meals*. They were part of the sacrificial ceremony and a way of sharing in it (1 Cor 10:18). They therefore made the people who took part in them holy, because taking part strengthened their belonging to God. While there is a difference between the old covenant and new covenant understanding of the holiness of God's people, the view that people share in holiness by partaking of a holy meal is common to both.

The action of giving a gift to God in sacrifice or making an offering had an important relational meaning. Gifts are, in fact, usually given to express something relational. When we come as a guest and give a gift to the host, we are expressing our appreciation of the meal that will be given to us and of the friendship behind it. We are not giving a payment for the meal or a bribe or advance tip to be treated well. The same could be said even of a sacrifice for sin. The old covenant sacrifices for sin did not count for much (Heb 9:13-14). They were chiefly the offering appointed by God so his people could express repentance.[18]

When Israelites or other contemporary people gave tribute to their overlords, they understood it as a gift to express their loyalty and submission. In a similar way, when they, and we, give sacrificial gifts and offerings to God, those gifts express something greater than the material value of the gift. They express our homage and submission, our desire to be in a certain relationship to God. If we are Christians, we express the gift of our whole life to God. We offer ourselves to him and express the fact that we are his. The gift, in fact, signifies our lives.[19]

A sacrifice, then, is a gift given to God to honor or glorify him as God and to worship him, that is, to acknowledge that he is our God and Lord, or it is the action of giving the gift to God. As an action, therefore, sacrificing is an act of worship of God. Sacrifices can be given for many specific purposes.[20] Some are given to take care of particular sins. Some are given to thank God for specific blessings or to pay vows that have been made. Many are given just to praise and honor and thank God because he is God and is good to his people. But whatever the reason, to sacrifice is to glorify and worship God as God and is the highest act of honor and worship.

The Sacrifice of Christ

The Book of Hebrews contains the fullest New Testament explanation of the death and resurrection of Christ as a sacrifice. We can find that teaching all through the New Testament, and it pervades Christian tradition.[21] The Book of Hebrews, however, is the place in the Scriptures where it is laid out in the most developed way.

In the course of the discussion, Hebrews (10:1) states a foundational principle:

Since the law has but a shadow of the good things to come instead of the true form of these realities, it can never, by the same sacrifices which are continually offered year after year, make perfect those who draw near.

"The law" means here the whole of the old covenant approach to God which was established by the Law of Moses. The sacrifices it refers to are the ones we just considered, like those at the celebration of Pentecost which were offered year after year. When the passage says that those sacrifices cannot "make perfect" those who draw near, it means that they cannot bring the old covenant worshipers to the full relationship with God and the fullness of God's presence and blessing which the full cleansing from sin would have allowed them to experience. That only can happen through the new covenant, where the "better things" planned for God's people are given.

The Letter to the Hebrews teaches that the sacrifices of the old covenant are shadows of what is to come. In the introduction we considered what it means to say that the old covenant realities are shadows that prefigure the new covenant realities (see p. 23). They are initial sketches, broad views, of what was planned. The "real thing" (RSV: "true form") is what the new covenant brings. In no other area is this so important as in the area of sacrifice. The old covenant sacrifices were an incomplete version of the kind of sacrifice God really had in mind: the sacrifice of the new covenant, the sacrifice which Christ offered.

In a sense to be treated later, the sacrifice of Christ is the only sacrifice of the new covenant. It therefore fulfils all the sacrifices of the old covenant. That which they were instituted for, that which they were intended to achieve, was fully accomplished by the one sacrifice of Christ.[22]

The treatment of sacrifice in Hebrews can chiefly be found in chapters 8 to 10. At the beginning of that section (8:3) we are told,

Every high priest is appointed to offer gifts and sacrifices; hence it is necessary for this priest also to have something to offer.

If, in other words, Christ was a priest, as Hebrews just finished explaining, then he must have a sacrifice to offer, because priests are appointed to offer gifts and sacrifices.

Christ, then, came to offer sacrifice so that he might save the world. A full explanation of this truth is beyond the scope of this book. Nonetheless, it is a foundational truth of the Christian faith and the reason why his death and resurrection are so central to Christian teaching. The "mystery of our faith" can be summarized as "Christ has died, Christ is risen, Christ will come again."

The death and resurrection of Christ was the culmination of his earthly ministry. He began by preaching and teaching, healing and casting out evil spirits. He did so to proclaim that the kingdom or reign of God was at hand and that those who heard him should accept his message as a message from God and repent so that they would be ready to enter the kingdom.

To accept the message, they had to accept the messenger, Christ himself, as someone sent by God. He had to be received as the one who could tell them what God was intending and what he wanted. He had to be accepted as having a special connection with God, at the very least as a prophet sent by God. In this case, he was the Son of God, the Messiah or anointed King, sent by his Father into the world to claim the allegiance of God's old covenant people. Many accepted him. Many did not, and among those were most of the rulers of Israel, the chief priests and the scribes and elders who made up the governing council of Israel. They decided to put him to death.

Jesus knew that he would be put to death. He forewarned his disciples, and much of his teaching toward the end of his earthly ministry was based on that expectation. He believed that it was God's will that he die for the salvation of the world. He believed that the salvific death of the Messiah had been prophesied in the Old Testament. Such prophecies could be found in many places but perhaps most spectacularly in Isaiah 52:13–53:12, where it was foretold that the servant of the Lord would "make himself an offering for sin" and so "make many to be accounted righteous."[23]

Jesus accepted such a death voluntarily and offered himself to God. As he put it in the prayer that concluded his Last Supper discourse, "For their [his present and future disciples'] sake I consecrate myself" (Jn 17:19). Here saying "I consecrate myself" probably means, "I give myself, make myself over to you, as a sacrifice."[24]

Christ, then, made an offering or gave a sacrifice to God. If a sacrifice is a gift, what is the nature of the gift Christ gave? We are given an answer in the ninth chapter of Hebrews (Heb 9:26–28):

> He has appeared once for all at the end of the age to put away sin by the sacrifice of himself. And just as it is appointed for men to die once, and after that comes judgment, so Christ, having been offered once to bear the sins of many, will appear a second time, not to deal with sin but to save those who are eagerly waiting for him.

We might be inclined to say that Christ gave his death to God to atone for the sins of the world, perhaps because of the tendency to understand sacrifice as death. Christ did die to atone for the sins of the world, but Hebrews does not say he gave his death. Rather it says that he "gave himself." He did not kill himself, but he obeyed his Father completely, knowing what the consequences would be. In doing so, he gave his life, himself, as an offering to his Father to atone for the sins of those who would believe in him.[25]

When Christ died on the cross, he paid the price for the redemption of the world. But the sacrificial action included more than that, just as old covenant sacrificial actions included more than the death of the sacrificial victim. The sacrificial gift had to be presented to God and intercession had to be made for those for whom the sacrifice was intended.[26]

Since the sacrifice Christ offered was a fulfilment of all the old covenant sacrifices, among them the sacrifice of the Day of Atonement, it had to include the presentation of his blood to God in the Holy of Holies. The ninth chapter of the Book of Hebrews (Heb 9:11-12, 24) speaks of that by saying,

> When Christ appeared as a high priest of the good things that have come ... he entered once for all into the Holy Place, taking not the blood of goats and calves but his own blood, thus securing an eternal redemption.... For Christ has entered, not into a sanctuary made with hands, a copy of the true one, but into heaven itself, now to appear in the presence of God on our behalf.

In other words, the Book of Hebrews tells us that Christ's resurrection and ascension were part of his sacrificial action. He rose again, ascended into heaven, and so entered into the true Holy of Holies, the true throne room of God, heaven itself, where he stood before the divine throne as the true High Priest. There he presented himself to his Father as a sacrificial offering so that he could intercede for us on the basis of what he had done to pay for our redemption.

This sacrifice God accepted. The resurrection and ascension of Christ was the acceptance of the sacrifice of the cross. By raising his Son and bringing him into his heavenly presence, God was receiving as an acceptable gift the sacrifice his Son had made.

But something more happened. The Gospel of Luke describes the last earthly appearance of the risen Christ by saying,

> Then he opened their minds to understand the scriptures, and said to them, "Thus it is written, that the Christ should suffer and on the third day rise from the dead, and that repentance and forgiveness of sins should be preached in his name to all nations, beginning from Jerusalem. You are witnesses of these things. And behold, I send the promise of my Father upon

you; but stay in the city, until you are clothed with power from on high."
Then he led them out as far as Bethany, and lifting up his hands he blessed
them. While he blessed them, he parted from them.

LUKE 24:45-51

Christ's concluding action was his blessing of his disciples. Probably this was
his high priestly blessing (Lv 9:22-24; Sir 50:20-21). He had offered the sacrifice for their redemption. Now he invoked upon them the blessing that sacrifice
had won. In this case, the blessing was the promised Holy Spirit, the gift of God
to those who entered the new covenant. The Holy Spirit would give them new
life and the blessings of the age to come. This promise, this gift from God to
them, would be received on Pentecost a few days afterwards.

There was another result of the sacrifice of Christ. To return to Christ's
prayer in John 17, his sacrifice would make his disciples, then and now, consecrated, offered to God.

I consecrate myself, that they also may be consecrated

JOHN 17:19

The word "consecrated" in the context of John 17 is a difficult one to translate confidently. In the above passage, the underlying Greek word is translated
"consecrated" in the Revised Standard Version. Yet in the preceding verse, in
which Jesus prays for the result of his offering, the RSV translation uses "sanctify [them]." Since "sanctify" and "consecrate" are synonyms, there might be
no difference in the two translations, yet the English words have different connotations. "Consecrate" more normally refers to the act of giving something to
God, "sanctify" to changing something by purification or filling with the presence of God, the Holy Spirit. In this case there is no substantial difference, since
new covenant people are given to God by being purified and filled with the
presence of God through the gift of the Holy Spirit. In both meanings, the
result of what Jesus does in his death on the cross is to make us holy, that is, an
offering or sacrifice consecrated to God.

In the Letter to the Colossians, this is put in a similar way:

And you, who once were estranged and hostile in mind, doing evil deeds, he
has now reconciled in his body of flesh by his death, in order to present you
holy and blameless and irreproachable before him.

COLOSSIANS 1:21-22

In Romans, speaking of his work as an apostle, Paul also used similar wording for the results of his efforts among Gentiles. He said that he was working so that "the offering of the Gentiles [might be] acceptable, [consecrated] by the Holy Spirit" (Rom 15:16).

As a result of Christ's sacrificial offering of himself, then, Christians are a sacrifice, people who belong to God because they have been offered to him. They therefore can and should live as a sacrifice. Paul exhorts them in Romans 12:1 to "present [yourselves] as a living sacrifice, holy and acceptable to God. This is your spiritual worship." They should now, in other words, make their lives sacrificial, not in the sense of involving self-denial and death, although both will come to disciples of Christ in this fallen world, but in the sense of being lives fully offered to God.[27]

Because the Christian people are sacrifices, offered to God, their individual actions may be as well. The particular actions they perform for God, in other words, can be expressions of a whole life given to God and so sacrifices. As it says in 1 Peter 2:5,

Like living stones be yourselves built into a spiritual house, to be a holy priesthood, to offer spiritual sacrifices acceptable to God through Jesus Christ.

Many actions can be sacrifices for Christians. The greatest sacrifice is a life given in martyrdom, because it is the closest possible imitation of Christ (Phil 2:17). Material gifts sent as contribution for Christian mission (Phil 4:18) or given to support poor Christians (Heb 13:16) are also sacrifices, genuine offerings to God. So, however, is prayer.

After treating the priesthood of Christ, the Book of Hebrews says something similar to what 1 Peter says but specifically mentions prayer:

Through him then let us continually offer up a sacrifice of praise to God, that is, the fruit of lips that acknowledge his name.

The same thing is said in the Book of Revelation when it interprets the incense offered to God in heaven as the prayers of the saints (Rv 5:8; 8:3-4). Prayer, then, can and should be a sacrifice or an offering as well.

The priesthood of Christ makes it possible for us to be priests. Like him, in order to be priests we have to have something to offer. For all of us it is our life, day by day or finally in martyrdom. But it is also many actions done in the service of God, including prayer.

Christians have traditionally spoken of *devotion*. In more recent years that word has come to mean something like zeal, often with the connotation of being emotionally or affectively felt. The word originally, however, came from one of the words used in making an offering to God. When something like gold or even a person was given to God for his service, it was said to be "devoted." From that, "devotion" was also used to refer to "the will to give oneself readily to things concerning the service of God," as Aquinas put it. "Devotion," then, at least as originally understood, expresses the sacrificial orientation of the Christian life, the willingness to live life and to perform particular actions as an offering or gift to God. Prayer, then, should be done "with devotion."

All this tells us something important about Christian prayer. It is not just something we do for our own benefit or spiritual growth. It is something we offer to God to honor him and acknowledge him as God. It is a gift we give him. The sacrifices of the old covenant show us how human beings can come to God—through the sacrifice of Christ. They also show us how Christians can pray in a way pleasing to God—by making their prayer and offering a sacrifice, a gift they give to him out of their devotion, their desire to honor or glorify him.

Meditation: The Heavenly Offering
Revelation 5:1-14

One of the most striking scenes in Scripture is the vision of John in the fifth chapter of the Book of Revelation. He is in exile on the island of Patmos in the Aegean Sea because of the persecution of Christians and because of his role as one of the main leaders of the persecuted people. His vision occurs on the Lord's Day, what we would call Sunday, the day that commemorates the resurrection of Christ.

John finds himself in heaven, and there he sees the throne of God. He sees God manifest as the ruler of the universe, the one who determines the course of human history. God is surrounded by the angels and saints, who worship and praise him as is fitting when God appears to his creatures.

John finds himself in heaven at a special moment. God is holding a scroll in his right hand. It is a special scroll and it is sealed. The seals have the mark of God on them and indicate that the scroll is not to be opened except by one authorized by God. The scroll has God's decree written in it—his decree for the fulfilment of human history and for the rescue of his people from the attack they are under.

A mighty angel, a minister of God, comes forward and proclaims to all who are assembled, "Who is worthy to open the scroll and break its seals?" No one, however, comes forward to take the scroll from God's hand, open it, and read it out, thus promulgating God's decree and setting in motion his plan. Mighty as the angel is, he himself is not worthy for such a role.

At this point John begins to weep. He has been shown heaven, but only to see that there is no hope. There is no one worthy to rescue the human race. God will simply have to let it be rejected and perhaps destroyed.

But one of the elders who is present turns to John and says,

Weep not; lo, the Lion of the tribe of Judah, the Root of David, has conquered, so that he can open the scroll and its seven seals.

The elder says, in other words, look over there. There you will see the one who is the Lion of the tribe of Judah, that is, the promised Messiah, the anointed King of Israel who is to establish the kingdom of God and bring people from all the nations of the world into the fulfilment of God's purpose for them (Gn 49:9-10). He has conquered, and so he can open the scroll.

"He has conquered." When did he conquer? He conquered when he rose from the dead. John, in other words, is having a vision of heaven when Christ arrives after having died and risen, having triumphed over death, Satan, and sin. The victor, the conquering hero, has arrived in heaven.

How did he triumph? The song of praise directed to him later on tells us.

Worthy are you to take the scroll and to open its seals,
for you were slain and by your blood ransomed people for God
from every tribe and tongue and people and nation.

He triumphed by his death, faithfully obeying his Father and offering his life in payment for the sins of the world.

Looking up at the elder's words, John sees an extraordinary sight:

And between the throne and the four living creatures and among the elders, I saw a Lamb standing, as though it had been slain, with seven horns and with seven eyes, which are the seven spirits of God sent out into all the earth; and he went and took the scroll from the right hand of him who was seated on the throne.

This is a picture. The Book of Revelation is written in picture language. That does not mean that John is describing something that could be drawn as one picture. We do not have to look forward to going to heaven and seeing Jesus turn his seven eyes upon us. But it does mean that each element of the description is a picture or image with a symbolic meaning.

This picture is of the Lion of the tribe of Judah who is now a Lamb. To say that he is a lion is to say that he is a warrior king. To say that he is a lamb is to say that he is a sacrificial victim. He is at once a conquering king and a slain sacrifice.

The Lamb has seven horns and seven eyes. Seven is the number of completion, the divine number. To say that the Lamb has seven horns is to say that he has the power of God. Horns are a sign of strength, as anyone who has seen a bull use his horns in a bull fight would know. Eyes are a sign of knowledge. To have seven horns and seven eyes, then, is to be divinely powerful or omnipotent and divinely knowing or omniscient. John is, in other words, saying that the Lamb is divine, the incarnate one. Because the Lamb's eyes are the seven spirits of God, John is also saying that the Lamb is the one who possesses the Holy Spirit of God, as only one who is God can.

The description of the Lamb contains a most unusual phrase. He is "standing as though he were slain." Slain lambs do not stand. John seems to be saying by that phrase that he is standing, but at the same time it is visible that he has been put to death.

Many of us have seen older paintings of such a scene, perhaps in a church, perhaps in a museum. These paintings present Christ standing before his Father. On his body are the five wounds. From those wounds stream rays of glory. He is standing because standing is the posture of priests. But at the same time he is showing his Father his wounds. He is presenting to his Father the fact that he has died and given his life in exchange for the life of the world.

One of the most famous medieval paintings is the Altarpiece of the Lamb by Jan van Eyck, now kept in the cathedral at Ghent in Belgium. It presents a scene that can be found in other paintings, but probably in none as beautifully as this. The scene is of a garden. This garden represents heaven, because heaven is the Garden of Eden, Paradise, returned to the human race.

In the middle of the garden is an altar. On the altar is a lamb. Behind the altar are angels holding the cross and other symbols of the passion of Christ. In front of the altar are angels incensing the lamb. From the lamb flows blood into a chalice that sits on the altar. Below the altar is a fountain from which water flows, the water of life, the gift of the Holy Spirit. The heavenly altar is the center of the events that bring the salvation of the human race.

The Altarpiece of the Lamb portrays John's vision—the Lamb standing before the throne of God. The Lamb is standing at the place where the altar would be in the temple. If we look at the Lamb in relationship to us, he is the atonement for our sins and therefore the source of new life and holiness. If we look at the Lamb in relationship to God, he is a priest, offering a sacrifice, and the sacrifice is himself.

Jesus died on earth. But he intercedes in heaven on the basis of his sacrifice. There he presented himself to the Father seated on the throne in the true Holy of Holies. When Jesus first arrived in heaven and came before his Father, he must have said something like this:

> Here I am, Father, having completed the task you sent me to do. I have suffered and died for human beings. I have paid the price. I have given myself completely. Now look upon these wounds, the sign of my life given to you as an offering. Look upon the sacrifice, which I know is acceptable to you, and be gracious to those below. Accept them as well. Forgive them. Cleanse them. Sanctify them. Pour out your blessing upon them, the gift of your Holy Spirit. Take them for yourself, holy to you. Free them from their bondage and bring them to yourself. May this offering I have made achieve the result for which it was given.

Then all the heavenly choir, "numbering myriads of myriads, and thousands of thousands," said with a loud voice,

> Worthy is the Lamb who was slain, to receive power and wealth and wisdom and might and honor and glory and blessing!
> Then the earthly choir, responding antiphonally, said, To him who sits upon the throne and to the Lamb be blessing and honor and glory and might for ever and ever!
> Then "the four living creatures said, 'Amen!' and the elders fell down and worshiped."

And likewise should we who have reaped the benefits.

FOUR

Eucharist and Covenant

Christ, our paschal lamb, has been sacrificed. Let us, therefore, celebrate the festival, not with the old leaven, the leaven of malice and evil, but with the unleavened bread of sincerity and truth.

1 CORINTHIANS 5:7-8

The death of Christ, according to the Gospels, occurred at the time of the Passover or Paschal celebration. As Paul put it, Christ is "our Passover," probably in the sense of "our Passover sacrifice," or, as the RSV translates it, "our paschal lamb." The death of Christ on the cross fulfilled all the sacrifices of the old covenant. It was, however, especially a fulfilment of the Passover sacrifice, and therefore the meaning of the Passover shows us the meaning of the death and resurrection of Christ and in consequence the meaning of the Eucharist.[1]

The Feast of Passover, which was normally understood to include the Feast of Unleavened Bread, was one of the great pilgrim feasts of Israel. It was held in the first month, the beginning of the year. Like all three of the pilgrim feasts, it was a harvest feast, a time for offering first fruits and of rejoicing in God's blessing. On the second day of Unleavened Bread the first sheaf of new grain was offered, signaling the beginning of the grain harvest. Passover, then, celebrated the blessings of creation which God gave to his people so that they might live.

Like all three of the pilgrim feasts, however, Passover was also a commemoration of what God had done to redeem his people. Pentecost, as we have seen, was the feast that celebrated the giving of the Law at Sinai. Passover celebrated the Exodus from Egypt, the beginning of the events that led to Pentecost.

The night before the Exodus was a special night, the night of the last of the ten plagues. Pharaoh had resisted God's demand, presented through Moses, to let the people of Israel leave. His resistance led to a contest of strength between himself and God. Each plague was another round in a kind of wrestling match.

The last was the plague of the firstborn, because God took the life of the first-born of all those who dwelled in the land of Egypt to force Pharaoh to comply.

The Israelites also lived in the land of Egypt and so they too could have lost their firstborn. But God gave them a means of deliverance. Each family was to take a lamb and sacrifice it. The blood of the sacrifice was to be put around the door. When the destroying angel passed through the land of Egypt, he would pass over and not enter into the houses of those who had the blood of the sac-rifice on their doors. The sacrificial blood would forbid him entrance and mark the family as belonging to God and so under his protection.

The Passover sacrifice, then, was the sacrifice of deliverance. It was the means by which the Israelites were spared and the Egyptians were defeated. It made possible the Exodus, because it allowed the Israelites to escape, and to escape intact, from Egypt. The Passover feast celebrated that deliverance, and the sac-rifices given at that feast were a thanksgiving for it.

Jewish teachers, however, saw more in the Passover celebration than simply the commemoration of the Exodus. One teacher summarized the celebration by saying that there were four events commemorated at the Feast of Passover:[2] the night of creation, when God delivered the world from darkness, the night of the "sacrifice" of Isaac, which "sealed" the covenant with Abraham;[3] the night of the Passover itself; and the night of the future coming of the Messiah. The three events, commemorated along with the Passover, give a fuller per-spective on the meaning of both the Exodus and the Passover sacrifice that made it possible.

First, the Passover gave effect to the covenant that God had made with Abraham. Just as a lamb replaced Isaac in the covenant sacrifice of Abraham, the Passover lamb delivered the people of Israel from death and made the definitive establishment of the old covenant possible. It effectively enabled the people of Israel, the descendants of Abraham, to become God's people. It opened the way for them to be brought by God to Sinai and there given the same covenant that was given to Abraham, but in a new way, as a people and with instruction on how to live as a people.

The Feast of Passover also involved a commemoration of the creation, pos-sibly originally because this feast occurred in the "first of months" and was the feast to celebrate the beginning of the yearly harvest. But since the Passover cel-ebrated the event that established the people of Israel, the participants were also celebrating an event that began the restoration of the world. As a result of the Passover sacrifice, the people of Israel were enabled to be the start of the new creation, the first of those who would be redeemed to belong to God from among all the nations of the earth.

Even in Jewish understanding the effect of the Passover sacrifice went beyond the people of Israel, because it would ultimately bring about the fulfilment of the promise to Abraham that in him all nations would be blessed (Gn 12:1-3; Gal 3:8). When the prophesied Messiah, the anointed King of Israel, would come, he would establish the rule of God over the nations of the earth, and then they would experience God's blessing as well. For this reason, the Passover looked forward to the coming of the Messiah, and most Jews at the time of Jesus expected the Messiah to come during the "night of watching" (Ex 12:42) at Passover time. The Passover, in short, celebrated God's creation of the world and of his people and looked forward to his completion of that work when the Messiah would come.

Over a millennium after the Exodus, the Passover season brought together the people of Israel in the year A.D. 33 (or possibly A.D. 30), at a time when they were ruled by the Romans. They hoped for deliverance again, this time from their Roman overlords. Many were expecting a Messiah who would proclaim an uprising and deliver them, and they were expecting him to come at this or a Passover in the near future.

The Messiah did come in the person of our Lord Jesus Christ. Most of the Jewish people did not receive him as the Messiah, in part because of how he came. He did not come as a conquering king but as a Passover lamb. He would begin a redemption that would be completed only when he came conquering from heaven to judge the living and the dead.

As we have seen, Jesus came to offer the sacrifice that would make a true deliverance possible, the deliverance from sin. He came to defeat the powers of darkness, so that when God judged evil, his people would be spared. He came to shed the blood that could be put on his people so that they could be recognized as God's, protected from the destroying angel. He came, in the words of the prophet Zechariah (Zech 13:1), so there would be "a fountain opened for the house of David and the inhabitants of Jerusalem to cleanse them from sin and uncleanness" so that they would be ready to serve the kingdom of God.

He was betrayed during Passover week, given over to be killed as the Passover lambs were. On the night of his betrayal he ate a supper with his disciples. There is some dispute as to whether he ate the Passover meal with them or ate some anticipation of the Passover meal.[4] But his farewell meal occurred as the first step in offering his life at Passover season for the deliverance of his people.

The sacrifice of Christ did not just free people from their sins. It also established the covenant of God with his people on a new basis, a basis that made it fully open to those who were not Israelites and would bring them God's kingdom and blessing. Involved in this was the outpouring of the Holy Spirit, who would make believers into new human beings and join them to the Church, the beginning of the new human race. In offering the sacrifice of himself, Christ completed the work of beginning the new creation, the work that would ultimately bring God's creation to the purpose for which it had been intended. When we celebrate the death and resurrection of Christ, the fulfilment of Passover, then we are celebrating the event by which the purpose of God's creation, the reason for which God made the human race, will be accomplished.

In this chapter, we will begin to consider the Eucharist as the fulfilment of the feast of Passover and as the celebration of "the paschal mystery." To do so, we will especially look at the two chief texts on the Eucharist in the letters of Paul. There Christ's death and resurrection are clearly presented as the event that established the new covenant and the Eucharist as the celebration of that event. In the next chapter, we will look at the way in which Christian tradition understands the Eucharist to be a sacrifice.

A Sacrificial Meal

Paul presents one of the most important New Testament instructions on the Eucharist in 1 Corinthians 10:14-22.[5] He is there discussing eating idol offerings (chapters 8–10). It was clear that Christians could not engage in idolatry. It was also clear that they could not eat food offered to idols (Ex 34:14). However, some questions had arisen that needed a resolution.

The concern seems to have been occasioned by the circumstances in the Greco-Roman world. Food that had been offered to idols was sold in the meat market for general consumption and also prepared by individuals and eaten in private meals, commonly with no overt intentional connection to a sacrifice. Could Christians who wanted meat for their meal buy and eat it (1 Cor 10:25-26)? Could they go out to dinner with a pagan acquaintance and eat a meal where the main course had been offered to an idol (1 Cor 10:27-29)?[6]

Before giving the Christians in Corinth directions about how to handle these situations, Paul began by restating the truth that, in principle, Christians could not partake of idol offerings because to do so was to engage in idolatry, one of the major sins forbidden by God. He then gave rulings that seem to have been based on the principle that they could eat meat that had been offered to idols as long as there was no direct association with an idolatrous ceremony. We are not interested here in the reasons for which he made this decision but in what his discussion lets us know about the Eucharist.

Paul laid out his overall view of the reason why Christians may not partake in a meal connected to a pagan sacrifice in the following passage (10:14-22, RSV; NAB in brackets):

Therefore, my beloved, shun the worship of idols. I speak as to sensible men; judge for yourselves what I say.

The cup of blessing which we bless, is it not a participation [sharing] in the blood of Christ? The bread which we break, is it not a participation [sharing] in the body of Christ? Because there is one bread, we who are many are one body, for we all partake of the one bread.

Consider the people of Israel; are not those who eat the sacrifices partners in the altar? [See if those who eat the sacrifices do not share in the altar.]

What do I imply then? That food offered to idols is anything, or that an idol is anything? No, I imply that what pagans sacrifice they offer to demons and not to God. I do not want you to be partners [sharers] with demons. You cannot drink the cup of the Lord and the cup of demons. You cannot partake of the table of the Lord and the table of demons.

Shall we provoke the Lord to jealousy? Are we stronger than he?

By "cup of blessing" Paul is probably referring to the cup at the end of a festal meal as celebrated in the Jewish tradition. The blessing over that cup of wine, drunk by all those participating in the meal, was the solemn concluding thanksgiving for the meal. By the bread which is broken, he is referring to the bread that was blessed and distributed at the beginning of the festal meal. When he says, "*We* bless ... *we* break," he is referring to the Christian Eucharist, understood as a festal meal.

In this passage, Paul is making a comparison between the Eucharist, Israelite sacrifices, and pagan sacrifices. All of them involve the kind of sacrificial ritual that includes partaking in a special meal of what was offered to a god. To make his point about idolatry and partaking of food offered to idols, Paul referred to the meaning of a sacrificial meal.

When Israelites ate a sacrificial meal, partaking of the body of the sacrificial victim and possibly of the bread that had been offered, they were being partners [RSV] or sharers [NAB] or participants in the sacrificial offering of the altar. "The altar" here refers to the place the sacrifices were put so that they could be given to God.[7] For the participants to partake of what had been offered, in other words, was to take part in worship of God by sacrifice. To do so meant that they were honoring God and receiving from him the benefits for which the sacrifices were offered.

As we have seen, not all Israelite sacrifices involved such a meal. There were no meals connected to burnt offerings or, for those making the offering, sin offerings. They were, however, connected to all peace offerings, in this case including the Passover offering. The sharing in the meal of a peace offering brought a strengthening of the relationship with God.

The same thing was true for those who took part in pagan sacrificial meals. To be sure, the idol to whom the sacrifice was offered was simply a block of wood or stone, a "nothing," no real god (1 Cor 8:4-7). However, behind the idols were demons. The result of taking part in a meal in which the sacrificial victims of an idolatrous sacrifice were being eaten was to participate in this sacrifice and so to become "partners" [RSV], that is, friends or associates, of demons. That was something no Christian should want to do. The consequences were grim.

Something similar, according to Paul, occurs during the Christian Eucharist. When we partake of the Eucharistic meal, we share in the Body and Blood of Christ which has been offered to God in sacrifice, the sacrifice of the cross. Therefore, when we take part in the Eucharist, we are expressing our status as partners, associates, friends of God by participating in the sacrifice of Christ and so sharing in the benefits that come from the offering of Christ's body and blood on the cross. We cannot do that and also participate in idolatrous worship, because the Lord has forbidden worshiping any god other than himself. We cannot be friends of God and friends of demons or false gods. In short, the overall flow of Paul's argument shows that he considers the Eucharist to be sacrificial.[8]

Even though Paul is concerned with idolatry and not the Eucharist itself, there are many things in this passage that give us understanding about the Eucharist. It says that:

1. partaking of the Eucharist is a participation in the Blood and the Body of Christ (1 Cor 10:16);

2. partaking makes or produces one body (v. 17);
3. partaking makes us partners or participants in the altar (v. 18);
4. partaking makes us partners with God, like the pagans who are made partners with demons by their participation in the pagan sacrificial meals (vv. 20-22).

The above phrasing is based on the RSV translation. The same truths, however, could be restated by saying that when we participate in the sacrificial meal of the Christian Eucharist by eating and drinking the blessed or consecrated bread and wine:[9]

1. we eat the Body and drink the Blood of the Lord;
2. we thereby become one body;
3. we thereby share in the sacrifice that has been offered and so get the benefit that it was offered for;
4. we thereby express and renew our relationship (communion, community, or fellowship) with God.

To rephrase the passage this way emphasizes that the Eucharist has to do with relationship, primarily relationship with God. This is the main understanding of the Eucharist the passage conveys, since Paul is making the point that partaking in the Eucharist rules out partaking in idolatrous sacrifices. It does so because partaking in the Eucharist is an expression of relationship with God, and relationship with God rules out relationship with demons. The Eucharist, then, is a means of renewing or strengthening relationship with God (or, to use current English theological terminology, a means of growth in communion).[10]

Paul is making his point that the Eucharist is a means of strengthening our relationship with God by saying that it is part of a sacrificial action. In so doing he presupposes the understanding that sacrifices are means of establishing or strengthening a relationship with God. That then raises the question of what sacrifice we are participating in.

The answer is provided by the truth that in the Eucharist we are partaking of the Body and Blood of Christ. The body and blood of Christ were offered on the cross. We are participating in "the sacrifice of Calvary," because Calvary is where Christ offered himself as a sacrifice to save us. There is, in fact, no other candidate. To partake in the Eucharist, then, is to partake of the Body and Blood of Christ, which have been offered for us in his death and resurrection, his Passover.

By "participation" [RSV] or "sharing" in the Body and Blood of Christ, Paul is referring to our eating the bread and drinking the wine. This is clear from the parallel case of the Israelites eating the sacrifices and pagans drinking the libation cup. He is therefore most likely simply saying that we eat the Body and drink the Blood of Christ (see John 6:53). Christ was put to death on the cross. There his body and blood were separated in death and so became a sacrifice, a gift given to God. That Body and Blood are present in the Eucharist so that we might partake of what was offered to God.[11]

If, as in the case of the old covenant sacrifices, God finds a sacrifice acceptable, those who take part in a sacrificial meal can expect the benefits of having offered that sacrifice to come to them, unless they participate in it in an unworthy state. We know that God found the sacrifice of Christ acceptable because God took the sacrificial offering to himself when Christ rose from the dead. Therefore, by partaking of the Body and Blood of Christ in the Eucharist, we know we are receiving the benefits of that sacrifice.

The main benefit for a Christian that Paul indicates in this passage is the renewal of our relationship with God. We become "partners" [RSV] with God. This does not mean, as the English word might imply to us, that God has formed a company, a business partnership, which allows us to invest some of our resources (our good works, perhaps) to produce salvation. Rather, it simply means that when we partake in the Eucharist we are renewing or strengthening our relationship with God. We are being received as "associates" or "friends" of God, to use a phrase that is sometimes used in Scripture (2 Chr 20:7; Is 41:8 [see Gn 18:17-1]; Jn 15:14-15), and we are having our friendship with God renewed.

We also become "one body." The body being referred to in the passage must be the Body of Christ, because the bread we partake of is the Body of Christ and Paul is making a link between the two. Partaking in the one Body of Christ (that is, by partaking of the consecrated bread) means we are being strengthened in being part of the relationship which is the body of Christ. As Hilary of Poitiers, a fourth-century Father, put it, "By receiving his holy body we receive a place in the communion of his holy body."[12]

Nowadays, many people would understand the body of Christ to be the Christian community or the Church, understood as the body of people who are Christians. "The body of Christ" is certainly one way of describing the Christian community or Church. Christians are in relationship with one another and form a community, and that community can be described as the body of Christ (see

1 Cor 12:27; Rom 12:5; Eph 1:23; Eph 5:23; Col 2:18; Col 2:24).

But to speak that way might leave out something very important. We commonly understand "the body of Christ" to be merely the Christians or the group of Christians (the Church). To use technical terminology, we understand the phrase to refer to the Christians exclusive of Christ. Paul, however, and most early Christian writers, use the phrase to include Christ, who makes their status as Christians possible. In other words, "the body of Christ" refers to Christ plus the Christians joined to him, and to become one body (in Christ) means to be joined to Christ as well as to other Christians.

The body of Christ is not something we create, even by coming together for the sake of Christ. We are only in relationship with one another as Christians because we are in relationship with Christ. We are only the body of Christ because we are joined to the head of the body, who is Christ. After all, if the body were severed from the head, it would be a dead body. One bread, therefore, makes one body, because the bread is the Body *of Christ*, the living Christ. By partaking of the consecrated bread, we are joined to Christ; we are strengthened in our relationship with Christ; and consequently we are strengthened in our relationship with one another.

Both aspects are important. It is true that before about fifty years ago, most Catholics emphasized the fact that partaking in the Eucharist unites us to Christ and neglected the fact that it unites us to one another. When, however, we go back to the Fathers of the Church, we find a strong emphasis on the fact that the Eucharist creates unity among Christians, and that emphasis should be central to our understanding.[13] But to emphasize solely the unity among Christians, as often happens now, without emphasizing the fact that it is unity with Christ that brings about the unity among Christians or that the body so united includes Christ, leaves us with the Church or Christian community as merely a human social group or organization, not as "one body [in Christ]."

The passage implies that there is more to what we receive from partaking in the Eucharist than participating in the Passover sacrifice of Christ and so having our relationship with God, and one another, strengthened. If we are eating the Body and drinking the Blood of Christ, presumably our eating and drinking must be somehow nourishing or strengthening us because that is what eating and drinking does. If we are being made one body in Christ, our partaking of the Eucharist must somehow be allowing us to be strengthened in the life of Christ because sharing a common life makes us living members of a body.

Such implications, however, are not directly addressed by Paul, who is mainly concerned with stressing that partaking in the Eucharist is incompatible with partaking in idol offerings, since relationship with God and with demons is incompatible. He therefore is mainly making the point that the Eucharist creates relationship without going further into why it does so. We will take up these further implications in the next chapter.

The Eucharistic Words

Paul's teaching about the Eucharist is based on Christ's own words, sometimes called his **Eucharistic words**. Paul presents these words, the words now enshrined in the center of every Eucharistic celebration,[14] in the eleventh chapter of 1 Corinthians (1 Cor 11:23-27). They allow us to grasp something more of Paul's understanding of the meaning of the Eucharist, but also allow us to consider the scriptural foundation of the Eucharist in the intention of Christ. They are presented in Matthew, Mark, and Luke as well (Mt 26:20-30; Mk 14:17-26; Lk 22:14-23). The following discussion will use Paul's version as the basis and refer to the other versions where the differences are important.

Paul has somewhat changed subjects between chapters 10 and 11. Chapter 11 does not continue the question of eating idol offerings but treats certain disorders within the Eucharistic assembly at Corinth. To underline the importance of care in how the assembly is carried out, care similar to that shown in the temple liturgy, Paul stresses the spiritual importance of the Eucharist.[15] To do so he quotes an account of the Last Supper and within it the Lord's own words:

> For I received from the Lord what I also delivered to you, that the Lord Jesus on the night when he was betrayed took bread, and when he had given thanks, he broke it, and said,
> "This is my body which is [given] for you.
> Do this in remembrance of me."
> In the same way also the cup, after supper, saying,
> "This cup is the new covenant in my blood [which is poured out for you].
> Do this, as often as you drink it, in
> remembrance of me."
> For as often as you eat this bread and drink the cup, you proclaim the Lord's death until he comes.

The Eucharistic words of Christ first occurred in the context of a special meal, as the Gospel accounts make clear. It was possibly a sacrificial meal, one in which the Passover sacrificial offering was eaten, but it was certainly a festal meal connected with the Feast of the Passover. At this meal, Jesus took bread and wine, blessed them, and then distributed them to his disciples. His "Eucharistic words" did not occur until after his blessing of the bread and wine and were intended to explain the significance of what he had done. Therefore, to understand them, we need to understand the meaning of blessing bread and wine, especially doing so in the context of a festal meal.

The Blessings

Contemporary English speakers would normally call a *meal blessing* a "grace." Our word "grace" for meal blessings comes from the Latin word for "thanks." Our form of the initial grace at meals is usually a prayer that the food be blessed ("Bless us, O Lord, and these your gifts which we have received from your bounty"). Early Christian "graces," both in Greek and Latin, usually began by thanksgiving or by praising God for his goodness in giving the food, and then asking him to bless it (We praise and thank you, O Lord, for this food and ask you to bless it).

The Jewish "grace," the "blessing" of the food, however, was different in form.[16] The key prayer for the blessing of the bread at a Jewish meal in the first century was, and still is, "Blessed are you, O Lord our God, king of the universe, who have brought forth bread from the earth." The one for the blessing of the wine was, "Blessed are you, O Lord our God, king of the universe, who have created the fruit of the vine." The actual food being blessed was not mentioned, but the person saying the blessing held the bread or cup in his hands and presented it to God, blessing him. In so doing he was thanking God for it. The fact that the food or drink was presented to God and God was blessed (or praised) for giving food meant that the presented food was blessed.

The presenting of the food or drink to God seems to have been an act of offering it to him in thanksgiving, much the way a first-fruits offering was presented (see Dt 26:1-11; also Rom 14:6).[17] It was *de facto* a prayer that God's blessing be on the food, because what was offered to God in an acceptable manner became his, that is, holy. Whatever was holy was spiritually purified, insofar as it needed to be, and brought God's blessing with it, if treated in an acceptable manner. In other words, it was unnecessary specifically to ask for the blessing to be on the food, because that followed from offering part of the food to

God and blessing (thanking) him for it. In Greco-Roman culture (and now in ours) the request for the blessing on the food had to be mentioned to be understood.

We see the view expressed that the blessing had a beneficial (sanctifying) effect in 1 Timothy 4:4-5:

> For everything created by God is good, and nothing is to be rejected if it is received with thanksgiving; for then it is consecrated [sanctified] by the word of God and prayer.

"Thanksgiving" (*eucharistía*, the Greek word from which "Eucharist" comes) here probably means "prayer of thanksgiving" or "grace." This was a prayer that, in Jewish custom, always included a reference to something in Scripture as its basis. If, as seems correct, the meal blessing is similar to the first-fruits offering, the offering to God of part of the food to be partaken makes the rest holy. As Romans 11:16, speaking of the dough offering, a first-fruits offering, puts it,

> If the dough offered as first fruits is holy, so is the whole lump.

The thanksgiving prayer which was the blessing of the food at the meal, then, made all the food "holy."

After the prayer of blessing, a part of the blessed food was given to those present at the meal. Distributing the blessed or consecrated food to the participants was a way of conveying God's blessing to them. It made them sharers in the blessing.[18] In an ordinary meal, the blessing probably just conveyed the blessing of God upon the use of his gifts and those who partook of them. It was a way of blessing and protecting the eating.

In a festal meal there was more to what happened. Those who partook of the food were taking part in a celebration and often a sacrifice. The blessing of the bread and wine at such a meal would have been a prayer that the benefit of what was being celebrated or of the sacrifice be conveyed to them during the meal. In short, the context of the eating and drinking, the nature of the meal, usually as mentioned in the prayers, expressed the meaning of the meal itself and of the blessing it was intended to convey.

There were special forms of meal blessings for feasts like the Sabbath or the Passover. These included longer prayers of blessing. They were mainly given over the concluding cup, "the cup of blessing" as Paul termed it (1 Cor 10:16), perhaps because at that point the meaning of the celebration had been expressed and God could be appropriately thanked, not just for the food but also for the event in honor of which the meal was held.

The festal prayers would praise and thank God for the feast being celebrated and, on the basis of what God had already done, would ask him to do more of the same or to bring about the full result his work was aiming at. For instance, after the destruction of Jerusalem by the Romans (and possibly after the one by the Babylonians) the Passover blessing prayers included petitions that Jerusalem and the temple be restored. In the time of Jesus, they included petitions that the Messiah come.

Jesus' Words

An understanding of Jewish meal blessings gives us a perspective on the Last Supper.[19] During the meal Jesus blessed or gave thanks to God for his goodness and his redeeming work.[20] He did so briefly over the bread at the beginning of the meal and more extensively over the wine at the end, the "cup of blessing." While he prayed, he held the bread and cup in his hands and raised them.[21] He therefore presented or offered them to God and praised God for his gift of food and therefore for his gift of the food at the meal.

Over the final cup of wine, Jesus thanked God for what he had done to redeem his people from bondage and make them a people. He likely also prayed that God would complete that work of redemption and that he would do so through the coming of the kingdom (as announced by his gospel). In short, in that prayer he would have expressed the meaning of the Passover celebration itself. Jesus would, however, probably have done so, like other teachers of the time, in accordance with his own understanding of the Passover. The prayers in the first century were not verbally prescribed as they are now, but allowed the one presiding to pray as he chose within a certain framework.

After each of the two blessings he distributed the blessed objects, the bread and wine, to his disciples. They conveyed a share in the sanctifying blessing Jesus prayed for. All these things we know from the accounts or can surmise with considerable probability from the fact that he celebrated a festal meal at Passover time in the first century.

Jesus, however, did something more. After having blessed the bread and wine, he gave some explanatory words in the process of distributing them to his disciples.[22] After the blessing of the bread he said, "This is my body [given] for you." After the blessing of the cup he said, "This is the new covenant in my blood [poured out for you]."

While for us the words stand almost alone for interpreting Jesus' intention, this would probably not have been the case for his disciples. Jesus had spoken about his approaching death and its connection with the Passover early in the meal (Lk 22:15–16; and probably Jn 14–16). To do so, he likely made use of the customary explanation of the meaning of the feast given by the leader at Passover meals (and probably at other festal meals in the first century). This was done after a first cup of wine and before the blessing of the bread.[23] Moreover, the prayer itself over the "cup of blessing" would have probably indicated something about his death in connection with the Passover (see Jn 17).

Jesus' Eucharistic words are somewhat different in each of the four accounts we have (Matthew, Mark, Luke, and 1 Corinthians). The words in brackets in the above quotation are added from Luke's account. They are almost certainly sacrificial words. Sacrifices were given to God, and the blood of the sacrificial victim, as well as drink offerings of wine, were poured out at the altar.

We do not, however, need to rely on the wording in Luke to see that the Eucharistic words make use of a sacrificial vocabulary. "The cup ... of the new covenant in my blood" or, as it is put in Matthew and Mark, "my blood of the covenant" is a reference to a covenant-sealing sacrifice (Ex 24:8; Zech 9:11; Ps 50:5). To be a body which is "for you" probably indicates something sacrificial. The phrase "for the many" also likely is an allusion to Isaiah 53:10-12, which expresses the atoning value of the death of a servant of the Lord.[24] Moreover, as we shall see shortly, "remembrance," in the command to repeat the ceremony, probably has a sacrificial meaning.

All four accounts, then, in slightly different ways, contain sacrificial wording. Each individual word or phrase (except "blood of the covenant") could be used in a nonsacrificial way. Nonetheless, the use of so many expressions in one ceremony that could be employed to describe sacrifices almost certainly indicates that they all are to be understood with sacrificial meanings.

These words allow us to see how Christ interpreted the celebration that occurred at the Last Supper and the meal blessings during it. In saying what he said on the night before his death on the cross, he was asserting that his death would be a sacrifice. His body would be given, that is, offered. His blood would be poured out, that is, offered like the blood of a sacrificial offering. The fact that the body and blood were separate[25] indicates that the meal symbolically expresses the manner in which the Passover lamb or any other animal sacrifice was offered—by being put to death with the blood separated from the body, each presented to God in a separate rite.

Put in the context of the meal, these words tell us that the meal, as a festal meal, was connected to the sacrifice of Christ on the cross. In identifying the blessed bread and wine with his body and blood that would be offered, he was indicating that the blessing he was praying for during the meal would be connected to the sacrifice of himself that he shortly would be giving. The result of that sacrifice would be the sealing of a new covenant with God by Christ's blood, and, as the account in Matthew makes clearest, the remission of human sins, by the sin offering he would be making (Is 53:1-12).

Since the festal meal was intended to celebrate the Passover, the meal also gives us the fuller context and therefore more of the meaning of Christ's sacrifice. The sacrifice of his body and blood would be a Passover sacrifice. What Christ said, in other words, implicitly tells us that the old covenant Passover sacrifice would be fulfilled by the sacrificial death of the Messiah, himself, that was even then in process. He would be "our Passover" (1 Cor 5:7), the new covenant Passover sacrifice, the replacement for the old covenant Passover lamb.[26] This meal was the first celebration of the new Passover.

Since Christ had not yet died, the meaning of the Eucharistic words is anticipatory. They indicate that his death would do what the original sacrifice of the Passover lamb had done—make possible the (imminent) redemption of those who were taking part in the meal. Probably the words "given" and "poured out" in Luke should be understood as meaning that the body *will be* given and the blood *will be* poured out.[27] Since the bread and wine being blessed were offered to God, Christ was offering his body and blood, himself, in anticipation of what was to occur on the cross and as a means of conveying something of the blessing of that sacrifice to those who partook of the blessed bread and wine (Jn 17:19). His offering was also a prayer that the blessing would be conveyed through them to those who would believe in him in the future (Jn 17:20).[28]

We are often mainly interested in these words as the "words of institution" we hear at the center of the Eucharistic Prayer. Probably that was not what most struck the disciples when they first heard the words. For them, Jesus was saying that he was about to die and his death would be a sacrifice "for" them, as well as for those who would come to believe through their word. The things he said at the meal, including the Eucharistic words, were, to use a term now common among Scripture scholars, "a farewell discourse," one that explained the significance of the death that was imminent.

Nonetheless, the words in their context were probably so carefully preserved because of the conviction that what Jesus did at the meal was to be continued by the apostles. Moreover, the versions in Paul and Luke contain the command to perform the same ceremony ("Do this in remembrance of me").[29] By "do this" Jesus is probably referring to performing the two ceremonies of blessing and distributing the bread and blessing and distributing the wine.

The command is to repeat those ceremonies, but at the same time "in memory of me," that is, making a memorial of himself and the death he was about to die. This was probably to be done primarily by means of the prayer of thanksgiving.[30] It was the intended memorial, likely expressed in the explanatory discourse and the prayers, as at other festal meals, that would indicate the meaning of the meal and the blessing it was intended to impart.

Such a command indicates, as other of his words at the Last Supper did, Jesus' conviction that the apostles would survive the upcoming trial in which he himself would be put to death. They should carry on his work, in part by ceremonially remembering him and his sacrifice. In commanding them to perform such a ceremony, Jesus' words were probably indicating that future participants would be sharers in his sacrifice, as Paul indicated in chapter 10 that the people of Israel were when they offered sacrifices, including the Passover sacrifices. They would be taking part in the new covenant Passover sacrifice.

In making a memorial or performing the ceremony in remembrance of the Lord, the apostles would be doing something more than just blessing the bread and wine at the beginning and end of a festal meal like the Sabbath meal. To "make a memorial" in this case could summarize the meaning of what they were doing. But what is a memorial or remembrance?[31] And who needs to remember?

The apostles themselves, and those who believe through them, we ourselves included, need to remember, to be sure. We need to call to mind what Christ has done for us so that we might put faith in it again. The Passover itself is a feast that is a "memorial," that is, intended to recall to the people of Israel what God has done for them (Ex 12:4; Ex 13:9). In the Eucharist, Christians need to make the same kind of memorial.

Very likely, however, the one who needs to remember is also God, to whom the prayers in the ceremony are addressed. God, of course, is not absent-minded, needing to be reminded of things he has overlooked. Rather, when we ask God to "remember" something, we are calling it to his attention. Jesus here is probably using a Hebraic way of speaking that we would not normally use ourselves, but that corresponds to our own understanding of a formal petition.

When we make a petition or send a formal "memorandum," we commonly begin with the reasons the people we are addressing should act the way we would like them to. The same thing was done by people in the Scriptures who prayed to God, as can be seen in the Psalms and other Old Testament prayers. For instance, the prayer "Remember, O Lord, in David's favor, all the hardships he endured" (Ps 132:1) meant, "be mindful of David because of his faithfulness to you, especially his sufferings on your behalf." It then went on to pray: as a result of what David did, be gracious to our king, his descendant, and so to us, the people he leads.

Equally important for our topic, at times when the Old Testament speaks about sacrifices, it also speaks about making a memorial or remembrance to God in connection with them. For instance, during certain sacrifices trumpets were blown at the moment of the offering for a "reminder [memorial] before the Most High" (Sir 50:16; Nm 10:10). This probably means that the priests were calling God's attention to the sacrifice they were offering so that he might act because they had offered a sacrifice. Such an understanding is expressed in the prayer in Psalm 20:2-3, addressed to the king of Israel,

> May he send you help from the sanctuary,
>   and give you support from Zion!
> May he remember all your offerings,
>   and regard with favor your burnt sacrifices!

If, as is likely, this is the kind of memorial or remembrance Jesus had in mind, then we find another sacrificial term used in connection to the Eucharist. Jesus is instructing his disciples to bless and so offer the bread and wine as a ceremonial prayer that the Lord might remember his death. The meal they then partake of would be a meal in which they participate in the benefits or blessings that come from the death he underwent "for" them—and for us.

Paul says the same sort of thing when he explains the command to perform the ceremony in remembrance of Christ by adding, "As often as you eat this bread and drink the cup, you proclaim the Lord's death until he comes." He probably does not mean here that in doing so Christians would proclaim the death of the Lord to non-Christians. Few if any non-Christians would have been able to make the connection, and they almost certainly would not have been allowed to be present, any more than non-Israelites were allowed to be present at the Passover sacrifice and celebration (Ex 12:43-49).

Rather, Paul is saying that the eating and drinking in the Eucharistic ceremony of the bread and wine are in fact a proclamation of the death of the Lord, because they are a ceremonial representation of his sacrifice and of the value of that sacrifice. They are primarily acts of worship, not evangelism, even as many proclamational psalms were acts of worship (for example, Pss 100, 103, 145 among many others). It is even hard to understand how watching a group of Christians eat some bread and drink some wine might be effective evangelism for someone who is an unbeliever.

Just as the Passover meal, celebrated year after year, "proclaimed" the Lord's deliverance of his old covenant people, so the Eucharist is celebrated to proclaim the deliverance of his new covenant people. Both proclaimed what God did, so that the participants might renew their appreciation of what came from it, and pray that that blessing might be increased. We can see that from the prayers of the Jewish Passover, as well as the prayers of the Christian Eucharist which was modeled on it.

The Eucharistic words of Jesus take us part way in our understanding of the Eucharist. They indicate that the Eucharist is a sacrificial meal and therefore that when we take part in the Eucharist we are participating in the sacrifice of Christ and in the blessing that comes from that sacrifice. They do not, however, tell us much more about the way the Eucharist is a sacrifice, especially how it can be a sacrifice when there is only one new covenant Passover sacrifice, the death of Christ on the cross. These questions will be taken up in the next chapter.

Meditation: The New Covenant
Exodus 24:4-11

In the twenty-fourth chapter of the Book of Exodus, we can read about the conclusion of God's manifestation to the people of Israel on Mount Sinai. They had come before him at the foot of the mountain, he had appeared before them in his glory, and he had spoken to them. He had given them the Ten Commandments and so made a covenant with them. They had agreed to accept the covenant and live by it.

Between the giving of the Ten Commandments and the events in chapter 24 is an extensive body of instruction now called the Covenant Code. Some commentators have understood this to have been given with the Ten Commandments. Some have understood it to have been given later and inserted here in the text. Either way, it is associated with the Ten Commandments and shows how the Ten Commandments are to be lived out by old covenant people. Then occurs the following passage in chapter 24,

> And Moses wrote all the words of the Lord. And he rose early in the morn-
> ing, and built an altar at the foot of the mountain, and twelve pillars, accord-
> ing to the twelve tribes of Israel. And he sent young men of the people of
> Israel, who offered burnt offerings and sacrificed peace offerings of oxen to
> the Lord. And Moses took half of the blood and put it in basins, and half of
> the blood he threw against the altar. Then he took the book of the covenant,
> and read it in the hearing of the people; and they said,
> "All that the Lord has spoken we will do, and we will be obedient."
> And Moses took the blood and threw it upon the people, and said,
> "Behold the blood of the covenant which the Lord has made with you in
> accordance with all these words."

The description above is of a sacrifice that is not strictly paralleled anywhere
else in the worship of the old covenant. First, a group of young men offers the
sacrifices, not the priests and Levites. That is an indication that we are reading
about a sacrificial ceremony that occurs before the temple worship is established.

The offering consists of burnt offerings and peace offerings. Moses takes the
blood of the offering, the way a priest would in a temple ceremony, and throws
half the blood on the altar as a way of giving it to God. He then reads the "book
of the covenant," and the people again commit themselves to be obedient and
keep the covenant. He then throws the blood on the people. When he does so
he says, "This is the blood of the covenant which the Lord has made with you,
in accordance with all these words." In other words, this blood establishes a
covenant relationship with God, your part of which is keeping the commandments stated in this book. This too is a special event that was not repeated in
temple worship.

Moses, in short, sealed the covenant with sacrificial blood, as many other
covenants at that time were sealed. The concluding sacrifices were part of the
process of making the covenant and so a means of reconciling the two parties
and uniting them together. The agreement in word was not enough for something as solemn as a covenant that would establish a lifelong relationship, but
needed to be sealed by the sacrifice. In this case the relationship was not simply
a friendship relationship between two human partners but between the people
of Israel and God.

"The blood of the covenant" are the words Jesus used as narrated in the

Gospel of Mark and then, in a slightly different phrasing, in 1 Corinthians, to describe the cup of wine that was drunk at the Eucharist. The Letter to the Hebrews refers to the same event in a similar way in chapter 9 (vv. 18-19). The phrase "blood of the covenant" tells us that not only was the death of Christ a fulfilment of the Passover sacrifice, which redeemed the people of Israel, it was also a covenant-sealing sacrifice.

The throwing of the blood by Moses was a sign of the joining of God and the people of Israel in a covenant relationship. Partaking of the Eucharist, then, is renewing the covenant relationship with God. Such a thing can, however, only be sealed, that is, fully accomplished, because of a sacrifice. In this case the sacrifice is the sacrifice of Christ, whose blood is given to us to drink, apparently as an equivalent of what happened when the blood was thrown on the old covenant people at Sinai.

The account in the chapter then continues.

Then Moses and Aaron, Nadab, and Abihu, and seventy of the elders of Israel went up, and they saw the God of Israel; and there was under his feet, as it were, a pavement of sapphire stone, like the very heaven for clearness. And he did not lay his hand on the chief men of the people of Israel; they beheld God, and ate and drank.

In other words, the elders, the representatives of the people, took a meal with God. This meal is probably the sacrificial meal that is associated with making a covenant (see Gn 26:30), a meal in which the two parties ate the peace offering. In so doing, they were like priests who were eating a sacred meal in the temple, in the place of God's presence. The conclusion of the covenant on Sinai and the sacrifice that sealed it was a meal that expressed the family bond between God and his people. During this meal, in some sense, the elders beheld God.

The Eucharist is such a meal, even though we do not partake of much food and drink. It is a meal in which the covenant relationship with God is renewed. As the body of the sacrificial victim was eaten and the blood was put on the worshipers in Exodus 24, so in the Eucharist the Body of Christ is eaten and his Blood drunk. In this meal, the relationship with God is renewed through partaking of the Body and Blood of the Lord, offered on the cross to establish the covenant. As a result, we are renewed in our personal knowledge of God (Jer 31:34; Heb 8:11; 12:22-24).

The Eucharist is not, however, a meal to renew the old covenant. The blood is the blood of the new covenant. It is the new covenant which is established by the death and resurrection of Christ and which is renewed in the Eucharist. It is this new covenant relationship that will be consummated at the end of time when, in heaven itself, we take part in the festal meal of the marriage feast of the Lamb, celebrating his union with his people. Then those who come from east and west, from the rising of the sun to its setting, will "sit at table with Abraham, Isaac, and Jacob in the kingdom of heaven" (Mt 8:11) and will see God "face to face" (1 Cor 13:12).

What happened at the top of Mount Sinai foreshadowed the meal that we partake of in the Eucharist. That, in turn, will strengthen our covenant relationship with God "until [Jesus] comes" to take his people to the great feast in the kingdom of God (1 Cor 11:26). Then, God will be "everything to everyone" (1 Cor 15:28).

Eucharistic Prayer III

The Anaphora

The Lord be with you.
And also with you.
Lift up your hearts.
We lift them up to the Lord.
Let us give thanks to the Lord our God.
It is right to give him thanks and praise.

Preface: Father, all-powerful and ever-living God, we do well always and everywhere to give you thanks through Jesus Christ our Lord. Through his cross and resurrection he freed us from sin and death and called us to the glory that has made us a chosen race, a royal priesthood, a holy nation, a people set apart.

Everywhere we proclaim your mighty works, for you have called us out of darkness into your own wonderful light.

And so with all the choirs of angels in heaven we proclaim your glory and join in their unending hymn of praise:

> **Holy, holy, holy Lord, God of power and might,**
> **heaven and earth are full of your glory.**
> **Hosanna in the highest.**
> **Blessed is he who comes in the name of the Lord.**
> **Hosanna in the highest.**

Father, you are holy indeed, and all creation rightly gives you praise. All life, all holiness, comes from you through your Son, Jesus Christ our Lord, by the working of the Holy Spirit. From age to age you gather a people to yourself, so that from east to west a perfect offering may be made to the glory of your name.

Invocation: And so, Father, we bring you these gifts.

Epiclesis We ask you to make them holy by the power of your Spirit, that they may become the Body and Blood of your Son, our Lord Jesus Christ, at whose command we celebrate this Eucharist.

Institution
narrative: On the night he was betrayed, he took bread and gave you thanks and praise. He broke the bread, gave it to his disciples, and said: Take this, all of you, and eat it: this is my Body which will be given up for you. When supper was ended, he took the cup. Again he gave you thanks and praise, gave the cup to his disciples, and said: Take this, all of you, and drink from it: this is the cup of my Blood, the Blood of the new and everlasting covenant. It will be shed for you and all men so that sins may be forgiven. Do this in memory of me.

Memorial: Let us proclaim the mystery of faith:

Anamnesis **Christ has died,**
Christ is risen,
Christ will come again.
Dying you destroyed our death,
rising you restored our life.
Lord Jesus, come in glory.
When we eat this bread and drink this cup,
we proclaim your death, Lord Jesus,
until you come in glory.
Lord, by your cross and resurrection
you have set us free.
You are the Savior of the world.

Father, calling to mind the death your Son endured for our salvation, his glorious resurrection and ascension into heaven, and ready to greet him when he comes again, we offer you in thanksgiving this holy and living sacrifice.

(Invocation): Look with favor on your Church's offering, and see the Victim whose death has reconciled us to yourself. Grant that we, who are nourished by his Body and Blood, may be filled with his Holy Spirit, and become one body, one spirit in Christ.

May he make us an everlasting gift to you and enable us to share in the inheritance of your saints, with Mary, the virgin Mother of God; with the apostles, the martyrs, [Saint *N.*] and all your saints, on whose constant intercession we rely for help.

Intercessions: Lord, may this sacrifice, which has made our peace with you, advance the peace and salvation of all the world. Strengthen in faith and love your pilgrim Church on earth; your servant, Pope N.; our bishop N.; and all the bishops, with the clergy and the entire people your Son has gained for you.

Father, hear the prayers of the family you have gathered here before you. In mercy and love unite all your children wherever they may be. Welcome into your kingdom our departed brothers and sisters, and all who have left this world in your friendship. We hope to enjoy forever the vision of your glory, through Christ our Lord, from whom all good things come.

Doxology: Through him,
with him,
in him,
in the unity of the Holy Spirit,
all glory and honor is yours,
almighty Father,
for ever and ever.
Amen.

FIVE

The Eucharistic Offering

For from the rising of the sun to its setting my name is great
among the nations, and in every place incense is offered to my
name, and a pure offering.

MALACHI 1:11

There is a prophecy in the Book of Malachi in which God expresses his displeasure as to how the people of Israel had been offering sacrifice to him. They were doing it in a way that did not honor him. He then says,

Oh, that there were one among you who would shut the doors [of the temple], that you might not kindle fire upon my altar in vain! I have no pleasure in you, says the Lord of hosts, and I will not accept an offering from your hand. For from the rising of the sun to its setting my name is great among the nations, and in every place incense is offered to my name, and a pure offering; for my name is great among the nations, says the Lord.

MALACHI 1:10-11

In other words, it was prophesied that God would receive from the other nations the honor that his chosen people would not give him because they offered their sacrifices in an unworthy and unacceptable way. Central to this would be "a pure offering," offered to his name from the rising to the setting of the sun. Not just in the temple in Jerusalem would God be offered sacrifice that would please him but throughout the world and by members of all the nations of the earth.

The early Christians understood this prophecy to refer to the Eucharist. Citing this prophecy, among other Scriptures, one of the earliest Fathers of the Church, Irenaeus of Lyons, called the Eucharist "the new offering of the new covenant," the "pure sacrifice."[1] It was the one offering acceptable to God that would not just be offered by Israelites but would be offered all over the world by those who had entered the new covenant.

The Eucharist would not, however, be a sacrifice on its own.[2] It would be a commemoration and re-presentation of the one sacrifice of the Son of God. This was the sacrifice that redeemed the world and began the new creation. This was the sacrifice that paid the price of the redemption of the whole human race. This was the sacrifice that made possible the true exodus from sin and this world, dominated by the oppressive rule of Satan, to the Promised Land of life in the Spirit and of heaven itself. This was the true fulfilment of the Passover. The Eucharist would be the celebration of this one sacrifice of Christ.

The Eucharist, then, is a sacrifice, the new sacrifice of the new covenant. For centuries that was taken for granted,[3] but in the Reformation it was called into question.[4] The issue raised by the Reformation controversies is based on an objective difficulty. The sacrifice that saves us is the death of Christ on the cross. No other does. The Eucharist is a sacrifice and has a role in our salvation. But it is not a different sacrifice than the one Christ offered in his death and resurrection. But how can the Eucharist be a sacrifice, without being simply a different sacrifice, a further sacrifice, than the sacrifice that Christ offered with full success about two thousand years ago?[5]

With the progress in the ecumenical dialogues[6] and the renewal of the Catholic liturgy, we are perhaps now in a better position to understand the way the Eucharist is a sacrifice. Although in this chapter we are mainly concerned with how Catholics should participate in the Eucharistic celebration, especially the Liturgy of the Eucharist, we also want to give attention to the issue of how the Eucharist can be a sacrifice without adding to the sacrifice of the cross. To summarize in advance, there is only one sacrifice of the new covenant, Christ himself, who died and rose again. The Eucharist is the way that sacrifice is re-presented as a pure offering to God from the rising of the sun to the setting of the sun among all the nations of the world.

In Catholic theology, it has been traditional to speak of the nature of the Eucharist or Mass in two "articles" or chapters. In the first, it is treated as a sacrifice; in the second as a sacrament. The next two chapters of this volume will follow that order. They will be followed by a third chapter, which will consider how Christ is present in the Eucharist, especially in the "Eucharistic elements." Each of the next three chapters, then, will cover the same material, but from three different perspectives: sacrifice, meal-sacrament, presence. All three chapters will seek to see the Eucharist within the context of the liturgical worship of the Church, the new covenant people of God.

The Eucharistic Prayer

As we have seen, at the Last Supper Christ took bread, gave thanks for it, and then broke the blessed bread and distributed it. After the meal, he took a cup of wine, gave thanks for it, and then passed the cup around. He most probably gave thanks over the cup in a way that expressed the meaning of the celebration as a whole.[7] The fact that Christ gave thanks over the bread and cup makes the ceremony a "Eucharist," a special kind of thanksgiving. Our Eucharistic Prayer corresponds to Christ's prayer and is therefore a thanksgiving prayer or prayer for a thanksgiving offering. It is probably the same as Christ's in its main outlines.

The early Christians, following Jesus' instruction, repeated what Jesus did at the Last Supper. However, at least those living in Gentile cultures made notable changes in the ceremony used at the Last Supper. They soon joined the two meal blessings into one (perhaps before the writing of 1 Corinthians) and dropped the full meal (sometime after the writing of 1 Corinthians), or at least separated it from the Eucharist. A ceremony resulted that contains the essential "shape of the Eucharist": taking and giving thanks for bread and wine together and then distributing them.[8]

The Christian Eucharistic ceremony, then, has two foci. The first is taking bread and wine and saying over them a prayer of thanksgiving. The second is partaking of the blessed bread and wine. By the prayer of thanksgiving, the bread and wine are offered to God. When we speak of the Eucharist as a sacrifice, then, we are speaking of something that primarily happens through the Eucharistic Prayer, the prayer of blessing or thanksgiving over the bread and wine.

The *Catechism of the Catholic Church* (1352) tells us that "with the Eucharistic Prayer—the prayer of thanksgiving and consecration—we come to the heart and summit of the celebration." Today many Catholics are surprised that the prayer as a whole is the heart and center of the Eucharist, not the words of institution by themselves. For that reason alone we should understand the prayer and understand what it means to take part when it is being prayed.

The Eucharistic Prayer is also, however, a prayer that tells us what it means to say that the Eucharist is a sacrifice. We are supposed to believe according to the way the Church prays. The Eucharistic Prayers are the prayers of the whole Church for the Eucharistic sacrifice and so tell us the faith of the Church in this regard.[9]

Because the Eucharistic Prayers from the early Church show the same essential characteristics, we can be confident that in looking at one of our Eucharistic Prayers, which are modeled on the traditional ones, we are looking at the Eucharist as it has been understood by the tradition of the Church. Because the tradition of the Church in this matter points back to the apostles as its source,[10] we can therefore be confident that, in its main outlines, our Eucharistic Prayers can teach us about the Eucharist as it was understood by the apostles. We are, in short, seeing in our Eucharistic Prayers, and the prayers of the early Church that gave rise to them, authentic tradition which allows us to better understand the words of Scripture about the Eucharist.

Preliminaries. Three things happened in most early Christian liturgies at the beginning of the Liturgy of the Eucharist before the Eucharistic Prayer, and those three things give us an orientation to the meaning of the Eucharistic Prayer. First, those who were not Christians in good standing, either because they were catechumens being instructed or because they were doing penance, were dismissed. Sharing in the Eucharist was only for those who were in *full* union with Christ.[11]

Then those who were present gave one another the kiss of peace. Even today the peace is given at this point in all the liturgies in the Catholic Church except for the Roman rite. In giving the peace, the early Christians understood themselves to be fulfilling the commandment of the Lord, "If you are offering your gift at the altar, and there remember that your brother has something against you, leave your gift there before the altar and go; first be reconciled to your brother, and then come and offer your gift" (Mt 5:23-24). The kiss of peace was meant to express the fact that all who were present were in good relationship with one another as a community and now could offer the Christian sacrifice as one body. It was even considered wrong to give the peace when there was lack of reconciliation.[12]

These two preliminary actions show us that the Eucharist is intended to be a corporate action, the action of a body united in Christ.

Then the gifts were brought up. In the Western Church this was the time for the people to bring their offerings to the altar rail and give them to the deacon. In the Eastern Church they brought them before the assembly began, and this was the time when the bread and wine, selected from the gifts of the people, were brought to the altar in a solemn procession called the Great Entrance.[13] The Eucharist, in other words, was taken from the gifts of the people, their material offerings to the Lord. It was the offering of the people that became the offering of the Lord.[14]

The prayer. The Eucharistic Prayer (sometimes called **The** *Anaphora*) then begins. The prayer goes from the summons "Lift up your hearts" to the concluding doxology ("Through him, with him, in him ..." in the Roman rite). Because of the way it includes certain acclamations and, in some rites, changes of posture, and because of the particular emphasis put on the words of institution in the way some celebrate the current Roman rite, many people do not realize that this whole section of the Eucharistic celebration is one prayer and all of it is a prayer of consecration.

When Christ gave thanks, he gave thanks to God his Father (Jn 17:1). In following his example, our Eucharistic Prayers do as well. They are addressed to the Father through the Son. It is the Father who "so loved the world that he gave his only Son, that whoever believes in him should not perish but have eternal life" (Jn 3:16). It is the Son who offered himself in accord with the will of the Father to save us, and who, at the Last Supper, said a prayer of thanksgiving which was also a prayer of self-offering (Heb 10:5-10; Jn 17:19).[15] Our Eucharistic Prayer, then, is directed to the Father.[16]

All the liturgies in the Catholic Church have Eucharistic Prayers. In order to understand the meaning of the Eucharistic Prayer, and with it the meaning of the Eucharist, we will look at Eucharistic Prayer III from the current Roman liturgy.[17] This can be found at the beginning of this chapter. The different elements of the prayer as listed in the *Catechism of the Catholic Church* (1352-1354) and described in what follows are marked in the margin. If another Eucharistic Prayer had been chosen, especially one from the Eastern rites, the presentation would be somewhat different, but since all Catholic and Orthodox Eucharistic Prayers (and many Protestant ones now as well) have the same elements, all of them could serve as an introduction to the theology of the Eucharistic sacrifice.

A thanksgiving sacrifice. The Byzantine liturgy and other Eastern liturgies preface the Eucharistic Prayer with a proclamation, "Let us stand well [that is, stand erect]. Let us stand with reverence. Let us pay attention so that we may offer the Holy Eucharistic Prayer in peace." When the Eucharistic Prayer is prayed, we are in the middle of a liturgy, a worship service, and we are in the presence of God, offering him the most solemn worship Christians can offer.

The Byzantine liturgy then goes on (and the Roman liturgy joins it) with the proclamation "Lift up your hearts." This does not mean, "Cheer up," as the English words might be understood. These are the words that were used to begin a solemn blessing in Jewish and early Christian worship.[18] The word "heart" in Hebrew refers to what we would call "mind," so the invitation is to direct our minds, our attention, to where the Lord is, above in heaven.

Next comes the exhortation, "Let us give thanks to the Lord our God." We are, in other words, about to begin the Prayer of Thanksgiving. The Eucharist is a sacrifice offered to God. But, as the word "Eucharist" tells us, and Eucharistic Prayer I (the traditional Roman canon) and the Liturgy of St. John Chrysostom explicitly indicate, the sacrifice we are celebrating is primarily a sacrifice of thanksgiving (sometimes translated "a sacrifice of praise"). We are thanking God for what he has done through the cross and resurrection of Christ to redeem us.[19]

We might not immediately make a connection between sacrifice and thanksgiving. Many of us would more readily see sacrifice as something to be done for atonement (satisfaction for sin) or for petition, since we understand a sacrifice to be an offering to God so that he will respond to us in a certain way. To be sure, the Eucharist is atoning or propitiatory.[20] Moreover, we may ask God for favors during it and will do so in the course of the Eucharistic Prayer.

Sacrifices, however, were often offered in the old covenant to thank God for something he had done. A gift was given to express thanks, much the same way we would offer a gift in appreciation of someone who has performed a service for us. The gift is not a compensation. We are not paying the person back. Rather it is an expression of our gratitude.[21]

The Eucharist, then, as a sacrifice, is primarily a thanksgiving sacrifice that expresses our gratitude to God for what he has done in his Son to redeem us and give us new life. In this it has a somewhat different character than the death of Christ on the cross. His sacrifice on the cross predominantly was a sin offering, seeking the redemption of the human race. Our Eucharistic commemoration of that sacrifice predominantly has the character of a thanksgiving offering, thanking God for the redemption that has been granted us through what Christ did on the cross.

The Eucharistic Prayer begins with what in the Roman rite is called the *preface*. "Preface" here probably does not mean "introduction" but "proclamation." It is a proclamation of God's goodness to us, the goodness for which we are thanking him, a prayer of praise. The Eucharistic Prayers in the other rites start in the same way. Because the Eucharistic Prayer begins by praising and thanking God and speaks of what God did to redeem us, it is, as a whole, a prayer of praise and thanksgiving to God for his goodness to us, especially his goodness in redeeming us though Christ.

The Eucharistic Prayer is a prayer of thanksgiving but it is also a prayer for a sacrifice. As we have seen, in the old covenant, prayers were said in the temple when sacrifice was being offered. They praised God's goodness as the source of all blessing, but they also praised God for what he had done that occasioned the sacrifice that was now being offered. In so doing they expressed the purpose of the sacrifice being offered.

The prayers at a sacrificial meal also seem to have praised God for his goodness and for whatever occasioned the sacrifice, as we can see by considering the Jewish Passover meal. In so doing, they expressed the purpose of the sacrificial meal which was completing the sacrificial action. As we have seen, Christ's prayer of "thanks and praise" at the Last Supper, which the institution narrative refers to, must have done the same. Our Eucharistic Prayer, which is a prayer of thanksgiving for the sacrifice of Christ, does likewise. Our Eucharistic Prayer is therefore a prayer that expresses the meaning of the sacrifice in which those who take part in the celebration are participating.

The *Catechism* calls the Eucharistic Prayer a prayer of thanksgiving and consecration. *Consecration* has been used as a technical term for the change in the bread and wine—making sacramentally present the Body and Blood of Christ. The *Catechism* may be simply using the term in such a way.

"Consecration," however, has been used more broadly. As we saw in chapter 3, it is a translation of a Hebrew word for "making holy" and could be used for the offering and acceptance of a sacrifice.[22] When an acceptable gift was given to God in an acceptable way, it was made holy, that is, God's, and so consecrated to him (Ex 29:27; 28:38; 1 Chr 23:13; 2 Chr 30:17). It was thereafter called a "holy thing," that is, something specially God's (Lv 21–22; Ex 29:34; Ez 20:40; see also the Mishnaic tractate *Qadoshim*). It could in some sense sanctify or convey holiness (Lv 6:18, 27; Ez 46:20).

The word could also be used to speak of something becoming filled with God's presence or becoming the vehicle of God's presence. When God becomes present on a mountain or speaks through a prophet or the Scriptures, or dwells in a holy person, those earthly realities are consecrated or sanctified by God's presence, even though they have not gone through a ceremony of consecration. As Cyril of Jerusalem put it while speaking of the Eucharistic Prayer,

"Whatsoever the Holy Spirit has touched, is sanctified and changed."[23]

The Eucharistic Prayer, then, is a thanksgiving prayer that consecrates. It offers the bread and wine to God, thanking him for what he has done, and calling his blessing, the holy presence of the holy-making Spirit of God, upon them. As a result they become "holy things," as the Greek-speaking Christians called them,[24] holy because of being offered to God, but also intrinsically holy and conveyors of holiness. Such a prayer is, like Christ's own prayer at the Last Supper, a thanksgiving or blessing prayer that consecrates or sanctifies in accordance with the meaning of the feast.

The sacrificial memorial. The prayers at an old covenant sacrificial meal presented the sacrificial victim again to God and blessed him for what he had done that had occasioned the sacrifice. In offering or presenting the food of the meal to God, including the meat from the sacrificial victim, the sacrificial victim was not being sacrificed over again, but the meal became a part of the sacrificial action, the completion of an offering to God. The meal completed the sacrificial action in the sense that it allowed the worshiper to share in the sacrifice, as Paul said in 1 Corinthians 10:18.

As we have seen, the prayer at the sacrificial meal of our Eucharist begins with praise and thanks to God for what he has done. This includes thanksgiving for his creation, because that is the fundamental blessing he bestows on us. In this, the Eucharistic Prayer continues the Passover, a harvest feast and therefore a feast to thank God for the blessings of his creation. It was also the feast that began the year (Ex 12:2) and so celebrated the beginning of all years, the creation. The prayer, however, primarily praises and thanks God for his redeeming us, especially by the Passover sacrifice of the death and resurrection of his Son, which makes possible new life for those who belong to the new covenant.

Many Eucharistic Prayers, then, as we can see in Eucharistic Prayer III, move from praise and thanksgiving to the *invocation* or, to use the English version of a Greek word, the *epiclesis*. While the whole Eucharistic Prayer is an invocation, the word "epiclesis" has become a special term in modern liturgical theology to refer to special prayers of invocation within the Eucharistic Prayer. In these prayers God the Father is invoked or called upon to act in the Eucharist in a special way.

And so, Father, we bring you these gifts.
We ask you to make them holy by the power of your Spirit,
that they may become the Body and Blood
of your Son, our Lord Jesus Christ,
at whose command we celebrate this Eucharist.

When the bishop or priest, the ordained president, says these words so that we can celebrate this Eucharist, he is acknowledging that he is not just bringing the Eucharist about by his own power or his own action. Only if the power of the Holy Spirit is at work, taking the bread and wine and transforming them into the Body and Blood, the sacrifice, of Christ, can such a thing happen. Invoking God is a confession that we need God to bring about what we are seeking.

From the first invocation or epiclesis Eucharistic Prayer III moves to the *institution narrative*, which contains what we would call "the words of institution." These we looked at in the previous chapter when we considered the scriptural basis for the Eucharist understood as a sacrifice. They now are quoted or paraphrased in all Eucharistic Prayers. In the Eucharistic Prayers they are primarily used to refer to what Jesus said would happen "whenever" we do what he commanded us at the Last Supper, that is, celebrate the Eucharist.

We use the phrase *words of institution* to describe the nature of these words in this context. This expression contains the Latin theological term that indicates that when Christ used these words he established the Eucharist as a sacrament, something that was to be repeated.[25] We might, however, also call them the "charter" or the "entitlement."

In these words, Christ said that if his apostles took bread and wine, blessed them, and distributed them, they would be his Body and Blood that will have been offered for human salvation. When the bishop or priest, "the president of the brethren," to use the phrase of Justin Martyr,[26] the second-century apologist, speaks these words, he is referring to what Christ said and thereby claiming Christ's authorization for what would otherwise be a tremendously audacious action, perhaps even a blasphemous action. He is reminding God that Christ has commanded us to do such a thing. As some Christians put it, he is claiming the promises of Christ for the celebration of the Eucharist.

The prayer of invocation (the epiclesis) and the institution narrative, together in whatever order they occur in a given Eucharistic Prayer, express the result that the Church, presided over by the bishop or priest, is seeking. We, the Christian people, are offering bread and wine, a small part of his gifts to us and an expression of the offering of our whole lives in return. We are asking God to receive them and, in accord with the words of Christ, transform them into something better, the Body and Blood of Christ.[27]

Since Christ is no longer on earth but in heaven, we are asking God to make our offerings heavenly. We could say that, as some prayers do, by asking him to take them to his altar in heaven. We could say that, as other prayers do, by asking him to send down his heavenly presence upon them. We are, however, in either case asking him to transform them so that our material gifts become the Body and Blood of the glorified, heavenly Lord. We are asking God to transform them so they become Christ himself in a form that sacramentally represents the fact that he has given himself as a sacrifice.

Eucharistic Prayer III then moves to the memorial prayer, or the *anamnesis*, to use the English version of another Greek word that now has also become a technical term in modern liturgical theology. The memorial prayer contains a short summary of the meaning of the whole Eucharist.[28] The prayer is as follows:

> Father, calling to mind the death your Son endured for our salvation, his glorious resurrection and ascension into heaven, and ready to greet him when he comes again, we offer you in thanksgiving this holy and living sacrifice.
>
> Look with favor on your Church's offering, and see the Victim whose death has reconciled us to yourself. Grant that we, who are nourished by his Body and Blood, may be filled with his Holy Spirit, and become one body, one spirit in Christ.
>
> May he make us an everlasting gift to you and enable us to share in the inheritance of your saints.

The prayer is called the memorial prayer, because it "calls to mind" the death, resurrection, and ascension, the basis of the Eucharist.

The sacrifice we are offering is Christ himself. We are not offering the sacrificial action but the sacrificial victim. "Victim" here is being used in the technical sense of something that has been sacrificed.[29] To be sure, we are offering the victim who died on the cross and was raised again and in that death and resurrection was offered to God. But that happened two thousand years ago. The sacrifice we are offering now is the Lamb who was put to death as a sacrifice in the past. As Aquinas put it, "The Eucharist is the perfect sacrament of our

Lord's passion, because it contains Christ himself who endured it."[30]

We are, however, not offering a dead victim. As the prayer says, we are offering "a holy and living sacrifice." We are offering the sacrificial victim who has died and come back to life. Moreover, that sacrificial victim is not only living but also holy, probably in the sense that this sacrifice has already been accepted by God and so is his—holy.

Since the sacrifice being offered is a holy and living sacrifice, we are not putting him to death again. It is Christ who once died and now is alive who is the sacrifice. To be sure, he only is now a sacrifice, because he was once given to God through his death. But he himself, the living victim, is being offered to the Father at this point in Eucharistic Prayer III as our sacrifice, the sacrificial victim who has saved us and continues to save us.

This brings us to the question of why, if the sacrifice has already been accepted, we are offering it again. The answer is that we are offering it, presenting it again to God, at the beginning of our sacrificial meal, because we want to ask God again to give us the benefits that come from such a sacrifice. As Eucharistic Prayer III says, we are asking him to fill us anew with the Holy Spirit. We are asking him to strengthen our union with him and with one another in him. We are asking again for the blessings or benefits that come from our redemption in Christ.

We are also asking that those benefits have their effect in us. We are asking that we become truly a gift to God. We are asking that we, as the body of Christ, be made an acceptable sacrifice or offering to him, something he truly wants because of the way we live our lives (see Rom 12:1; 15:16). We are also asking that sometime in the future we be allowed to receive our heavenly inheritance.

Finally, we are praying for others who are not present. We are praying that God may "strengthen in faith and love" his "pilgrim Church on earth." We are also praying that he may "unite all [his] children wherever they may be" (see Jn 17:22). We also pray for "our departed brothers and sisters" who have "left this world in your friendship" that they may be "welcomed into your kingdom." In addition, we are praying that "this sacrifice, which has made our peace with you, advance the peace and salvation of all the world." We are, in short, not just praying that we might receive the benefits of the sacrifice of Christ but that the whole Christian people, even the whole world, might receive them.

We are not repeating the sacrifice of Christ to obtain all these blessings. As the Letter to the Hebrews said, that sacrifice has been offered "once for all" (Heb 7:27; 9:12; 10:10; 9:26-28; see also Rom 6:10; 1 Pt 3:18). Christ does not need to die again. Once was enough, probably more than enough. He will never die again. He is, however, standing before his Father, as in the vision of the Lamb in Revelation (Rv 5), and he is presenting to his Father the fact that he has died. He is interceding for us in heaven on the basis of what he did for us on earth (Rom 8:34).

We too are joining in that intercession. We are gathering together on earth and asking God to renew the gift he has already given us when he made us Christians. We are asking him to grant that gift to others as well or to strengthen them in it. We are asking him to do so because of the death of Christ on the cross, which is being sacramentally represented on the altar by the separated Body and Blood.

There is a technical theological term that describes what is happening in the Eucharistic Prayer. We are *re-presenting* the sacrifice of Christ.[31] "Representation" could refer to what a sign or image does in relationship to the reality it points to and, in this case, contains. In this sense the Eucharist is a sacramental representation of Christ and his death. "Representation" could also mean present again. In this sense we are presenting Christ's sacrifice to God again and in that sense offering it to him (see Heb 9:25). There are not two sacrifices, the sacrifice of Christ at Calvary and the sacrifice of Christ in the Eucharist. There is only one sacrifice of Christ, offered on the cross by Christ when he gave himself and now sacramentally represented and re-presented to God in the Eucharist.[32]

We are, to use a phrase somewhat common among certain Evangelical Christians, "pleading the blood." We are placing Christ and what he did before the Father, not just in words but sacramentally, and making that our plea in the legal sense of "plea," the grounds on which we are asking him to act. And we are confident that those grounds are so adequate that he will do nothing else but act the way we ask him to.

The prayer we have quoted begins by saying that we are "calling to mind" Christ's death, resurrection, and ascension. Because it follows on the words of Paul quoted in the institution narrative, the prayer is indicating that we are fulfilling Christ's command to "do this in remembrance of me." As we have seen in the last chapter, such a prayer is likely the kind of prayer that expressed a formal petition, especially the kind of petition that accompanied a sacrifice.

Our Eucharistic Prayer is addressed to God the Father. We are praying that God might remember Christ's sacrifice and grant the blessing for which it was offered. We are, however, calling his attention to a sacrifice that has already been accepted in Christ's resurrection. Moreover, we recognize that the blessing he sought has already, in germ, been granted by the outpouring of the Holy Spirit. We are therefore praying that what he died for might be fully completed by our sanctification and by the second coming.

During the Eucharist, then, we make a formal petition and call to God's attention the basis on which we want him to act. That basis is the death and resurrection of Christ, the sacrifice offered for our redemption. The memorial we make in the Eucharist is a sacrificial action, because it is presenting again to God something that is a sacrifice, calling God's attention to it, and asking God to be favorable to us because of it. The connection is well expressed in the Chaldean liturgy when the priest prays, "[Glory to God who has chosen me] that I might offer to you this lifegiving, holy, and acceptable sacrifice, which is the memorial of the passion, death, burial, and resurrection of our Lord and Savior Jesus Christ, in whom you are well pleased and by whom you have decreed to efface the sins of all men."

The Eucharist is, to use the term in the *Catechism of the Catholic Church,* a sacrificial memorial. It is a feast we hold that includes a sacrificial offering which is the memorial of the death and resurrection of Christ. When we re-present that sacrifice we are recalling to ourselves the most important event of our salvation and thanking God for it. But we are also calling that event to God's attention so that he might renew in us, and others, the blessing for which Christ has offered it and is even now offering it.

The ones who offer.[33] This brings us to the question of who is offering the sacrifice of the Eucharist. The first and easiest answer is that "we," God's people, are, to use the words of the Eucharistic Prayers. We are offering to God the bread and wine. We are giving him an offering that is a kind of first-fruits offering. We are taking what he has given us, the bread and wine made from grain and grapes that grew by God's power, and we are giving part of it back to him to acknowledge our dependence on him for life and our thanksgiving for his blessing. In so doing, we are offering our lives in homage to him our Lord.

Bread and wine are not much. They are just expressions of our worship. We come, however, with a further purpose in mind. We come to seek from God more than his continued blessing of earthly life. We come to seek from him a renewal of our new covenant, spiritual, eternal life. For this to happen an earthly sacrifice is not enough. Only a heavenly sacrifice will do. Only if our earthly gifts are received by God and made into heavenly gifts can we receive what we seek.

One alone can offer such a sacrifice, and that is Christ. In a certain way then, according to Catholic theology, Christ is offering the sacrifice. He is the one standing before his Father, showing him the basis on which redemption should be given to us. He is in the Eucharist sacramentally present in our midst. He is present in our midst without leaving heaven. Therefore he is present the way he is in heaven, as the Lamb who "by his blood purchased us for God and made us a kingdom of priests to God" (Rv 5:10), not the way he was on the cross, suffering and dying over again. He is, however, interceding on the basis of his death and resurrection so that we might become what he died to make us (Rom 8:34; Heb 9:11-12, 24; 10:12).[34] We might say that he has offered and is still offering for us the sacrifice of Calvary, which is being sacramentally re-presented in the Eucharist.

But, as we have seen in the memorial prayer, we, his church, under the sacramental presidency of the priest, are also offering the sacrifice of Christ. We are not offering it in the sense that we are making it possible for Christ to be offered. We are offering it in the sense that we, part of Christ's body, are presenting again what Christ did for us so that we might become more fully, confidently, and successfully what he died to make us. We are pointing to Christ himself, who died and rose again and is now standing before the Father interceding for us.[35]

We cannot present Christ in the presumptuous sense that we can decide or could ever have decided how Christ offers himself or that we are making his sacrifice on the cross a sacrifice. Rather we are "memorializing" his own sacrifice, that is, calling it to the attention of God the Father. We are "reminding" God that we belong to Christ, and therefore we can claim the benefits of what he did. We are his body, him in a certain way, so we are entitled to receive what he and those who belong to him should have and to intercede for others that they too might receive it.

In doing this we are also offering ourselves "through, with, and in him." We are not offering ourselves in the Eucharist in the same sense that we are re-presenting Christ's sacrifice. Rather, we are praying that his sacrifice might make us truly God's, truly holy. We are asking, in the words of Eucharistic Prayer III, that as a result of the sacrifice of Christ, we become "an everlasting gift" to God. We pray, in other words, that our re-presentation of the sacrifice of Christ and the renewal of our union with him that it is intended to accomplish should renew our own lives as "living sacrifices, holy and acceptable to God" (Rom 12:1). In making such a prayer, we give ourselves to God once again.

The Eucharistic sacrifice today. There are now three common approaches to this "heart and center" of the Eucharistic celebration. The first one is what we could call the "Here, People" approach. According to this approach, in the institution narrative Christ is offering the elements to his disciples. This is represented by the priest acting out the words of Christ by presenting the elements to the people, as if he were saying, "Here, take this." The image behind this is Christ looking at the congregation, welcoming and affirming those who are present, and offering them the food and drink for a meal.[36]

The second is what we could call the "Come, Adore" approach. In this approach the crucial thing that happens during the Eucharistic Prayer is that Christ becomes present. When he does, we come to him and adore him. The image behind this is Christ present on the altar, looking at the congregation, presenting himself for their worship.

While these images focus us on aspects of the truth of the Eucharist, neither is the image conveyed by the Eucharistic Prayers themselves. There we see what has been termed a "Look, Father" approach. The prayer is addressed to the Father, and he is asked to look upon his Son and his offering. To take part in the liturgy in the spirit of the Eucharistic Prayers, which express the meaning of the liturgy, this is not as much the time to focus on adoring the presence of Christ, much less to focus on his offering of a meal to the congregation, as to re-present the offering of Christ to the Father.

What Christ did at the Last Supper is repeated in the Eucharistic celebration.[37] The priest, presiding over the assembly as the representative of Christ, takes bread and wine, gives thanks for them, breaks the bread, and distributes the consecrated elements. The Eucharistic Prayers occur at the point of taking and giving thanks, where the focus is on praising and thanking God for his goodness and on offering the memorial of Christ's death to him. The distribution of the elements, with the confession that it is the Body and Blood of the Lord that we are receiving, comes during the Communion service. During the Eucharistic Prayer, our focus should primarily be on the Father and on the offering that we are making to him as the Lord of the universe and the source of all that is good.

The Eucharist is perhaps the most "evangelical" moment of Catholic life. It is evangelical because it brings us before a representation of the central gospel reality—what Christ has done for us through his death on the cross and through his resurrection and ascension. It is the time when our only "plea" is Christ's sacrifice.[38]

The Eucharist is also the main place in Catholic life where we come before the fact of our human insufficiency and need for God's grace. It is a sign, icon, objective representation, of God's commitment to give us that grace because of what Christ did for us if we come to him in faith and confidence. The sacraments in general, but especially the Eucharist, are what has kept most Catholics from being Pelagians or from falling prey to discouragement about their ability to please God and to be saved.

To be ecumenical, we do not need to downplay the Eucharist as a sacrifice. We do, however, need to clearly and emphatically see the Eucharist as a representation of the one sacrifice of Christ, not something we are adding to that sacrifice. That may also help us to come to a deeper understanding of the fact that in the Eucharist we are gathering to celebrate the event that saved us and to receive renewal in our Christian life as a result of it.

Meditation: The Fire From Heaven
2 Chronicles 5–7

There is a prayer of thanksgiving and consecration in the Old Testament, the prayer of Solomon at the dedication of the temple described in 2 Chronicles. The prayer occurs at an important point in the spiritual history of the people of the old covenant. God had commanded them to make the tabernacle in the wilderness, an earthly representation of his heavenly throne room. There they were to offer their animal sacrifices by the ministry of Aaronic priests, and if those sacrifices were offered rightly, they would be accepted.

God had also, however, instructed them that in the future he would "put his name," his earthly presence, "and make his habitation" at a certain place in the Promised Land (Dt 12:5). There, in other words, they were to build a temple. That temple would then be the only place where they might offer sacrifices that would be accepted. When God chose David to be his anointed king, David conquered Jerusalem and made it his capital. God then indicated that Solomon, David's son, should build the temple there.

Solomon's prayer was a prayer for God's acceptance of the building he had constructed for a temple. He prayed that God would accept it as a dwelling place and so accept it as the place where sacrifices acceptable to him could be offered. Solomon began by praying:

Blessed be the Lord, the God of Israel, who with his hand has fulfilled what he promised with his mouth to David my father, saying, "Since the day that I brought my people out of the land of Egypt, I chose no city in all the tribes of Israel in which to build a house, that my name might be there, and I chose no man as prince over my people Israel; but I have chosen Jerusalem that my name might be there and I have chosen David to be over my people Israel."

Solomon followed by citing God's promise to David that his son would build the temple and said,

I have built the house for the name of the Lord, the God of Israel. And there I have set the ark, in which is the covenant of the Lord which he made with the people of Israel.

By "the covenant" he referred to the tablets on which the Ten Commandments were written. The ark contained, in other words, part of what we would call the Scriptures, the Word of God, as a testimony to God's promise of his covenant with his people. Solomon then confessed God's faithfulness.

There is no God like you, in heaven or on earth, keeping covenant and show-ing steadfast love to your servants who walk before you with all their heart...

Solomon then went on to ask,

Now therefore, O Lord, let your word be confirmed, which you have spoken to your servant David.

He continued by petitioning for the various blessings that should come from God accepting the sacrifices that would be offered at the temple and hearing the prayers of the people that would accompany them. He concluded with,

Now, O my God, let your eyes be open and your ears attentive to a prayer of this place.

Second Chronicles then narrates what happened.

When Solomon had ended his prayer, fire came down from heaven and con-sumed the burnt offering and the sacrifices, and the glory of the Lord filled the temple.... When all the children of Israel saw the fire come down and the glory of the Lord upon the temple, they bowed down with their faces to the earth on the pavement, and worshiped and gave thanks to the Lord, saying, "For he is good, for his steadfast love endures for ever."

Like many of the accounts of miraculous events in the Scriptures, this occurred at a point when God needed to manifest that his hand was behind a new beginning, in this case the beginning of temple worship. The fire at the dedication came upon the sacrifices that were being offered and consumed them. God thereby indicated that he himself was accepting the sacrifices and taking them to himself, as he did at other points in the history of his people (Lv 9:23-24; 1 Chr 21:26; 1 Kgs 18:28). In this case the fire showed that the temple in Jerusalem was indeed the place where acceptable sacrifices could be offered to him.

Fire is a sign of God's glory. When the Lord came down on Mount Sinai, it was in the form of fire. When the Holy Spirit came down upon the disciples at Pentecost, it was in the form of fire.

When God comes down, heaven, the place of his presence, comes down. As a result, earthly things are brought up to heaven. Here spatial language fails us. Perhaps we might say more neutrally, heaven and earth are brought into a new relationship with one another, so that earthly things are brought to God and there become in a new way his—holy. An acceptable sacrifice, then, is one that has been taken by God and so made his—holy.

When Jesus died on the cross, his body was laid in the tomb. On the third day God's glory came upon his body. Corruption, mortality, was taken away. His body was glorified. His resurrection or glorification was a manifestation of the fact that the sacrifice he offered according to what God had commanded was received by God and was acceptable.

When our offering of bread and wine is presented to God, when God's promise is recalled and he is asked to fulfil it again, then the fire of the Holy Spirit comes upon our offering, and the glory of God fills it so that it becomes a truly acceptable sacrifice—holy, glorious, and lifegiving. It becomes the glorified Body and Blood of our Lord Jesus Christ, the Lamb who was slain to ransom human beings for God. The earthly fire that came down from heaven to receive Solomon's sacrifice gives us an image, a type, of the heavenly, spiritual fire that comes down during the Eucharistic Prayer to receive our own offering. What that results in for us, we will consider in the next chapter.

SIX

The Eucharist as Life-Giving

He who eats my flesh and drinks my blood has eternal life, and
I will raise him up at the last day. For my flesh is food indeed,
and my blood is drink indeed. He who eats my flesh and drinks
my blood abides in me, and I in him.

JOHN 6:54-56

Various events narrated in the Old Testament have traditionally been
applied to the Eucharist. One of the more mysterious is the story of
Melchizedek, the king-priest of Salem, the city that later became Jerusalem.
After Abraham had defeated Chedorlaomer, the king of Elam, who had just led
a raiding party on the part of Palestine in which Abraham was living, he came
to meet Melchizedek. The meeting is described in Genesis 14:18-20:

And Melchizedek king of Salem brought out bread and wine; he was priest
of God Most High. And he blessed him and said,
"Blessed be Abram by God Most High,
maker of heaven and earth;
and blessed be God Most High,
who has delivered your enemies into your hand!"
And Abram gave him a tenth of everything.

Although the event is only briefly referred to, we are probably reading about
a thanksgiving meal to praise God for the victory he gave through Abraham,
then still called Abram. The Letter to the Hebrews refers to this passage to
instruct us about Christ. It also refers to Psalm 110:4, which addresses the
anointed king (the Messiah) as "a priest according to the order of Melchizedek." On the basis of these two passages, Hebrews speaks of Melchizedek as a
type of the Messiah (Christ) and concludes that Christ, the Messiah, is a priest.

Priests need something to offer (Heb 8:3). According to the Fathers, what
Melchizedek offered was bread and wine. As Cyprian, the early Latin Father,

147

put it, "In Melchizedek the priest, we see the sacrament of the sacrifice of the Lord prefigured according to the witness of Scripture; Melchizedek, king of Salem, offered bread and wine" (*Ep.* 58, 4). The Roman canon (Eucharistic Prayer I), written probably in the fourth century, puts it even more forcefully: "Look favorably upon [the bread and cup we have offered] and find them acceptable as you found ... the holy sacrifice and immaculate victim which your high priest Melchizedek offered to you" [translation by the author]. The bread and wine of the Eucharist, then, typologically understood, is the offering of Christ, the priest after the order of Melchizedek, in a thanksgiving meal.[1]

We do not often think of bread and wine as sacrifices, yet most of the sacrifices of the temple worship in the old covenant were offered with bread (grain ground into flour or made into a bread or cake) and a libation of wine. On occasion offerings consisted of only bread, as for instance the first-fruits offering or part of the consecration offering (Lv 2:1-16; 6:19-23). Moreover, the peace offerings, including the thanksgiving offerings, which were always part of the great feasts, were completed by holy meals in which bread and wine formed a part (Lv 7:11-36; 21–22).[2]

The offerings of sacrificial animals could even be described as "the bread of God" (Lv 21:6, 8, 17, 21, 22; 22:25). The use of such a phrase indicates the ability of bread to stand for the "food" offered in sacrifice (see Nm 28:2; Lv 3:11), and so indicates that "bread" was thought of as a fitting sacrifice. It was even fitting to stand for sacrifices in general, or at least for peace or communion sacrifices. The phrase is especially significant for our purposes because it is used to refer to food offered to God in sacrifice, which will then be eaten by human beings in a sacrificial meal.

If "sacrifice" only refers to the killing of an animal as a way of offering it to God, bread and wine cannot be a sacrifice. If, however, "sacrifice" can also refer to anything given to God through presentation on the altar, bread and wine can be sacrificial offerings. They were so regarded in the old covenant.[3]

At the Last Supper, as we have seen, bread and wine were offered to God, as they would have been in any festal meal, so that they might be vehicles of the festal blessing. In the Christian Eucharist, following what happened at the Last Supper, bread and wine were the sole offerings. In one way, they were offered for the blessing of the meal. But in this case, as we have seen, the meal was special, and the ceremony at the meal was performed "in memorial of" the Lord. The sharing of the blessed food conveyed a blessing to the participants, and the meaning of the meal (as expressed in the prayers) indicated the nature of the blessing that was conveyed. The bread and wine, in other words, had a special significance, especially because of the blessing they were intended to convey.

The Christian Eucharistic celebration was a sacrificial meal, a meal to complete and take part in a sacrifice. The sacrifice, a festal offering since it was a Passover sacrifice, was made on the cross in the death of Christ. It was, however, presented to the Father at the true temple in heaven, not the earthly temple in Jerusalem. The bread and wine in our sacrificial meal, therefore, are a means for thanking God for what Christ did when he gave himself for the remission of sins on earth and presented his offering to his Father in heaven. They are therefore a means for our participating in that sacrifice and receiving the blessing that comes from it.

In the last two chapters we have looked at the Eucharist as a sacrificial action that creates or strengthens a relationship between God and his new covenant people, the Church of Christ. We saw the importance of our re-presenting the sacrifice of Christ, his Body and Blood offered in sacrifice. We now have to look at the way we take part in that sacrifice by receiving the Body and Blood. To do so, we first need to consider the meaning of what we present to God in thanksgiving and then receive in the sacrificial meal in order to receive the blessing. Then we need to consider the nature of the blessing we receive, the new covenant life that comes to us through what Christ accomplished.

Bread and Wine

As we saw in the last chapter, the Eucharist, understood as a sacrificial offering, strengthens the new covenant relationship between God and his people. The new covenant relationship is established "in Christ." As a result, Christians are united with one another and with God because they are united to Christ. Because their union with Christ is renewed as a result of the offering, their new covenant relationship with God and one another is strengthened. In this way the Church is built up by the Eucharist.

But to speak that way possibly could make the process sound external and even somewhat natural. The union with Christ, however, is not created or strengthened simply by taking part in ceremonies. It becomes real through a spiritual impartation that occurs through means that can be described as "sacramental" (see p. 25), to use the Western word, or which are *mysteries*, to use the Eastern one.[4]

The Eastern (Greek) term conveys something helpful that the Western (Latin) one might not. The Greek word we have taken over as "mystery" indicates something hidden or in some way unknown that has been made known or revealed, at least partially. Pagan Greeks used the term "mysteries" for ceremonies or rituals that established some kind of connection to a god. Greek-speaking Christians made use of the term very early to refer to Christian ceremonies. The term can be used to refer to all aspects of the ceremonies in the Eucharistic celebration, including words and symbols, because in various ways they mediate the presence and grace of God.

Greek-speaking Christians, then, make use of the term for ceremonies that impart divine life to us in a special way: ceremonies that include what Western Christians refer to as sacraments and sacramentals, to use Anglicized Latin terms. These ceremonies have a spiritual aspect that is somewhat hidden because they make use of human things that are part of our spatial-temporal world but are connected to God and convey his presence and action. Because of their divine aspect, there is something more to them than we can experience through our senses. Moreover, even when we come to know or recognize their divine aspect, it cannot be fully comprehended by us, because God is above us. "The mysteries," then, allow us to participate in something that we can experience but that transcends our understanding, the life and blessedness of God himself. Of all the mysteries, that of the bread and wine becoming the Body and Blood of Christ is the chief.

There are still other ways of speaking about them. They can be referred to as "spiritual" food and drink (1 Cor 10:3-4), probably in the sense of food and drink that imparts something from the Holy Spirit, spiritual life.[5] We could also say that they are "heavenly," because something is taken from the earth and becomes a bearer to us of something from heaven. As Irenaeus put it:

> For just as bread from the earth, receiving the invocation of God, is no longer common bread but a Eucharist consisting of two elements, an earthly and a heavenly, even so, our bodies, partaking of the Eucharist, are no longer corruptible, possessing as they do the hope of resurrection unto life eternal.[6]

We will begin by considering the earthly elements and their significance and then see what happens when they "receive the invocation of God."

Bread, to use a scriptural image, is the "staff" of life (Lv 26:26; Ps 105:16; Ez 4:16; 5:16; 14:13). It is a support that allows us to stand up and move. In other words, it feeds us so that we might live and function in a normal way. In societies where potatoes are the main sustenance or where grain is made into some kind of pasta or porridge and no longer called bread, we do not make the connection between bread and life so easily. However, bread in the form of a baked loaf was the main food of the people of Israel and their neighbors in scriptural times. Without bread there would have been no life.

Unlike bread, the ordinary food, wine was for celebrations. Poorer people could not afford much wine, if any. In fact, it was considered a responsibility to help the poor to have enough wine that they could celebrate feasts.[7] We might be inclined to take a sterner approach to the poor, recognizing the responsibility to help them stay alive but expecting them to work for anything more. However, the Scriptures, and Jewish and early Christian tradition, recognized the responsibility to provide wine so that the poor and needy could also share in the joy of the community celebration (Dt 16:1-17; 1 Cor 11:20-22).

Wine, according to a Jewish prayer, is a symbol of joy. In the Scripture, it can also be a symbol of hostility. Too much wine can knock people down, make them reel as if struck by a blow. It can be degrading, making people act like animals or act sinfully. But a moderate amount, drunk in the context of a meal, makes people joyful. As it says in the Psalm, "The Lord gave us wine to make the heart glad" (Ps 104:15). According to an important prophecy in Isaiah (Is 25:6-8), when the restoration of Israel comes, God will give a feast on Mount Zion for everyone and serve wine:

> On this mountain the Lord of hosts will make for all peoples a feast of fat things, a feast of wine on the lees, of fat things full of marrow, of wine on the lees well refined.... He will swallow up death for ever, and Lord God will wipe away tears from all faces.

The miracle of Cana is one of the signs of the fulfilment of this prophecy, and it centered on water turned into wine at a feast (Jn 2:1-11). Jars holding water for the Jewish rites of purification were transformed by the Lord into good wine in great abundance, a sign of the messianic age (Am 9:13-15). In fact, Jesus produced the best wine, and because he had only been asked "late in the day," the best wine ended up being served last, contrary to what many would find customary but an apt symbol of the blessing he came to bring "in the last days" (Acts 2:16-17).

The wine that resulted from Jesus' miracle, given to make a feast possible, was a sign of the new covenant. New covenant people are not purified by external washings with water, as would have happened had the water in the "jars" been used for Jewish rites of purification, but by drinking "new wine." The new wine of Cana was a symbol of the Holy Spirit, who purifies and sanctifies us (see Mt 9:14-17; Mk 2:15-22; Lk 5:33-39, where the wine serves as a symbol of the new covenant). That wine of the Holy Spirit enters into us and changes us.

It is for such reasons that the Fathers of the Church often say that the blessed wine of the Eucharist "inebriates" us. Leo the Great, for instance, talks about our keeping the Passover of Christ (Easter) by "the inebriating and feeding of the new creature with the very Lord."[8] The earthly wine, in other words, is a vehicle for something divine.

The wine of the Eucharist does not inebriate us in the sense that we become less capable of functioning in a good way, as happens when we have too much ordinary wine. Rather, receiving the Eucharist changes us so that we can function in a better way, a way that is above the capabilities of our fallen nature.[9] It helps us to become joyful in the Lord. It elevates us spiritually, raises us above ourselves, so that we can readily and worthily celebrate the goodness of the Lord. It is, in the words of an older prayer in the liturgy, "a sobering inebriation with the Holy Spirit."[10]

Bread and wine are both in their own ways symbols of life. As we saw, the main elements of a Jewish sacrifice were domestic animals, bread, wine, and oil. Offered in sacrifice, these made up a meal given to God to honor him. They expressed the life of the people offered to God.

As we also have seen, in some sacrifices part of those gifts were returned to the people after the offering so that they could have a meal in which they celebrated with God. When the Jewish people could not come to Jerusalem, either because they lived far away, as most Diaspora Jews did, or because they did not accept the validity of what was done in the temple, as was the case with the Essene Jews, they still could celebrate the feasts in honor of the Lord and make offerings to him. The meal as a whole, but especially the bread and wine, blessed and offered to God, expressed their offering to God and God's gift to them.

As in so many other areas, the new covenant takes things from the old covenant and makes them the vehicle of new realities. With the Eucharist we are at the heart of the newness of the new covenant. Food and drink are given us, but they are spiritual food and drink. They are food and drink that enter into us and strengthen the new, spiritual life inside of us.

Some of the Eastern liturgies describe the Eucharistic elements as "glorious, holy, vivifying, and divine." The Eucharistic elements are glorious because they have the power and presence, the glory, of God in them. They are holy because they belong to God and are from him. They are vivifying because they give life to us. They are divine because the life they give us is the divine life. They have, in the words of Irenaeus, become heavenly.

Bread and Wine From Heaven

The True Manna (Jn 6:1-71)

The multiplication of the loaves and fishes, one of the most important events in the earthly life of Christ, occurs at the midpoint of Christ's earthly ministry. Christ has attracted much attention because of his miracles. He has not been completely pleased with the attention he has been given, because much of it has missed the point. Those who have flocked around have seen him as a miracle worker and have wanted some personal benefit. But too many failed to come to a real faith in him as the Son of God and to see his miracles as signs of the new life he came to bring.

His miracles also provoked his opponents. They had applied their own tests to what he was doing and had come to the conclusion that he was not from God. They had also been offended by some of his critiques of them, their devotional practices, and their scriptural interpretations. But they could not refute his miracles. Those were convincing to too many people. So his opposition was increasingly decided that force would be needed to eliminate him.

A crisis point had been reached, one that indicated that a conflict was at hand. It was a crisis that Christ himself took as an indication that the moment he had expected had arrived and he should prepare for death. Moreover, John the Baptist had just been put to death by Herod Antipas (Mk 6:14-29). To Jesus that was a spiritual event of great importance. His forerunner had been put to death and de facto rejected. Now he would follow.

Jesus had just taken his disciples away for a kind of retreat (Mk 6:30-34). For this purpose he had crossed the Sea of Galilee to a deserted place, expecting to leave behind people who knew his reputation and who mainly wanted healings. Many of them, however, followed. When he saw their need, not only for healing but even more for the word of God, he gave in and taught them.

At a certain point, it became clear that he needed to do something for these people; otherwise they would have to go away hungry. Given how far away they were from any settlement and the necessity of returning on foot in a hot sun, going hungry could be dangerously weakening. A search revealed that only one person, a boy, had brought food, and he had only brought five barley loaves and two fish. Thousands were present.

Jesus simply instructed them to sit down. He took what was given him, inadequate though it was, blessed the bread, then the fish, and distributed food to those who were present. All who were present had enough and some food was left over, exactly twelve baskets of bread.

The Gospel of John tells us that at that point the people recognized Jesus as "the Coming One," the prophet (predicted in Dt 18:15-18) "who is to come into the world." As a result they wanted to make him king and start a messianic uprising. Jesus knew that was not what God sent him to do, so he escaped to the nearby hills, leaving his disciples to return home.

We might not understand why the crowd would go from seeing a wonder-worker multiply loaves and fish in a deserted place to deciding that he should be proclaimed the Messiah. However, at the time of Jesus Jewish teachers looked for the Messiah to renew the wonders of the Exodus when he restored the people of Israel. Consequently, when the crowd saw Jesus provide bread miraculously in a deserted and arid area where they could not get any food, they concluded that he was the expected Messiah who was giving out "bread from heaven to eat," a renewal of the miracle of the manna.

The Gospel writers and patristic interpreters looking back to the multiplication of the loaves and fish did not see the miracle merely as a renewal of the giving of manna. They also recognized that Jesus had been giving the people, and even more, his disciples, a new covenant sign. To be sure, he was showing them that he was the Messiah and could feed people in the wilderness. But even more, he was showing them that he had come to give not just physical life but spiritual life, new covenant life. He had come to bring them the abundant life of the messianic age (Jn 10:10).

These early Christian interpreters also saw something else in the accounts of the multiplication. Fragments were gathered up, and twelve baskets were left over. These probably symbolized the tribes of Israel. The multiplication therefore was a sign that Jesus was creating a new Israel. He was at work to give new spiritual life to people—Israelites and the Gentiles that would join them—life that would sustain them in the wilderness of this fallen world. In the process he would create a new covenant people for God.

Finally the early interpreters saw something else. What Jesus did in the desert was very similar to what he later did at the Last Supper. He took, gave thanks, broke and distributed bread. As a result, people who could not provide food for themselves were satisfied with what he gave them. The multiplication fore-shadowed what he would do in the Eucharist. The discourse in the Gospel of John appended to the account of the multiplication makes that even clearer.

According to John, when some of those who had been present at the multi-plication made their way back and found Jesus in the synagogue at Capernaum on the other side of the Sea of Galilee, a discussion between them and Jesus ensued.[11] Perhaps it was a discussion connected with a scriptural reading in the synagogue about the manna.[12] Certainly Jesus cited the scriptures about manna to explain what had happened when he multiplied the bread and fish.

Jesus' words, like so much the Gospel of John reports him as saying, were extraordinary and somewhat incomprehensible to his Jewish audience. He acknowledged that Moses had brought them bread, manna, in the wilderness journey. But he said that the Scripture passages that say, "He gave them bread from heaven," should not be understood as referring to Moses. They should be understood as referring to God, Jesus' heavenly Father. God, not Moses, is the one who gives bread from heaven. And the bread his heavenly Father gave them was Jesus himself. He was God's true provision for them, and now they were experiencing the fulfilment of the promises of the old covenant in what he was doing in their midst.

Jesus *was* the bread from heaven, the Bread of Life. This means, in the lan-guage we often find in John, that he was the "bread" who could *give* them life. He would therefore provide them divine, spiritual life—if only they would believe in him.

There then follows a passage (verses 51-58) that speaks about the Eucharist. It begins with a verse that contains a conclusion to what Jesus has said so far but also a transition to something further:

I am the living bread which came down from heaven; if any one eats of this bread, he will live for ever; and the bread which I shall give for the life of the world is my flesh.

Instead of speaking about himself as the Bread of Life in this verse, Jesus speaks of himself as the living bread. He is bread, but unlike manna or bread baked from grain, he is alive. That likely indicates that he intends to share with those who "eat of this bread," that is, himself, the life that he himself has. He intends to share with them the special life that is in him as the Word made flesh.

He then goes on to refer to the bread that he will give not as himself but as his flesh. He will give this bread, his flesh, for the life of the world. His words provoke the Jews to ask, "How can this man give us his flesh to eat?" Jesus then replies:

> Truly, truly, I say to you, unless you eat the flesh of the Son of man and drink his blood, you have no life in you; he who eats my flesh and drinks my blood has eternal life, and I will raise him up at the last day. For my flesh is food indeed, and my blood is drink indeed. He who eats my flesh and drinks my blood abides in me, and I in him.
>
> As the living Father sent me, and I live because of the Father, so he who eats me will live because of me. This is the bread which came down from heaven, not such as the fathers ate and died; he who eats this bread will live forever.

In an already unusual set of statements, this is still more striking. It was so difficult to accept, such a "hard saying," that even some of Jesus' disciples left him because of it. They seem to have thought he was proposing a kind of cannibalism.[13] But in these words we find truths that provide a further understanding of the meaning of the Eucharist.

When John writes "flesh," he is using a Greek word that can mean the same as "body." When the passage speaks about "flesh and blood," it is therefore speaking about "body and blood." By using "flesh and blood" rather than "body and blood," the Gospel of John is using possibly just a different Greek translation of the Hebrew or Aramaic original, possibly emphasizing the fact that Jesus was talking about something physical, not immaterial. But for whatever reason a different word was chosen, "flesh and blood" seems to mean the same as "body and blood."[14]

More important, Jesus shifted from speaking of himself as the source of new life to speaking of something he will give so that people may have life. The two are closely related, because what he will give is his own Body and Blood, something that cannot be separated from him. Nonetheless there is a difference. The most credible way of understanding this shift is that he changed from speaking of himself as the Son of God come into the world to give life to people to speaking of the Eucharistic elements as giving life to people. The Eucharistic elements are distinct from him, yet at the same time the Eucharist only gives life because it is Christ's Body and Blood.

As we have already seen, the word "give" is a sacrificial term. Both Old and New Testaments speak about "giving" a sacrifice to God, and a sacrifice is very commonly described as a "gift." Jesus, therefore, is likely beginning this part of his discourse in verse 6:51 by saying that he will be "giving," that is, offering, "his flesh" to God in sacrifice "for the life of the world."[15] Since he is about to speak about eating his flesh, there is probably a second meaning of "give" here. He will also "give" his flesh (to those who come to him) to be eaten.

These two meanings of "give" are linked in an important way. Just as a peace or communion offering is given as an offering to God, it is also given for people to eat in a sacrificial meal so that they might strengthen their union with God. Partaking of what has been offered is a way of becoming a sharer in the sacrifice, a "partner in the altar," as Paul puts it in 1 Corinthians 10:18. It is important that what is given to us was first given to God as a sacrifice, because only when it has been offered to God is it holy, something that belongs to God and can communicate to us a strengthening of our relationship with God.

Jesus then goes on to emphasize that eating his body and drinking his blood is the key to having life, eternal life. In the Gospel of John, eternal life is a kind of life that people can have now. It is "eternal" in the sense that it will last forever, not in the sense that we will not get it until after we die.

Jesus' audience had not eaten his flesh or drunk his blood, but even those who did not yet believe in him had life of a certain sort. They were not totally dead, even if they were spiritually dead because of the effects of the Fall. So when Jesus said they would "have no life in them" unless they ate of his flesh and drank of his blood, he was speaking of a needed transformation of the life they had in order to have the better kind of life he came to bring. He was speaking, in other words, of their receiving what we might call new life or spiritual life, the kind of life that would bring them through death to the Promised Land of heaven. Partaking of his flesh (body) and blood would be the means of receiving that life.

Jesus goes on to say that when we partake of his body and blood, we abide in him. The word "abide" is one that John often uses and that seems to be the equivalent of "dwell" in the Old Testament. When we partake of the Body and Blood of Christ, then we dwell or live in him and he in us. This is sometimes referred to as "mutual indwelling" or "union."

Partaking in the Eucharist therefore results in union with Christ. Paul said the same thing when he said it makes us "one body" with him. But as the discourse in John makes clear, being one with Christ must mean that he lives in us and we in him. John states more explicitly what was implied in Paul's Eucharistic teaching—the new covenant relationship with God that the Eucharist strengthens is not just an external union but comes from an interior union, a mutual indwelling.

Many of us have read this passage often enough that we do not notice the strange wording anymore. If someone were to talk of abiding or dwelling in another human being, a friend for instance, they would get a puzzled look. How can someone abide in or live in a friend?

We cannot live in another human being. The fact that Jesus talks about his living in us and us in him indicates that he is not talking about a relationship he has with us as one human being to another. He is rather talking about a relationship he can only have with us because of his divinity. He is talking about a spiritual relationship.

Partaking of Jesus' Body and Blood is a physical action. We eat and drink physically. But that produces a spiritual relationship with Christ. Our partaking strengthens our union with him, the Son of God. Consequently the Eucharist also strengthens our union with Jesus' Father, because he and his Father are one, inseparable (Jn 10:30), and he has come to bring us to the Father (Jn 14:6). Moreover, the strengthening of our union with Christ happens through the action of the Holy Spirit in us (Jn 14:16-17). In other words, even though the Eucharist centers on uniting us with Christ who has been offered for us, it unites us with the Trinity.

The indwelling of the Son in us, then, connects us to God and the life of God, the divine life. Second Peter (1:4) speaks of this connection using different words when it says, "He has granted to us his precious and very great promises, that through these ... [we might] become partakers of the divine nature." Using the terminology of this passage, we can then say that by partaking of the Body and Blood of Christ we become partakers of or sharers in the divine nature. Because of the union of the earthly and heavenly in Christ, when we unite ourselves sacramentally to his flesh we strengthen our participation in his divinity.

Cyril of Alexandria was one of the great patristic teachers about the Eucharist. Much of his teaching was given as a commentary on the passage we have been considering. In his *Commentary on the Gospel According to John,* speaking about verse 6:35, he clearly states the link between partaking of Christ's flesh, receiving the Holy Spirit, and participating in God's own nature:

When then we were called to the kingdom of Heaven by Christ (for it is this and nothing else, I believe, that the entry into the promised land points to), then the manna which was given as a type no longer belongs to us (for not by the letter of the law of Moses are we any longer fed) but the Bread of Heaven, i.e. Christ, feeds us for eternal life, both through the supply of the Holy Spirit, and the participation of his own flesh, which infuses into us the participation of God and wipes out the deadness that comes from the ancient curse.[16]

The True Vine (Jn 15:1-17)

The new covenant life can only be ours if we remain united with Christ. It is not something he can just give us and we can carry off. It depends on what we might call an organic union with him in which we constantly draw life from him. This is expressed by the parable of the vine and the branches that he uses in the Last Supper discourse in John 15, a passage that many would understand as concerning the Eucharist.[17]

> I am the true vine, and my Father is the vinedresser. Every branch of mine that bears no fruit, he takes away, and every branch that does bear fruit he prunes, that it may bear more fruit. You are already made clean by the word which I have spoken to you. Abide in me, and I in you. As the branch cannot bear fruit by itself, unless it abides in the vine, neither can you, unless you abide in me. I am the vine, you are the branches. He who abides in me, and I in him, he it is that bears much fruit, for apart from me you can do nothing. If a man does not abide in me, he is cast forth as a branch and withers; and the branches are gathered, thrown into the fire and burned.

When Jesus begins by saying that he is the true vine, he is referring back to a parable in the prophets about a vine that God has planted (Is 5:1-7; Jer 2:21; Ez 19:10-14). In the parable, the vine is Israel, so Jesus is claiming that he is the true Israel. He with those who belong to him, therefore, are the new people of God.

The parable speaks about the vine and the branches, not the trunk of the vine and the branches. Christ is the vine as a whole, and his disciples are joined to him and make up one vine in him. They need to stay properly connected to him. Once they no longer "abide" in him, that is, stay joined to him in such a way that they can draw life from him, they wither and die, because life circulates within the vine.

Many understand this parable as a passage about the Eucharist, partly because the context is the Last Supper, but partly because wine is the "fruit of the vine" according to the Jewish prayer used to bless the wine at festal meals like the Last Supper. It would be natural to see wine, fluid drawn from a vine, as something that passes on the life of the true vine to human participants in the Lord's Supper once they have been "grafted into" that true vine.

The connection is perhaps even stronger since the wine in the Eucharist is a symbol of blood, the life of a body. Moreover, in a messianic prophecy wine was described as "the blood of grapes" (Gn 49:11). In terms of both understandings (body or vine), to partake of the Eucharist is to tap into the life which circulates through the whole body (vine) of Christ. Christ's own life, divine life, the life of the Holy Spirit, is shared with those who are one with him.

The image of the vine and the branches in John, then, is similar to the image of the one body in Paul. Christians are members of Christ's body. They only remain members by being joined to Christ. Separated, a member or part of a body will die. But as in the image of the vine and branches, the simple physical connection of parts connected to one another externally, in this case by joints, is not enough. The members have to be tied into the body in such a way that the flow of blood through the body can bring the life of the body and with it those things that sustain life.

Images have their limitations. We need to stay constantly connected to Christ, like a branch to the vine or a leg to the body, but we do not need to constantly partake of the Eucharist. In this something like a laptop computer is probably a better example. The computer battery will go dead after a period of time if left to itself. In order to keep functioning, it needs to be plugged into a source of energy periodically but does not need to stay plugged in all the time. Similarly, we only have to eat regularly for our bodies to stay alive and have energy to function.

The computer image illustrates another truth about the process. It is not actually the wire itself that is so important. The wire only makes a certain kind of connection. The computer does not absorb more metal from the wire so it can function. Rather, the wire is a conduit of power which flows through it into the computer, and that power allows it to function.

Something similar is true of the Body and Blood of Christ in the Eucharist. The blessed bread and wine are not so important in themselves as physical realities. When we eat a small piece of bread, all it can do is give us a small amount of physical energy. But because it is Christ's body, because Christ is therefore united to it and his life is present in it, it has become a conduit for strengthening the new life inside of us. By partaking of the Eucharistic elements we become partakers of the divine life, because we are connected to a source of divine power which energizes us so that we can function in a new way.

Both truths are important. Like a branch of a vine or an arm of a body, we need to stay constantly connected to Christ. Yet, like bread that we eat or wine that we drink, the external sacramental source of spiritual life is given to us from time to time, enters into us, and strengthens something inside of us so that we can function in an ongoing way. The Eucharist strengthens our relationship with the Lord, as we saw in the last chapter, but it does that by feeding and strengthening the life inside of us that now is our own new life in him.

The Blessing the Eucharist Brings

There are many ways of describing the life that we have received through being joined to Christ, and that is strengthened in us when we eat Christ's flesh and drink his blood. It is new life, new covenant life, divine life, eternal life, spiritual life, true life. It is also grace, the favor or gift of God, sanctifying grace, the grace that makes us holy. It is also sharing in the divine nature, divinization, participation in the life of God.

The first Eucharistic Prayer of the Roman rite prays that as a result of partaking of the Eucharist, we "be filled with every grace and blessing." "Every grace and blessing" here probably refers to the graces and blessings of the new covenant. The Eucharist gives us all the blessings that the death and resurrection of Christ brings to the human race.

These blessings are not primarily material blessings. We do not necessarily become guaranteed of health, for instance, so that we will never die of cancer or any other disease. Nor do we get infused knowledge about engineering or geography. We certainly are not guaranteed that we will live tranquil lives, freed from all persecution. It is "through many tribulations we must enter the kingdom of God" (Acts 14:22). The graces and blessings the Eucharistic Prayer speaks about are the ones that come with new life in Christ.

The chief blessing we receive is the gift of the Holy Spirit. We take part in the Eucharist so that we might be filled with the Holy Spirit. The memorial prayer from Eucharistic Prayer III that we looked at in the last chapter prays:

Grant that we, who are nourished by his body and blood, may be filled with his Holy Spirit, and become one body, one spirit in Christ.

We might think that it is not the function of the Eucharist to fill us with the Holy Spirit. The Sacrament of Confirmation (or perhaps Baptism) fills us with the Holy Spirit. Or maybe we need to be "baptized with the Holy Spirit" or have an "outpouring of the Holy Spirit" so that the Holy Spirit might fill us. Most modern Catholics find it strange to speak of being filled with the Spirit in the Eucharist. To be sure, the Eucharist is not intended to be the means of our being filled with the Spirit for the first time, but it is one of the main ways, perhaps the main way, of maintaining our filling with the Holy Spirit.

Paul uses an image that helps us understand what it means to be filled with the Spirit in an ongoing way in the Letter to the Ephesians. There, at the end of an exhortation to live in a way that is fitting to being a Christian (Eph 5:17-20), he says:

Therefore do not be foolish, but understand what the will of the Lord is. And do not get drunk with wine, for that is debauchery; but be filled with the Spirit, addressing one another in psalms and hymns and spiritual songs, singing and making melody to the Lord with all your heart, always and for everything giving thanks in the name of our Lord Jesus Christ to God the Father.

Here we see Paul exhorting those who already are baptized Christians to be filled with the Spirit, probably in the sense of "maintain your filling with the Spirit" but possibly in the sense of "renew your filling with the Spirit."

Paul introduces the exhortation in an unusual way by saying that those he is speaking to should not get drunk with wine. That might raise a question of why he is suddenly interested in encouraging them to avoid drunkenness when he is giving a general exhortation on good Christian living. In fact, he is not specially interested in drunkenness, but he is making a comparison. He is indicating that being filled with the Spirit is somewhat similar to being "filled with" wine.

We ourselves speak in a similar way about what may happen when people drink too much wine. They are "loaded" or "tanked," that is, filled full with alcohol. We also, however, speak of them as "under the influence." When wine is in us, it does not just sit there, as if our body were a convenient place of storage like a bottle. Rather it enters into our bloodstream and begins to influence our actions. We can tell people who have drunk too much by the fact that they walk differently, talk differently, act differently. What has filled them has changed their behavior.

The same thing is true of the Holy Spirit. When he fills us, he does not just sit in us so that we might worship him. Rather he enters into us and begins to transform us and the way we behave. Paul uses a similar image in Galatians 5, one close to that used in the parable of the vine and the branches, when he speaks of the fruit of the Spirit. When the Spirit enters into us, he produces love, joy, peace, patience, kindness, goodness, faithfulness, humility, self-control, and the like. Something, in other words, begins to grow under his influence, and what grows is certain character traits. He makes us people who handle the various situations in life in a "spiritual" way.

We might speak in a different way and say that the gift of the Holy Spirit sanctifies us. *Sanctification* is perhaps the most common term used in English to describe what the Holy Spirit does to change us. It simply means "making holy" or "imparting holiness." In this context, "holiness" refers to God's own holiness of character which is shared with us. When the Holy Spirit dwells within us, he makes us "holy as God is holy" (Lv 19:2; 1 Pt 1:16). This involves the taking away or purification of our sinfulness. It also, however, involves our sharing in God's own holiness, becoming like him. It is the Holy Spirit who enables us to participate in God's nature or to become like God. That means that our character, the way we behave, becomes God-like or holy, because he dwells in us.

Another way of describing the result of being filled with the Spirit is to say that we are given love or charity. We receive love, because "God is love and he who abides in love abides in God, and God abides in him" (1 Jn 4:16). If, through the presence of the Holy Spirit in us, God abides in us and we in him, then love is strengthened in us.

We certainly do not become perfectly loving Christians simply by receiving the Holy Spirit. Love does grow in us, as Paul indicates, as a fruit of the Holy Spirit in us. But at the same time we have to "walk in love as Christ loved us and gave himself up for us, a fragrant offering and sacrifice to God" (Eph 5:2; see Gal 5:25). That is, we actually have to act in a loving way, even at personal cost. We also have to "by the Spirit put to death the [sinful] deeds of the body" so that we might live the life of God (Rom 8:5; Gal 5:24). We have to "kill" our sinful ways. Nonetheless, the spiritual life that makes us want to live a loving life and makes us capable of it comes to us through the presence of the Holy Spirit in us. Therefore we can say that the Holy Spirit gives us love.

The gift of the Spirit is in fact the chief blessing of the new covenant, the chief benefit that comes to us from the sacrifice of Christ. As Christ put it right before his ascension (Lk 24:49), *the* promise of the Father, that which the Father specially promised through the prophets, is the gift of the Spirit. In the new covenant the Holy Spirit enters into us, dwells in us, and gives us the new life that Jesus was speaking about in John 6. He is the life-giver (2 Cor 3:6). Since, as we have seen, the Eucharist gives life, and since the Holy Spirit is the source of our new covenant life, when we receive the Eucharist we are filled with the Spirit. The source of life inside of us, the life-giving presence of the Holy Spirit, is strengthened.

At the same time the Eucharist takes away or forgives our sins. This is the opposite side of the coin, so to speak. As the *Catechism of the Catholic Church* puts it (1393), "The Eucharist cannot unite us to Christ without at the same time cleansing us from past sins and preserving us from future sins." In the Liturgy of John Chrysostom we pray:

> that to those who partake of [the body and the blood of Christ], they may be for the purification of the soul, for the remission of sins, for communion in Your Holy Spirit, for the fullness of the heavenly kingdom, for confidence before You, not for judgment or condemnation.

In possibly the earliest full Eucharistic Prayer we have, the *Anaphora of Addai and Mari* from the East Syrian tradition, still used with some modifications in the Chaldean rite, we pray:

> May your Holy Spirit come, Lord. May he rest upon this offering of your servants. May he bless and sanctify it, so it may win for us, Lord, the forgiveness of offenses and the remission of sins, the great hope of the resurrection of the dead, and new life in the kingdom of heaven with all those who have been pleasing to you.[18]

We might think that it is not the function of the Eucharist to give us forgiveness of sins.[19] The Sacrament of Penance (Reconciliation, confession) does that, not the Eucharist. To be sure, for someone who has fallen into serious, mortal sin, the Sacrament of Reconciliation or Penance (repentance) is an indispensable step in being restored to God and so being free to receive the Eucharist again. It is also used devotionally by people without mortal sin who desire a help to grow in repentance and so to be freed from sin in their lives.

However, the Eucharist, as the above prayer indicates, has been seen through the centuries as the primary way to be freed from sin. The "taking away" or "remission" of sin is helped by confession of our sins, but it is helped even more by having the sinfulness of our life replaced by the positive presence of the grace of God in Christ. It is the new life in the Holy Spirit that frees us from sin, because it changes us so that we share in divine life and as a result sin is taken away.

When we paint a wall white, it is no longer black. When we pour water into a bottle, it is no longer empty. When we are filled with the life of Christ, to the degree that that life of Christ transforms us, we are freed from sin. Partaking of the Eucharist fills us with the life of Christ and of the Holy Spirit, and so takes sin away or sanctifies us in the sense of purifying or cleansing us from what is displeasing to God.

As Ephesians 5:2 shows, the same reality can be spoken of in still a further way, a way that connects with the truths we looked at in the last chapter: the Eucharist makes us into a living sacrifice. In Eucharistic Prayer III we pray:

May [the Holy Spirit] make us an everlasting gift to you and enable us to share in the inheritance of your saints.

In Eucharistic Prayer IV we pray:

Lord, look upon this sacrifice which you have given to your Church; and by your Holy Spirit, gather all who share this one bread and one cup into the one body of Christ, a living sacrifice [sacrificial victim] of praise.

As we have seen in chapter 3, the idea of our being a sacrifice is scriptural and patristic. When we are an offering or sacrifice, we are given to God. We have been made over to him and so belong to him. Another way of saying this is that we have been sanctified or consecrated or made holy, because a sacrifice is consecrated, made holy, when it is offered to God.

In this context, however, another feature of this truth should be clearer. Being holy as a new covenant sacrifice is not just a matter of an external relationship with God, simply belonging to him. We are not like a car that sits in a garage until the owner wants to use it. We become holy, a sacrifice, when the Holy Spirit himself comes and dwells in us, sharing with us his own holiness, transforming us so that we can live in a new way (see Rom 15:16). We can then be a genuine offering, something that belongs to God not just by legal possession but also by interiorly sharing in his life, and so able to live a life that is holy like his.

All this raises a question. When the Eucharistic Prayers speak about our being filled with the Holy Spirit, having our sins taken away, being made a sacrifice for God, they seem to speak as if we become Christians when we receive the Eucharist. When we pray, for instance, "Grant that we, who are nourished by his Body and Blood, may be filled with his Holy Spirit, and become one body, one spirit in Christ," it might seem that we were praying to become a Christian or join the Church for the first time. This can be disorienting. What, then, does it mean that all these things happen to us when we receive the Eucharist?

We do not get the gift of the Holy Spirit for the first time when we first share in the Eucharist. Nor do we get it over again each time we share in the Eucharist, as if we lose the Holy Spirit and then have to get him back. Nor do we become one body in Christ for the first time. Rather, the Eucharist fills us with the Holy Spirit in the sense that it renews or strengthens the presence of the Holy Spirit in us. That in turn strengthens spiritual life in us, because the Holy Spirit is the giver of that life. That strengthens our union with Christ so that we can be one body and one spirit in Christ.

The way of speaking we see in the Eucharistic Prayers shows us an important truth about the Eucharist. If we ask what the Eucharist does for us, we could answer that it gives us Christianity, new covenant life.[20] This is in one way the same answer we would give to the question of what Baptism does for us. Baptism gives us Christianity, new covenant life. "All" both Baptism and the Eucharist do, in other words, is convey the grace of God to us, which enables us to be Christians. Of course there is a difference between the two, because Baptism normally gives us the beginning of that life, while the Eucharist feeds that life in us in an ongoing way. But both are concerned with "making us" Christians.

What the Eucharistic Prayers tell us about the blessing the Eucharist brings is confirmed by the Last Supper discourse in John 14–17. This discourse is presented as a version of the instruction that Jesus would have given during his last meal with his disciples. The central theme is similar to what we have seen so far.

Jesus is about to die but also to "go to the Father." His death and resurrection will make something possible—the indwelling life of the Father, Son, and Holy Spirit. Because the Lord will consecrate himself to the Father as a sacrifice (Jn 17:19), his disciples will be sanctified, made holy by receiving new life, participating in the divine glory (Jn 17:20-22). If the Eucharist in some way perpetuates what happened at the Last Supper, then it must be the means for fulfilling the promise and prayer of Jesus. It must be the channel for bringing the blessing of the new covenant in the blood of Jesus, the covenant in which the law is written in the hearts of the disciples of Jesus by having God put his Spirit into them (Jer 31:31-34; Ez 36:26-28).

The Eucharist, then, is food and drink, food and drink that "makes us" Christians. Bread and wine were chosen as the signs in the Eucharist, because they were the two items blessed at a festal meal, the kind of meal eaten after a sacrifice like the Passover. In any festal meal they are symbols of God's blessing to us. As the Body and Blood of the Lord, however, the bread and wine consecrated as the Eucharist are a special blessing. They have become "the bread of eternal life and the cup of salvation." They are spiritual food and drink, the food and drink that strengthen our new covenant life by strengthening the life-giving presence of the Lord in us.

Meditation: The Eucharist as Paschal and Pentecostal
Acts 2

Jesus died and rose again at Passover. He ascended to heaven for the last time forty days later. On the tenth day following, the day of Pentecost, his disciples were gathered together in one place and the Holy Spirit came on them. As Acts 2:2-4 recounts:

> Suddenly a sound came from heaven like the rush of a mighty wind, and it filled all the house where they were sitting. And there appeared to them tongues as of fire, distributed and resting on each one of them. And they were all filled with the Holy Spirit and began to speak in other tongues, as the Spirit gave them utterance.

Many who heard the noise came and were impressed with what they heard. Some, mocking, said, "They are filled with new wine." The effects of the out-pouring of the Spirit had a certain similarity to the effects of drinking wine. The disciples had experienced something happen to them in a way that was visible.

Peter then stood up and explained what had occurred. He preached the gospel, because what had happened could not be explained in any way other than by telling about the death and resurrection of Christ. As Peter put it:

> This Jesus God raised up, and of that we all are witnesses. Being therefore exalted at the right hand of God, and having received from the Father the promise of the Holy Spirit, he has poured out this which you see and hear.

Those who believed Peter's words were baptized and received "the gift of the Holy Spirit," which gave them "the forgiveness of sins" and new life.

People sometimes think that the disciples then scattered and preached the gospel everywhere. Acts tells us something different. They came together in a greater unity than God's people had ever had before because the same divine Spirit had filled each one of them and now dwelled in them. As a result:

> They devoted themselves to the apostles' teaching and fellowship, to the breaking of bread and the prayers.... And all who believed were together and had all things in common; and they sold their possessions and goods and distributed them to all, as any had need. And day by day, attending the temple together and breaking bread in their homes, they partook of food with glad and generous hearts.

Pentecost, then, brought a greater unity. The heart of that unity was expressed in a common life, in their assembly. That assembly probably included their own "synagogue service" in which the apostles taught. It also included "the breaking of the bread," what we would call "the Liturgy of the Eucharist."[21] Their unity and the preaching of the gospel, along with the accompanying wonders and signs, brought about the addition of many more disciples.

In English, the words "Passover" and "Easter" are different. Passover is for Jews, Easter for Christians. In fact, in most languages and certainly in Greek, the language of the New Testament, there is only one word for the two feasts. Easter is the Christian Passover. When we celebrate Easter, we are celebrating Passover. We are, however, celebrating it as fulfilled in Christ.

As we have seen, the Feast of Passover was more than a one-day feast. It lasted for a week, the week that could also be described as the Feast of Unleavened Bread. But not only did Passover introduce a feast of seven days, it introduced a season of seven weeks. Seven times seven days later came the end of the Passover season, and the fiftieth day, the jubilee day, was the Day of Pentecost. Its Hebrew name was the "Feast of Weeks," that is, the feast that concluded the seven weeks of Passover. The Greek name was "Pentecost," that is, the Fiftieth Day (of the season of Passover). Pentecost, in short, can only be understood as the completion of what the Passover (Easter) began.[22]

Pentecost, like Passover, was a harvest feast. During Passover week, the first sheaf of the grain harvest was offered in thanksgiving. At Pentecost, the first-fruits offerings of the completed grain harvest were offered. Christians understood the first sheaf to be a type of Christ (who rose on the day it was offered), the first of the harvest of the human race for God (1 Cor 15:20-23). They considered Pentecost to be the first-fruits offering of people from every nation, a promise and type of the Christian people, the harvest that Christ came to bring (Rv 14:4; see Jas 1:18).

As we have also seen, Pentecost was the feast of the giving of the Law. This too was fulfilled in Christ. As the old covenant Passover and Exodus celebrated the bringing of the people of Israel out of bondage into freedom, so Easter, the new covenant Passover, celebrated the bringing of the new covenant church out of the bondage of sin into the freedom of the gospel through the death and resurrection of Christ. As the old covenant Pentecost celebrated the giving of the old covenant and its Law, so the new covenant Pentecost celebrates the outpouring of the Holy Spirit, which writes the Law in the hearts of Christians (2 Cor 4:3). What we celebrate at Easter, the Christian Passover, is completed in what we celebrate at Pentecost.[23]

The result of the Day of Pentecost, then, was the establishment of the community of the new covenant, a body of people who had been given new life through the death and resurrection of Christ. They still prayed in the temple, because they were Jews. They were, however, "completed" Jews who had experienced "the fulness of the blessing of Christ" (Rom 15:29).

At the same time, those first Christians also came together by themselves to worship God. When they did, they had their own Liturgy of the Word like the one in most synagogues. In that service they learned to understand the Word of God as it was fulfilled in the new covenant. They also had a meal, a meal that was based upon what had happened at the Last Supper. In that meal they celebrated and renewed the blessing of the new covenant.

The Eucharist is a commemoration. It is first of all a commemoration, a "proclamation," of the death of Christ, because we are saved by Christ's offering his life on the cross as a sacrifice for the sins of the world (1 Cor 11:26). It is also a commemoration of the resurrection, because he rose for our justification (Rom 4:24). Had he not risen, we would not be saved (1 Cor 15:16-18). But in addition it is a commemoration of Pentecost, because on Pentecost the disciples first received the gift of the Holy Spirit, which gives us new covenant life.

In the Liturgy of the Eucharist, Christ is present. He is present in bread and wine, his Body separated from his Blood to represent the death by which he atoned for sin and saved us. He is not, however, dead. The risen and glorified Christ is present because there is no other.

In the Eucharistic service in the early liturgies, and to this day, the bread and wine are mingled together before the communion. Their mingling is intended to indicate that we receive a living, risen Christ whose body and blood have been reunited through his resurrection. In some liturgies, hot water is added to the wine to indicate that with faith we receive a cup filled with the Spirit. Earthly things have been glorified, made heavenly, through the death and resurrection of Christ and the outpouring of the Holy Spirit. Earthly things that become heavenly gifts bring new covenant life to us.

Some people call the Eucharist a Pentecost. That phrase has a misleading aspect to it, because it makes us think of the Eucharist as a dramatic event that should bring about something new. It can, however, convey a truth. Although the Eucharist is not the first giving of the Holy Spirit to us, it is a strengthening of the life-giving presence of the Holy Spirit in us. It is truly spiritual food and drink, the food and drink that renew the life of the Spirit in us. We at least can call it Pentecostal.

SEVEN

The Eucharistic Presence

Then they told what had happened on the road, and how he
was known to them in the breaking of the bread.

LUKE 24:35

After Jesus rose again, he appeared to his disciples and taught them. He
"opened their minds to understand the scriptures, and said to them,
'Thus it is written that the Christ should suffer and on the third day rise
from the dead'" (Lk 24:45-46). He also instructed them to preach the
gospel and promised them the gift of the Holy Spirit to give them a new
power (Lk 24:47-49).

Jesus' disciples needed to understand why his death had not been a condemnation for sin or a defeat by Satan but part of the plan of God, a necessary step for their salvation and for the salvation of the world. Even more,
they simply needed to see that he was alive. He had not been defeated by
death but had triumphed over it. Nor had he become a different kind of
creature, especially not simply a spirit. He was still fully human, with a body
(Lk 24:39-43). But he had a glorified body. The existence he now had
allowed him to function differently than he could before his death. By seeing him risen and glorified, his disciples were enabled to comprehend that
the new covenant in his blood would bring to them a glorified life that
would last to all eternity, a life like the one he had entered into by his resurrection.

Jesus appeared to his disciples a number of times. Some of those accounts
were preserved and told over again so that those who came after could realize what had happened. One of the more striking ones is his appearance to
two disciples who were walking on the road to Emmaus (Lk 24:13-35).[1]

These two disciples knew that Jesus had been crucified, and they had
wavered in their faith in him as a result. They had, however, just recently
heard stories about appearances of the risen Lord. Without warning Jesus
approached the two and spoke to them without their recognizing him. As

171

he walked with them he explained to them the necessity for the Christ to "suffer these things and enter into his glory." He then went through Old Testament writings and interpreted to them the way those writings spoke about himself and about his death and resurrection.

They still did not seem to recognize who he was until something else happened:

> So they drew near to the village to which they were going. He appeared to be going further, but they constrained him, saying, "Stay with us, for it is toward evening and the day is far spent."
>
> So he went in to stay with them. When he was at table with them, he took the bread and blessed, and broke it, and gave it to them. And their eyes were opened and they recognized him; and he vanished out of their sight. They said to each other, "Did not our hearts burn within us while he talked to us on the road, while he opened to us the scriptures?"

They promptly returned to Jerusalem, to the place the apostles were gathered, and according to the account in Luke,

> Then they told what had happened on the road, and how he was known to them in the breaking of the bread.

The turning point occurred for these disciples when the risen Lord stayed in their home. There, at the meal, he took the bread, blessed it, broke it, and gave it to them. They had begun to recognize him as he interpreted the Scriptures about himself, but they finally saw that it was the risen Lord present with them "in the breaking of the bread."

Many interpreters think that Jesus celebrated a Eucharist with these disciples, because the same words are used to describe his actions here that are used in the accounts of the Last Supper: he took, blessed, broke, and distributed bread. Moreover, the Eucharistic celebration is sometimes simply referred to in Scriptures as "the breaking of the bread." Others hold that this breaking of the bread was not a Eucharist. They observe that these words could be used of any meal blessing, especially at a meal without wine. Some also hold there was no need for him to celebrate a Eucharist with them since he was already there with them. Moreover, this meal could not be a Eucharist because the gift of the Holy Spirit, which would make the breaking of the bread a true Eucharist, had not yet been given.

Many of those who would hold that he was not celebrating a Eucharist would say that he only celebrated with them the kind of meal, the kind of "breaking of the bread," that he was known for when he held special meals with his disciples. He no doubt blessed the bread in a particular way. Such a meal would be transformed into the Eucharistic meal after his final ascension and Pentecost. These disciples, then, had recognized something characteristic that they had seen him do before and only seen *him* do.

Whether a Christian Eucharist or just the kind of meal of Jesus with his disciples that would later become the Eucharist, the disciples realized that the Lord himself was present with them. The two disciples went back to tell the apostles that they had seen the risen and glorified Lord. He was different from what he had been, and so did not look exactly the way he did before his resurrection. Yet he was recognizably the same once someone accepted the fact that he was still alive. He also could do things he did not do before, such as appear in rooms and disappear from them when he wished. Yet he could still be touched and could eat normal food. The conversation and the meal were the means for them to realize the fact of the glorified Christ's new presence among them.

English speakers who actually believe in the resurrection would commonly use the word "real" to describe Christ's presence in such events. They would say that he was "really" there, not just present as he would be if people were remembering what he had done and were somehow affected by that recollection or having a vision or dream. Likewise, someone who has had a genuine experience of Christ, as happens in retreats or Cursillos or Life in the Spirit Seminars, will often say afterwards, "I found out that he was real." By that they mean that they realized he is a living person who is present to them, not simply an historical figure or a doctrine.[2]

As a result of what happened to the disciples at Emmaus, they were able to say that the Lord was alive and related to them as a person with whom they could interact. They knew that something had happened to them when he spoke about the scriptures, when he "gave the homily," so to speak. They recognized something spiritual had worked in their "hearts"—meaning not just in their feelings but also their minds. He had given them spiritual light as well as faith and hope and love. They also reported that he blessed the bread in a way that allowed them to recognize the person they were speaking with as "the Lord." In other words, they were able to say that he was real, a living person, because they had encountered him present with them.

It is probably no accident that the way the Lord came to these two disciples was similar in form to what happens during a Eucharistic celebration. He first spoke to them in what we might call a Liturgy of the Word. He then distributed blessed bread to them in what we might call a Liturgy of the Eucharist. In this event he was coming to them in something of the same way he would come later to the disciples in the Eucharistic celebration. But these disciples did not go to the apostles to tell them about how the risen Lord conducted liturgy. They went to tell them that he was "really" alive and had been with them.

He was really alive. And he still is. Moreover, he is seated at the right hand of the Father. That is, he is enthroned in his human nature there. Therefore his physical body is there, glorified, but still a human body. Nonetheless he reigns on earth. He is at work, and he comes to people in our world.

There are many ways the Lord comes to people and makes contact with them so that they know he is alive. Occasionally he does so immediately and unexpectedly, as he did to Paul on the road to Damascus. Most commonly he comes to people for the first time through some kind of preaching of the Word. But he has come to his disciples during the ages in a regular way through the reading of the Scriptures and "the breaking of the bread" in the Eucharistic celebration.

We are the heirs of over a millennium of controversy about the way Christ comes to his people in the Eucharistic liturgy. That controversy has centered on the nature of Christ's relationship to the bread and wine that are blessed or consecrated during the Eucharist.[3] The issue has been discussed in terms of questions about the nature of "his presence" in the Eucharistic elements. The *Eucharistic elements,* or as we sometimes say, "consecrated elements" or "consecrated host (sacrificial victim)" in the case of the bread, are phrases that refer to the bread and wine in the Eucharistic celebration after they are blessed or consecrated. "The Eucharistic elements" is the term that seems to be chosen most commonly as a technical term for discussions of Christ's presence in the Eucharist.

Catholics have been noted for being defenders of the "real presence" of Christ in the Eucharistic elements. The emphasis on the presence being "real," however, especially in the midst of controversy, has often produced an imbalance in understanding, so that at times some Catholics speak as if the Eucharist only exists to produce a real presence.[4] They do not seem to have an effective understanding that Christ is present sacramentally under the form of bread and wine in order that his sacrifice can be presented to the Father and in order that his people can be renewed in the divine life he came to bring.

Moreover, Christ is not present exclusively by means of the Eucharistic elements. He is also present in the assembly, because he is present whenever his people gather in faith. In addition he is present in the Scriptures, because they are the Word of God and his Word. He is also present acting in the ordained priest's words as Christ's sacramental representative. All of these presences are "real." As the *Catechism of the Catholic Church,* quoting Paul VI about Christ's real presence in the Eucharistic elements, says:

> This presence is called "real"—by which is not intended to exclude the other types of presence as if they could not be "real" too *(Mysterium Fidei,* 39).

Christ is present in the Eucharistic celebration as a whole, the sacred mysteries, really present in various ways, working through various aspects of it, so that he can renew in us his presence and the life that comes from that.[5] Nonetheless, Christ is present in a special way through the Eucharistic elements. When we understand that truth and when we understand how to approach that reality, our ability to receive life from him can be strengthened. It can be another way of enabling the blessing of the Eucharist to come to us.

The Real Presence

Paul treats the Eucharist incidentally to other concerns. Had Paul not heard of significant difficulties at Corinth, his letters would not have told us that the churches he founded had Eucharistic celebrations.[6] That means that his comments on the Eucharist are unsystematic and incomplete, even though he gives us the most developed New Testament teaching on the topic.

We have already considered what Paul said about the Eucharist in 1 Corinthians 10 when he exhorted the Corinthian Christians to avoid eating idol offerings. There he spoke about partaking of the Body and Blood of the Lord, that is, eating his Body and drinking his Blood. Some think that is the most unambiguous reference to what we would term the real presence.[7] The next chapter, however, gives us another reasonably clear reference to the real presence.

Paul had to correct the way the Corinthians celebrated the Eucharist itself. At the time, the early Christians seem to have celebrated the Eucharist as part of a meal like the Last Supper. In Corinth, however, instead of sharing the same food at a common meal, each family group began eating in an individualistic manner before the common gathering started (v. 21). Moreover, the poor ended up with little to eat (v. 22) because all they had was what they themselves could bring. The Corinthian gatherings were not a good manifestation of the one body that the one bread was supposed to produce (10:17).

Paul addressed this problem in an important discussion in 1 Corinthians 11:17-34. He began by stating the problem. He then gave his account of the Last Supper to remind the Corinthian Christians that the Christian Eucharist is not just an ordinary meal but involves partaking of the Body and Blood of the Lord. This should have made them understand they needed to behave differently when they came together for the Eucharist.

After giving his account of the Eucharistic ceremony, Paul then said (vv. 27, 29-30):

> Whoever, therefore, eats the bread or drinks the cup of the Lord in an unworthy manner will be guilty of profaning the body and blood of the Lord.... For anyone who eats and drinks without discerning the body eats and drinks judgment upon himself. That is why many of you are weak and ill, and some have died.

For our purposes here, the key phrase is "guilty of [profaning] the body and blood of the Lord." The RSV translation adds the word "profaning" for clarification. Some would hold that "guilty of the body and blood of the Lord" refers to the civil crime of attacking the ruling authority, what would have once been referred to as *lèse majesté*. It therefore means that the action of the Corinthians was de facto insulting of the Lord of the universe and consequently a major crime expressive of an attitude of rebellion. Some would even say that the phrase indicates that the Corinthians who relate to the Eucharist in a disrespectful way are actually guilty of his death.[8]

The RSV translation, however, gives us a more probable understanding. The guilt Paul speaks about is guilt in regard to the Body and Blood of the

Lord. That indicates the guilt does not directly refer to the Lord in his person, independently of the ceremony, but of desecrating a sacrificial offering or "holy thing" (see Lv 22:1-9). That would have been a serious sin in respect to the old covenant sacrificial offerings, and Paul is saying that it is a cause of condemnation in respect to the new covenant offering, the Body and Blood of the Lord. This interpretation is strengthened by the observation that the penalty in the old covenant for profaning a holy thing is "cutting off" (Lv 22:3),[9] sometimes translated "excision" or "extirpation," which means death directly inflicted by God (Lv 22:9), often through sickness (Nm 8:19 with Nm 18:22). That is the penalty Paul warns the Corinthians about.

If Paul can say that someone who eats the bread and drinks the cup of the Lord in an unworthy way is guilty of profaning the Body and Blood, he likely does not think we are merely dealing with a symbol that is designed to help us call to mind some Christian truths. He must believe that the symbolized reality is actually the Lord's Body and Blood offered for us. This is especially true if such behavior merits the death penalty. In other words, the seriousness of the way Paul speaks about the failure to treat the Body and Blood of the Lord as something holy, in this case by treating the meal as an ordinary meal and by disregarding the poor Christians, those with whom partaking of the Eucharist unites us (1 Cor 10:17), indicates that he views the Eucharistic elements as objectively holy, the real Body and Blood of Christ, the sacrificial offering of the new covenant.

As we have seen, Paul says in 1 Corinthians 10:16 that we partake of the Body and Blood of the Lord when we receive the Eucharistic elements, and he speaks as well of profaning the Body and Blood when we partake unworthily. That implies that what looks or appears to us like bread and wine is now the Body and Blood of the Lord. At the same time, Paul describes the same event in 1 Corinthians 11:26-28 (see 10:17) as "eating the bread" and "drinking the cup." In both, he is clearly referring to the Eucharistic elements after what we would term the consecration.

The Eucharistic Prayers sometimes handle the difficult question of bread and wine (in a cup) that are Body and Blood by referring to them as "the Bread of Life" and "the cup of salvation." They are bread that gives life (see Jn 6:48-51) and the cup of salvation in the post-resurrection thanksgiving offering (see Ps 116:13, 17). They convey life and salvation because now they "contain" the true presence of Christ.[10] He is united to them in such a way that they communicate spiritual, eternal life, because they are his Body and his Blood.[11]

We now most commonly use the phrase *real presence* to speak about Christ's presence through the Eucharistic elements. "Presence" is readily understood as indicating the fact that he is somehow there. "Real," however, has an older meaning that is no longer commonly used.

In current English, we usually would contrast "real" with "illusory" or even "false." If we then say, Christ is "really present" in the Eucharist, we would be adding "really" to give emphasis. We would be simply affirming that he is there and we are not making a mistake. "Real," however, when we refer to the real presence, bears an older technical sense that is slightly different in meaning. It contrasts something present as something existing independently of our minds to what is only mentally present, like an idea or a memory.

For example, if we are at home thinking about an aunt who has died recently, we might say that when we remember her she is present in the room. But we would only mean that she was present as a memory or thought, not that she was present in objective reality. Her presence is not a "real presence," to use the technical term. The doctrine of the real presence,[12] then, asserts that Christ is present by means of the Eucharistic elements as an objective reality and not just as an idea or memory, something that only exists in our minds.

This means that his Eucharistic presence is not merely symbolic. The bread and wine are not just symbols of his body and blood that call him to mind and call his sacrifice on the cross to mind. He is present in objective reality, or, to use traditional technical terminology, "in truth."

Nor is his presence simply a matter of our faith, so that he is present as long as we have faith that he is there or "there for us." Such an understanding would have the consequence that if we do not have faith, he is not there. Or he might be present to one person, who had faith he was there, but not to another, who did not have that faith. However, if a chair, or a seeming ghost, were "present" in a room to one person but not to another, we would likely conclude that the presence was not an objective reality. It would be something in the mind of the person who thought or believed it was there. It would be, in other words, a merely subjective presence, not a "real" presence.

Still more could be said about the way Christ is really present by means of the Eucharistic elements. He is not just present by his power the way he is in Baptism or ordination, working in and through the ceremony to produce an important result. Nor is he just present the way he was in the burning bush, using the bush to manifest his presence but not becoming a bush. He is not even present along with the bread and wine. To use the traditional technical term, he is "substantially" present. The bread and wine have *become* his Body and Blood and are no longer "really" bread and wine.[13] To use another traditional technical theological term for the change, we could describe what has happened as "transubstantiation," although to develop the technical meaning of this term in a way that would be comprehensible would go beyond what can be accomplished in this book.[14]

The doctrine of the real presence is important, because it means that when we come to the Eucharist, Christ is objectively present. We may be low in faith or in desire, but he is simply there. We can respond to him adequately or poorly, but he is there.

On the other hand, the real presence of Christ in the Eucharistic elements is an unusual presence, as is well expressed in Thomas Aquinas' hymn *Lauda Sion,* used as the sequence in the Roman rite feast of Corpus Christi. When we partake of the Eucharist, we do not become cannibals. Nor is Christ torn into pieces when we chew the bread. Nor would he be hurt if the church were bombed or burned down with the consecrated elements in it. Nor is he dead because his Body is in one place and his Blood is in another. Nor would he be farther away from us if the only piece of consecrated bread in the church were carried away from us and put in the sacristy.[15]

Even more important, when the priest takes some of the consecrated bread and breaks it and gives it out, he is not giving only part of Christ to each person. Only the sacramental sign of the bread is being broken and made smaller. Each person is receiving the whole Christ, and the Christ they receive is no smaller in size than he would be if they had received a larger piece of bread. If there are thousands of people receiving Communion, all of them will receive Christ fully. The very point of the distribution is that the same Christ and his life is given to each one fully so that one bread may make one body.

Many people have come to an awareness of what it means to say that Christ is really present through their participation in some Eucharistic devotion. They see the sacramental elements in the form of bread, believe it is Christ, and so come to the awareness that he is now present in a way similar to the way other things in our space-time world might be present. It often convinces them, in fact, that he is a real person.

The mindset Eucharistic devotions produce can, however, also be misleading in certain respects.[16] We might imagine a situation in which instead of there being one monstrance there were two, each containing a consecrated host. In both Christ would be really present. But there would not be two Christs in the church, only one. He is present as a real person, but not the same way he was when he walked the earth before his resurrection.

A group of people were once having a discussion about a church burning down. They postulated that the consecrated host and a baby were in the church. The issue was whether, if someone had to make a choice, he or she should save the host or the baby. The participants in the discussion should not have hesitated but should have decided for the baby. That would be to save a life, while Christ himself would have remained perfectly alive and completely unharmed even if the host were burned up. Yet they could not solve the problem, because their theology led them to conceive of Christ's real presence as if it were the same as when he was preaching in Galilee. Consequently they discussed at length which of two people to "save," the Lord or the baby. Inadequate theology can potentially have bad consequences.

Christ's Eucharistic presence is real. Moreover, he is not just spiritually present in the sense of immaterially present. The consecrated bread is the means of his presence in this space-time world. It is his Body, and bodies are corporeal. Yet, as we have seen, Christ's presence is an unusual presence. For this reason it is often termed a *sacramental presence,* or in this case a sacramental real presence.

The phrase "sacramental presence" does not indicate just the special nature of Christ's presence but even more that Christ makes use of the Eucharistic elements for a particular purpose.[17] He is present to strengthen his people with the spiritual life won by his death and resurrection. This result is brought about by re-presenting his offering to the Father so that the grace and blessing might be given again. It is also brought about by his people partaking of the sacrificial offering, his body broken for them and his Blood poured out for them, and so having his life renewed in them.

The bread and wine are signs, signs of what Christ will do for us when we partake in the Eucharist. But they are sacramental signs, not merely symbols. They are signs that point us to effects that taking part in the Eucharistic action can or will produce. When we eat the consecrated bread and drink the consecrated wine, we are fed with the Body and Blood of the Lord. We do not just think of the Body and Blood of the Lord and appreciate how helpful his atoning sacrifice was for us. Nor do we simply exercise faith that his atoning sacrifice will have its intended effect. Rather, we actually receive, or at least can receive, the grace it was intended to bring to us.

It is partly for this reason that the Eucharistic elements look like and are experienced like bread and wine, that is, food and drink. They indicate to us that we are being supplied with the means that nourish spiritual life, the life of Christ. We are being strengthened in the life that comes from the presence of Christ and the Holy Spirit in us.

For Christ to be present in our parish church in the way he was with the disciples in Galilee would only be of limited help to us. We could see that he really exists and is alive, and that would help our faith. We might be able to talk to him more easily. However, he probably would not have much time for individual conversations. He would have to speak to everyone else in the parish and then move on so he could speak to billions of other Christians. If he started somewhere else, in Palestine, say, he would not even get to most of us before we died.

But he is not present at the Eucharist the same way he was when he was on earth before his death, nor even in the way he was after his resurrection until his ascension. He is present sacramentally. That means, first of all, that he can be present to all of us all over the world at the same time. More significantly, it means that he does not just relate to us externally, as he would if he were talking to us the way he did with Philip or Peter at the Last Supper, answering their questions. Through his sacramental presence, when we partake of the consecrated bread and wine, he puts his Spirit and his life into us, so that we can live in a better way.

The Eucharist was not given so that we could talk to Christ or worship him the way we might if he were still on earth before his resurrection. To be sure, he should be worshiped when the Eucharistic elements are present because he is God and the elements are his Body and Blood. But that is not the main purpose of the Eucharist. The Eucharist was given so that the sacrifice of Christ might be re-presented to the Father to worship him and to ask him that the blessing that Christ won for us be given to us again. And it is given so that we might receive that blessing anew, the strengthening of the presence of the Holy Spirit in us, who strengthens in us the presence and life of Christ.

Eucharistic devotions, like Benediction of the Blessed Sacrament or "Eucharistic Adoration," are devotions, not the participation in a sacramental action. Consequently, we can only consider such devotions in this book in a brief way. In such devotions, we are making use of the consecrated elements as an aid to our prayer or contemplation, our subjective appreciation of Christ, of his presence, and of what he has done for us and our desire to give ourselves to him in turn. For many, such a devotion is an effective help and so strengthens their spiritual life. It is, however, when we participate in the offering of the consecrated elements in the Eucharistic sacrifice and especially when we partake of them in Communion that we are using them as sacraments. We are then making use of them as signs that objectively give grace.[18]

Moreover, as a result of receiving Communion, we are strengthened in our ability to take the presence of Christ with us when we leave the church. As Leo the Great said (Sermon 63, 7):

> For nothing else is brought about by partaking of the body and blood of Christ than that we pass into what we take and both in spirit and in body carry him everywhere, him in whom we have died and risen again.

The Eucharist was given so that we might go to our home, to our work, to our school, and have Christ in us and with us. We are strengthened spiritually so that we might live as Christians in all the circumstances of our life. We also should be strengthened in our faith so that we can pray wherever we are with the confidence that God is truly there and we are spiritually in contact with him.[19] Although it may help us, we do not need to be in church to pray, nor near the Eucharistic elements, nor in a room with the Eucharistic elements exposed. The heavenly temple is open to us, and in Christ we are in the presence of God and can worship him "in spirit and truth" (Jn 4:24).

The Change

As Paul says, we partake in the Body and Blood of the Lord in the Eucharist. For us to do so, the bread and wine must have undergone some change so the things that once were merely bread and wine now are the Body and Blood of the Lord. In few places is the change in approach of Catholic teaching since the Second Vatican Council more visible than in speaking about the transformation in the elements, "the consecration."

Before the Second Vatican Council the tendency was simply to emphasize that the transformation was due to the priest's speaking the words of Christ. The role of the priest in the consecration had been under attack. It therefore had to be emphasized.[20] An unintended side result was that Catholics often seemed to think no more needed to be said on the subject. Even more problematic, by isolating one aspect of the process and treating it in independence of the rest, the change was made to seem almost magical. It might seem that the priest could simply summon Christ at will and make him appear.

Catholic theology still upholds the truth that a validly ordained priest, one with powers passed on by apostolic succession, is needed for sacramental consecration (CCC 1566). It also upholds the truth that the words of Christ are an integral element in the consecration (CCC 1375-76). But, in the course of the Eucharistic Prayer, God acts, and the priest is not in charge of God. He is only God's minister. He is the one appointed by the Lord as his representative to preside over and represent the assembly of the local church.[21]

The presence of Christ in the Eucharist is primarily an action of God. Christ joins himself to the bread and wine in such a way that it can be accurately said to be his Body and Blood. The elements are not physically changed in our sense of "physical." If they underwent a chemical test, they would appear to be simply bread and wine, and no trace of divinity would appear. Just as we cannot make use of a psychological test to ascertain whether the red liquid before it has been drunk contains alcohol, so we cannot make use of a chemical test to determine whether it "contains" divinity. Divinity transcends space, time, and matter and so cannot appear in chemical tests or physical tests, but must be "tested for" in a different way.

The Eucharist celebration, then, is primarily a divine action. It is, however, a divine sacramental action. It is a celebration of the divine mysteries.[22] In it, God the Father, Son, and Holy Spirit act within our world to strengthen the life of the new covenant people of God. They do so by receiving the offering of bread and wine and uniting them to the glorified Christ so that he can re-present his sacrifice on the cross and give life to his people. In so doing, they work through the ministry of the priest presiding over the worship of the whole people assembled.

The Divine Action

The Eucharistic celebration is the work of the Holy Spirit. In Eucharistic Prayer III, the one we have been considering, we pray:

> And so, Father, we bring you these gifts. We ask you to make them holy by the power of your Spirit, that they may become the Body and Blood of your Son, our Lord Jesus Christ, at whose command we celebrate this Eucharist.

This prayer states that the Holy Spirit brings about the consecration. He acts on the bread and wine in such a way that they become Christ's Body and Blood.

Then, after the institution narrative, we pray:

> Grant that we, who are nourished by his body and blood, may be filled with his Holy Spirit, and become one body, one spirit in Christ. May he make us an everlasting gift to you and enable us to share in the inheritance of your saints.

This prayer states that when we receive the Body and Blood of the Lord, the Holy Spirit enters into us and fills us, strengthening us so that we might become what God wants us to be.

It is, in other words, the Holy Spirit who transforms the bread and wine into the Body and Blood of Christ. He brings heaven to earth. He enters into the bread and wine and changes them "from within." He unites the bread and wine to the divine Son of God, in such a way that they become his Body and Blood. He does so, however, so that they might become the means of sharing divine life with us.

But the Holy Spirit comes because God the Father sends him. The Eucharistic Prayer is addressed to God the Father. We call upon the Father to send the Spirit so that the Body and Blood of Christ may be really present in our midst. As Cyril of Jerusalem put it in his *Catecheses* [XXIII (V), 7]:

> Then having sanctified ourselves by these spiritual hymns [the "Holy, Holy, Holy"], we call upon the merciful God to send forth His Holy Spirit upon the gifts lying before Him; that He may make the bread the Body of Christ, and the wine the Blood of Christ.

The sections quoted above from Eucharistic Prayer III are called "epicleses." As we have seen, "epiclesis" simply means "invocation." To invoke God is to call upon him. The word "invocation" is usually used to refer to a prayer of petition. When we invoke God, we call upon him to do something for us that we cannot do ourselves. While there are sections of the Eucharistic Prayers called invocations, the prayer as a whole is also spoken of as an invocation. It is a petition to God for his blessing that includes special prayers that invoke the work of the Holy Spirit upon the bread and wine.[23]

We cannot sanctify ourselves. Even less can we turn the bread and wine into the Body and Blood of Christ. No human being can do that. A priest, therefore, cannot do that, unless God works through him. Only God can bring about such a transformation, and he acts when he wishes, not when we wish. The epiclesis expresses the truth that only if God the Father deigns to accept our offering and bless it, only if the Holy Spirit enters into our celebration and works in it, can the bread and wine become the Body and Blood of Christ. And only if God the Father deigns to accept our prayer and bless us when we partake of the Bread of Life and the cup of salvation, only if the Holy Spirit works through our partaking of them and enters into us to work in us, can we receive life through them.

We therefore should not just listen to the Eucharistic prayer being prayed by the priest, waiting for it to accomplish its effect. Nor should he recite it as if all he needed to do was say the words. The prayer is an invocation or petition that he is reciting as the Lord's appointed representative speaking on behalf of the congregation. We, and the priest, should therefore pray with faith while it is being spoken for the outpouring of the Holy Spirit on the bread and wine and through them on us when we receive them.

The consecration of the Eucharistic elements is a means to an end, our filling with the Holy Spirit. The action of God in the Eucharistic celebration can be greater or less depending on the preparation and spiritual disposition with which we corporately and individually participate. The gift may be objectively given but received without much result. The more a body of Christians turns to the Lord in the Eucharist and seeks his grace, the more that grace will act in us effectively. That truth is a key to personal Eucharistic renewal.[24]

The Sacramental Action

To say that the presence of Christ in the Eucharistic elements is real is to say that it is objective. That means it does not depend on us. It does not matter how little we believe, how ineffectively we participate, Christ is still there.

On the other hand, it would not be true to say that Christ's presence is independent of any human beings other than himself. His sacramental presence is not the same as a resurrection appearance. He does not just appear of his own accord so that we realize it or do not realize it as the case may be. Nor is it the same as his incarnation, where he announces to unsuspecting human beings that he is about to take flesh and does so with their cooperation but without their fully understanding what is happening. A sacramental action is something that occurs "at his command" and is carried out by human beings who do what he told them to do for the reasons he told them.

Christ becomes present in the Eucharist because a part of his Church, his body, is assembling. Moreover, it is assembling in order to have a Eucharistic celebration. In this sense, faith is essential. A group of pagans could not bring about a Eucharistic celebration, no matter what they did. Only a group of people with faith and united with Christ can. Once Christ becomes present, a pagan who happened to be attending the celebration would be objectively in Christ's presence as much as Christians are, whether he realized it or believed it or not. That presence, however, comes about through Christian faith.

According to Catholic teaching, not any set of members of the Church can have a full Eucharist. There needs to be a priest present. Only with the priest present and presiding over the assembly can the group of Christians do all that is possible for an assembly of Christians, especially celebrate a Eucharist in which the bread and wine become the Body and Blood of Christ. Christ is really present when a group of Christians gathers to pray without a priest. "Where two or three are gathered in my name, there am I in the midst of them" (Mt 18:20). But he does not become sacramentally present without an ordained priest.

Just having a priest present, however, is not enough. He has to hold a Eucharistic celebration. He has to take bread and wine and pray over them in such a way that he expresses the fact that he is presiding at a Eucharist. He needs to intend to fulfil Christ's command, "Do this in memory of me." To use the technical phrase, he has to do what the Catholic Church intends to do at a Eucharist. He has to say a Eucharistic Prayer, not as a quotation as he might when teaching a theology course or by reciting it as he would when trying to memorize it, but intending the words to do what they say.

The "words of institution" have to be spoken in such a way. Following the pattern of Jewish blessings, where divine commands are often cited, the priest, the president of the assembly, repeats the words that Christ spoke. He does so because it is the Lord who brings about the Eucharist and he brings it about when his people do what he commanded them to do. The president of the assembly refers to that command to authorize his action.

Catholic theology uses the Latin term *ex opere operato* to express how the bread and wine become the Body and Blood of Christ. Those words mean "by the work performed." In other words, just by the celebration of the Eucharist the bread and wine become the Body and Blood of Christ, even if the priest is living an immoral life or is generally ineffective as a priest. To "perform the work," the priest needs to call to mind the authorization that comes through the command of Christ and to invoke the Holy Spirit, but he does not need to be especially holy or faith-filled.[25] Moreover, those who receive those consecrated elements receive the Body and Blood of Christ, even if they do not believe it or realize it. In this sense, what happens is objective and independent of subjective dispositions—"real."

On the other hand, when a valid Eucharist is celebrated the participants do not necessarily receive the blessing or grace that receiving the Body and Blood is intended to give. The benefit or fruit does not come *ex opere operato*. The participants may, in fact, receive condemnation if they receive unworthily, as Paul indicated in the passage in 1 Corinthians 11 on the Eucharist. Or they simply may not receive much benefit if they receive without much faith or desire for the Lord.

Behind the understanding of the objectivity of the gift given is what could be called an "evangelical truth." The Eucharist depends on the word of the Lord, the command and promise of Christ. The priest and assembly of the people do not bring about a genuine Eucharist by themselves. If, however, a body of Christians, assembled in one locality, does what Christ told them to do, fulfilling all the conditions he stated or implied, the result is God's action.

Confidence in the effectiveness of claiming God's promises is a fundamental truth of the Christian life and the foundation behind the effectiveness of proclaiming the gospel as well as celebrating the Eucharist. As

Ambrose, perhaps the chief patristic teacher about the Eucharist in the Latin Church, put it in *On the Mysteries* (IX, 52):

> If a human blessing [that of Moses or Elisha] was powerful enough to change nature, what do we say of the divine consecration itself where the very words of the Lord and Savior act? For the sacrament which you receive is consecrated by the word of Christ. But if the word of Elijah was powerful enough to bring down fire from heaven, will not the word of Christ be powerful enough to change the characters of the elements?

We live in an individualistic age. Many preachers speak of what can happen if we "claim the promises of Christ." Sometimes they fail to mention any conditions that need to be met to do so, but not always. Often they present important truths in a way that is very beneficial. But almost always they apply their message to individuals. If individuals claim the promises of Christ, meeting the conditions, they will be blessed by the God acting in or for them. But some promises are corporate. Some can be claimed by any individual Christians, some only by bodies of Christians who meet all the conditions to be the Church and act as the Church.

The word "institution" is used to describe Christ's words at the Last Supper, in the conviction that he was not speaking of a promise that any individual could claim but of one that only the Church could claim, and only if it met all the conditions. Moreover, it is a promise that is meant to be claimed in a regular way year after year until he comes again. It is meant to be a stable, corporate support and source of life for the Christian pilgrimage throughout the centuries.

The Catholic teaching on the objective nature of the Eucharistic action does not take away from the need for faith, either for the Church as a body or for the individual who seeks to benefit from the Eucharist. Rather, it indicates that the Eucharist primarily depends, not on our subjective dispositions, but on the intention and promise of Christ. When we are gathered together, with a priest presiding, in order to celebrate the Eucharist, Christ acts in such a way that the bread and wine become his Body and Blood, offered to the Father and given to us. We can count on that. We can put faith in that. That truth gives us a key to personal Eucharistic renewal.

Eucharistic Renewal

When we talk about "Eucharistic renewal," we are speaking about the renewal of a sacrament in our lives and in the life of the Church. Not every way of honoring sacraments or emphasizing them is a means of sacramental renewal. Perhaps one way of describing some recent problems among Catholics is that there has been too much speaking about sacraments—renewing our Baptism, renewing our marriage, putting symbols of the sacraments in churches and homes, but too little real renewal of the sacraments. When we focus on the sign, we can too easily fail to focus on the reality to which the sign is meant to bring us.

We are heirs of centuries of polemics. The Catholic side has seen the sacraments as under attack, both by Protestants and unbelievers, and has "dug in" to defend them. To some Catholics, it has almost seemed that it was impossible to emphasize the sacraments too much. The result has unfortunately been at times an approach to the sacraments that has focused on them as important in themselves rather than on what the Lord does through them.

We might be driving along, trying to find our way, and finally come across a sign that says "Krakow" with an arrow pointing down the road. Most of us would not then say, "What a nice sign." Nor would we say, "Let's take some time to contemplate the sign and to think about how good it is to go to Krakow." If we are Canadians or Hondurans, we might need some instruction in Polish signs to know which way to set off. If we had not been thinking of going to Krakow, perhaps we might need instruction as to why someone would want to get on the road to Krakow. But if all was working well, we would mainly respond to the sign by saying, "Thank God, there's the road to Krakow." Our focus would be on what the sign was pointing to, not on the sign itself.

The sacraments, although, as we have seen, they are special signs that "contain grace," are not intended to be ends in themselves. They are intended to be means. They are intended to be means that lead us to the grace of God, signs that show us that the grace of God is present and available, signs that allow us to receive it. The grace of God ought to be our primary focus. We should mainly say, "What a wonderful thing God has done for us!" We ought to receive the grace of God, thank him for it, and thank him for what his Son has done to make it possible.

Sacraments are given for a purpose. We have not renewed a sacrament unless something has happened to produce greater effectiveness in achieving the purpose for which the sacrament was instituted. To renew the Eucharist is not the same as to increase the attendance at Sunday or daily Mass, to get more people involved in Eucharistic devotions, to verbally stress more often the importance of the Eucharist, however much those things may be helpful. The Eucharist is renewed when, as a result of celebrating the Eucharist, God is more fully worshiped, when the sacrifice of the Son is represented to the Father with greater faith, and when those who receive Communion are strengthened in their life in Christ by the power of the Holy Spirit so that they might live faith, hope, and charity in all the circumstances of their daily lives.

The Eucharist follows on Baptism (and Confirmation). Nowadays Catholic theologians often teach about the Eucharist as the final step of Christian initiation. They are following the practice of the early Church, when mainly adults became Christian. At that time, the Eucharist was the final part of one ceremony of Christian initiation which began with Baptism and Confirmation, so it was truly part of Christian initiation. It is, however, somewhat artificial to simply approach the Eucharist now as the last step of Christian initiation, because most Catholics do not receive the Eucharist until many years after they have been sacramentally initiated into the Church and are considered full members. Moreover, in contrast to Baptism, the Eucharist is mainly experienced as something ongoing in the Christian life.

On the other hand, there is an important reason for considering the Eucharist in its place in the initiation process if we are concerned with Eucharistic renewal. The Eucharist depends on what happens in earlier stages of Christian initiation, just as our appreciating good literature depends on our first learning to read. If people have not learned how to read well, they will not likely make good students of literature no matter how important they have come to think it is. If they try, they will often, in fact, simply repeat words whose meaning they do not really understand or at least do not fully understand. Similarly, if people's Christian initiation has been defective, their approach to and experience of the Eucharist will likely also be defective, even if they think the Eucharist is very important and can repeat a certain amount of Eucharistic doctrine.

The key to sacramental renewal, then, is Christian initiation. Unless the basic connection with God in Christ has been established, Eucharistic experience will be weak at best. This is not the place to treat the elements of Christian initiation. We can, however, briefly look at the rite of initiation in the early Church, see what was involved in it, and then consider what that shows us needs to happen for Eucharistic renewal.

In the early Church (as we can see, for instance, in the *Apostolic Tradition* of Hippolytus, written about A.D. 215)[26] most people were baptized and confirmed on Easter. Easter was the day of the resurrection. They were to be made sharers in the risen and glorified life of Christ, the result of what was celebrated in the Christian Passover, Easter.

When they entered the baptistery, they took their clothes off, faced west, and renounced Satan and all his works. In this they expressed the fact that they were rejecting their former life, not in the sense that they thought there was nothing good about it but in the sense that it was formed and shaped by living in the kingdom of darkness. In other words, they rejected a way of life dominated by sin and Satan. What they said in the baptismal ceremony expressed the fact that they had completed a process of repentance and exorcism, had ceased to practice serious sin, and had left occupations or activities that would lead them to sin.

They then turned to face east, the place from which the sun rises and from which Christ would come in his second coming. They acknowledged or confessed their belief in God the Father, the Son, and the Holy Spirit and in what the triune God has done for us by creating us, by redeeming us, especially through the death and resurrection of the Son, and by sanctifying us. What they said expressed the fact that they had completed a process of instruction in which they came to understand and accept the foundational Christian truths.

They were then baptized, going down into the pool and having water poured over them completely. In doing this, they were buried in the water and so the old person was put to death, the power of sin in them was destroyed and washed away, and they were raised up to begin a new life. Then they were anointed with oil, and the bishop laid hands upon them as he prayed that they might be filled with the Holy Spirit for the first time.

They were then clothed in white garments, symbolizing the newness of life they had entered into, and were brought into the church to join the whole body of Christian people. There they were present at the Eucharist for the first time and joined with everyone else in offering the Eucharistic sacrifice. At its conclusion, they received the Body and Blood of the Lord, along with milk and honey to express the fact that they had truly entered into the Promised Land of life in Christ and were now being fed like a newly born infant. As a result of all this their life was now given to God, made spiritual and holy, through Christ by the power of the Holy Spirit.

If we were to make a list of the elements of Christian initiation preliminary to sharing in the Eucharist, it would include:

- true conversion, including deliverance from bondage to evil spirits and repentance from a sinful way of life
- instruction in Christian truth, resulting in understanding and accepting the elements of the gospel and the Christian way of life
- an experience of God acting in the catechumens, so that the power of the old life was destroyed and they were filled with the Holy Spirit
- joining the Christian people, a body of people who had gone through the same process and were one in mind and heart in their worship of God.

This list reveals the main problem that one category of Catholics experience in relationship to Eucharistic renewal. They are not converted people. They have not turned from the old, turned to the new, and received the action of God resulting in change of life. Nowadays bishops and theologians often say that Catholics are sacramentalized but not evangelized. Properly understood, that is true. They have undergone valid sacramental actions, but without the orientation that would make them effective for personal change. They lack the Christian conversion that comes from responding to the gospel preached to them. Perhaps they have never heard it effectively preached. As a result, the sacraments they receive do not have much effect.

There is, however, a second category of Catholics. They keep the commandments. They believe the creed and catechism. They attend church regularly. They do all the things they are expected to do and do those things as sincerely as they know how. They would even want to die for the faith if that were required. Yet they do not experience the presence and power of the Holy Spirit within, or at least not in a way that is very conscious and helpful. They can easily practice a Eucharistic devotion, because there they worship Christ's presence as something external to them. They do not, however, receive communion as something that will genuinely strengthen and transform them. It is a mainly a chance to be "physically" closer to Christ and to talk to him and ask him for favors.

Conscious Christian experience is not the most important thing in being a Christian. What "avails" or counts, as Paul put it, is "keeping the commandments" (1 Cor 7:19). What counts is "faith working through love" (Gal 5:6). What counts is being "a new creation" (2 Cor 5:17). Normal good Catholics are truly Christians, not pagans, despite what certain preachers, including at times Catholic preachers, might lead us to believe.

Yet Christian life is meant to be experiential. The apostles taught that Christians should recognize the experience of the presence and power of the Holy Spirit inside themselves as a way of knowing that they truly are Christian and living new covenant life. Paul, in expressing the superiority of the new covenant to the old, said in Galatians 3:1-5:

O foolish Galatians! Who has bewitched you, before whose eyes Jesus Christ was publicly portrayed as crucified? Let me ask you only this: Did you receive the Spirit by works of the law, or by hearing with faith? Are you so foolish? Having begun with the Spirit, are you now ending with the flesh? Did you experience so many things in vain?—if it really is in vain. Does he who supplies the Spirit to you and works miracles among you do so by works of the law, or by hearing with faith?

Paul clearly expected the Galatians to know how they had received the Holy Spirit.

John, in giving people a criterion to know that they were Christians, unlike the Gnostics they had to deal with, said in 1 John 4:13:

By this we know that we abide in him and he in us, because he has given us of his own Spirit.

And again, in 1 John 3:24, he said:

All who keep his commandments abide in him, and he in them. And by this we know that he abides in us, by the Spirit which he has given us.

In short, he expected the presence of the Spirit to be conscious enough in them that they would know that they had received him.

For Christians who are converted enough so that the basics are present, ordinary "good Catholics," something more is needed if they are to experience a true renewal of the Eucharist. They need a renewal in faith, both belief in the fact of what Christ is doing in the Eucharist and confidence in receiving the results that the Lord intends should come from that fact.

For such a renewal we first need to believe in the objective truth of Christ's presence. Before we receive Communion, we are told, "[This is] the Body of Christ. [This is] the Blood of Christ." We say, "Amen." That means, "Yes it is." The foundation of any true and not illusory or imaginary experience of Christianity is the truth, objective reality, and recognition of that reality.

When we say, "[This is] the Body of Christ," however, we are not just expressing belief in the real presence. We are expressing belief that this Body and Blood of Christ has been presented to the Father for us and that it is the perfectly acceptable offering. We can therefore claim the blessing that it has been offered to win. We are also expressing belief that this Body and Blood of Christ is given to us as spiritual food and drink. It will fill us with the Holy Spirit. It will strengthen us and "inebriate" us with new life. We are, in short, believing that what God has promised in his Word will come to pass in us and come to pass effectively.

"Belief" and "faith" are two different English translations of the same Greek word, but they have different connotations in English. If we say that we believe that new life will be given to us in the Body and Blood of Christ, we usually are referring to mental acceptance of the fact. If we say we have faith that new life will be given to us, we usually mean that we believe something will actually happen to us when we receive the Body and Blood. Both are needed, and for renewal of the Eucharist faith is needed as well as belief.

Doctrinal belief, important as it is, is not a full response to the gospel. Those whose faith is not active or expectant will usually miss something Christ is offering them. A friend might give us a ticket to a football game that will allow us to sit in a box seat. We may think he is playing a practical joke on us and so not use it. We may also, however, forget we have it or not want to go to the effort to go to the stadium and likewise not use it. As a result, although we have everything we need to experience the foot-ball game firsthand, we may end up just watching it on television or listen-ing to it on the radio. In other words, if we do not actively respond to what is given us and use it in the appropriate way, confident that by using it we can obtain what we want, we will not receive the result for which it was given. This latter response is often referred to as expectant faith.

If we have expectant faith, we will respond to what Christ has done for us so that we begin to experience something new in the Christian life. We will not just accept the fact that Christ has done something for us "in invisible Graceland," but we will confidently expect that he is working in us now and begin to make use of the grace he has given. As a result we will begin to experience his presence and power in us more consistently as we live our daily lives. That experience may not be dramatic. It may grow on us slowly. But an expectant faith will bring us to a deeper, more "real" experience of the Christian life.

Active or expectant faith is often more easily caught than learned. The easiest way to get it is to be with a group of people who have it. It can often be gotten by attending Life in the Spirit Seminars or some other event designed to help us come to a living faith in the reality of the Holy Spirit working in and through us.

There is still a third category of Catholic, the "renewed Catholics," who also face a problem in experiencing renewal of the Eucharist. There have been many programs of renewal that have helped such Catholics. Some may have had a charismatic experience or been changed by a powerful retreat like a Cursillo. Some have gone through special courses that have proceeded in a slower manner. Some have even experienced a personal renewal by a special action of God during an ordinary Eucharistic celebration.

Such Catholics may have come away with a conviction that they have experienced the presence of the Holy Spirit in themselves and consequently find Christian living much easier and more effective than previously. But often they have seen their new experience fade, so that a few years after their experience of renewal they do not live as Christians much differently than they did before. They now know it is possible. They now know Christ is real, not merely a doctrine or a historical personage. But they do not experience the power in that truth or only do so sporadically or weakly.

Such people can be tempted to think that they need to have the same initial experience over again. They need to be baptized again, rebaptized, rebaptized in the Spirit. They need to attend another Cursillo, go through another Life in the Spirit Seminar, go to a meeting where they can "rest in the Spirit."

Such things may help, but the problem will recur. It will recur because they have been renewed in the beginning steps of the process of Christian initiation but not in the last step. The last step is the Eucharist. The last step is the regular Christian assembly in which we participate with a group of people of faith in re-presenting to God the death and resurrection of Christ, which saves us and in which we receive the spiritual food and spiritual drink that sustain us.

To experience life from the Eucharist, we need the same faith we had in our first spiritual renewal, but it has to be more "routine" faith. When we encounter something for the first time, the experience of it is often very conscious, even dramatic. The first time we experience the reality of God's presence in us can be stirring and exciting. It may even be something like falling in love.

Some experiences, however, are more quiet and, paradoxically, might even be something we do not notice. All of us are aware in a semiconscious way that we are breathing. If suddenly we could not breathe anymore, we would become vividly conscious of the fact that we had been breathing and now no longer were. If all goes well, however, our experience of breathing will be steady and somewhat routine, something we normally pay little attention to, but not something we are tempted to doubt. It is something we simply rely on as we go through daily life, even though we do not notice it.

In a similar way, there are many people we have good personal relationships with and love deeply, but we are not always conscious of that fact. We may not even realize the importance of the relationship to us until we lose the person through death or lose the regular interaction because the person moves away. Nonetheless, as we live with them or work with them and speak with them, we are having an experiential relationship with them, often a very good one.

We cannot live excited all the time, especially as we get older. We cannot fall in love over and over again. Likewise, we cannot be constantly excited by knowing the Lord and having the Holy Spirit in us. If, however, we have come into an experiential relationship with the Lord, we can have a steady confidence of our personal relationship with him and a confidence that his Spirit is in us and will strengthen us and act through us.

We can also learn to renew what we have. We can renew our experiential relationship with God by having our "filling with the Holy Spirit" (Eucharistic Prayer III) strengthened regularly through receiving the spiritual food and drink which the Eucharist provides. We can be confidently thankful for it, act on that basis, and live with the joy that comes of knowing we belong to God and that he has blessed us in Christ with new life here and for all eternity—if we have faith.

Meditation: Personal Thanksgiving
Luke 17:11-19

In the last year of Jesus' life, we find him healing some lepers. The incident is described in the seventeenth chapter of the Gospel of Luke:

> On the way to Jerusalem he was passing along between Samaria and Galilee. And as he entered a village, he was met by ten lepers, who stood at a distance and lifted up their voices and said, "Jesus, Master, have mercy on us." When he saw them he said to them, "Go and show yourselves to the priests."
>
> And as they went they were cleansed. Then one of them, when he saw that he was healed, turned back, praising God with a loud voice; and he fell on his face at Jesus' feet, giving him thanks. Now he was a Samaritan. Then said Jesus,
>
> "Were not ten cleansed? Where are the nine? Was no one found to return and give praise to God except this foreigner?"
>
> And he said to him,
>
> "Rise and go your way; your faith has made you well."

We may be accustomed to reading this passage and thinking about it as an exhortation to gratitude to God for his benefits to us. It is that, but it is also a lesson in faith. It is not an accident that Christ says to the Samaritan who came to express his thanks to God, "Your faith has made you well."

Catholics can be like the Jews in this story. They get used to what God does for them and in a certain way take it for granted. They then can fail to give thanks for it. The story does not tell us what happened to the nine Jews who had been healed. It does, however, tell us that the Samaritan who gave thanks experienced the full effect of his cleansing and healing—because of his faith.

Faith is concretely expressed in thanksgiving. If we give thanks to God for what he has done, we thereby confess that he has done it. This is an appropriate response to anything God has done for us. However, in addition, giving thanks, especially if deliberate, often activates our faith. We then can experience more of the results.

An important step towards Eucharistic renewal is thanksgiving for the fact of what has happened to us. This has, in fact, traditionally been the last part of the Eucharistic service. Our prayers after Communion are not supposed to mainly be a time to talk to the Lord because he is now really present in us or to ask him for favors. Rather, it is mainly a time to thank him for the fact that he has strengthened his presence in us and strengthened the life of the Holy Spirit in us. We therefore praise and thank him for what he has done to us and pray that the grace he has given will have its full effect in us.

The Byzantine liturgy has preserved a set of prayers after receiving Communion that express the response we should make to receiving Communion. The first of those prayers (along with the directions for praying them, here given in italics) presents a good summary:

Immediately, after having worthily partaken of the life-giving Mystical Gifts, raise your voice in acclamation. Be very grateful and recite the prayers to God with heartfelt fervor:
  Glory be to you, O God!
  Glory be to you, O God!
  Glory be to you, O God!
Then recite this Prayer of Thanksgiving:
  I thank you, O Lord my God, that you did not reject me a sinner, but deemed me worthy to be a partaker of your holy mysteries. I thank you that, despite my unworthiness, you made me worthy to receive your most pure and heavenly gifts.

  O Master, lover of mankind, you died and rose for our sake and favored us with these, your awesome and life-giving mysteries for the benefit and sanctification of our souls and bodies. Grant that they may be for the healing of my soul and body and for the rout of every adversary, for the enlightenment of the eyes of my heart, for the peace of my spiritual powers, for an undaunted faith, for an unfeigned love, for the fullness of wisdom, for the keeping of your commandments, for growth in your divine grace, and for belonging to your kingdom, in order that, preserved by them in your holiness, I may always remember your grace and no longer live for myself, but for you, our Master and benefactor.

  Thus, when I depart from this life in the hope of life eternal, may I attain that everlasting rest where the sound of those celebrating never ceases, and where there is no end to the delight of those who behold the ineffable beauty of your face. For you are the true object of desire and the indescribable gladness of those who love you, O Christ our God, and all creation sings your praises for ever. Amen.

The prayer is a prayer of praise and thanksgiving. We praise God for his goodness and thank him for what he has given us. We mainly thank him for the gift of the Body and Blood of Christ, the heavenly gifts. These are the mysteries or, as the English translations of the Roman liturgy would more likely say, the sacraments, which give us life. They renew the life of Christ in us and sanctify us.

We then pray that our reception of these gifts might take effect. We pray that the life of Christ in us might strengthen us interiorly and transform us so that we might live the Christian life effectively. And we pray our Christian life will allow us to attain the everlasting rest, the unending feast in thanksgiving for God's victory.

When we thank God in this way, we thank him for what he has done. We confess that what he promised has been accomplished, the gift has been given. That, of course, does not mean that we will be totally transformed. But it means that we have something inside of us that will allow us to be transformed. We should have the confidence that the grace of God is at work in us, enabling us to be what God created us to be.

Now to him by the power at work within us is able to do far more abundantly than all that we ask or think, to him be the glory in the church and in Christ Jesus to all generations, for ever and ever. Amen.

EPHESIANS 3:20-21

EIGHT

Worship the Lord

Let us be grateful for receiving a kingdom that cannot be shaken, and thus let us offer to God acceptable worship, with reverence and awe; for our God is a consuming fire.

HEBREWS 12:28-29

The liturgy is "the summit toward which the activity of the Church is directed; at the same time it is the fountain from which all her power flows" (SC 10). As this book began, we focused on the Lord's efforts to communicate his truth to us so that we might have life. We then focused on the way he feeds us sacramentally, also so that we might have life. Throughout, however, we observed that true spiritual life only comes to us as we approach the Lord and worship him.

We also began by looking at the renewal of the liturgy which opened the Vatican Council. *Sacrosanctum Concilium* indicates how important the "renewal and fostering" of the liturgy is. There follows a paragraph that should orient us towards what we are about in the liturgical renewal of the Christian life and the renewal of the corporate life of the Christian people, the Church (SC 2):

For the liturgy, "through which the work of our redemption is accomplished," most of all in the divine Eucharistic sacrifice, is the outstanding means whereby the faithful may express in their lives, and manifest to others, the mystery of Christ and the real nature of the true Church. It is of the essence of the Church that she be both human and divine, visible and yet invisibly equipped, eager to act and yet intent on contemplation, present in this world and yet not at home in it. She is all these things in such a way that in her the human is directed and subordinated to the divine, the visible likewise to the invisible, action to contemplation, and this present world to the city yet to come, which we seek (see Heb 13:14).

201

This paragraph calls for a change of perspective from the one most of us are accustomed to. As human beings, especially as fallen human beings, we are inclined to begin (and, at times, end) with ourselves, our needs, and our desires. The subjective orientation is easy for us. However, a subjective approach leads us to see God as a means to ends we have, our help in life and the solution to our problems, especially the ones we cannot solve by ourselves. To be sure, God can be that, but such a view gives us a very misleading perspective.

The summit of the Christian life is standing in the presence of the Lord and glorifying him, so that he might be "all in all" (1 Cor 15:28), so that "in everything God may be glorified through Jesus Christ" (1 Pt 4:11). We were not created so God could help us, so that we could become the center of the universe and God could be our servant. One of the most astounding truths of Christian revelation is that God is willing, out of his mercy, to condescend to help us, even at great cost. Nonetheless, it is still Christian teaching that we were created "for God's glory." We were created for his sake. And as we glorify him and serve him, we come closer to the purpose for which we were created. We move towards the summit of the Christian life.

In what follows, we will look at the liturgy and the Eucharist in the light of the end. "The end" here is used both in the sense of the final point towards which God's plan is tending, the consummation, and in the sense of the purpose God is seeking to achieve. The two meanings come together, because "the end of time" will be the point at which God's purpose will be fully accomplished. The liturgy, our worship of God, is the place where we can come closest to that end in our earthly life, and where also, in God's presence, we are given the provisions, the *viaticum*, the traveler's meal, to accomplish the journey to its full consummation.

The Heavenly and Earthly Liturgies

The Scriptures end with the Book of Revelation, which contains several visions of the worship that takes place in heaven. The main vision occurs in chapters 4 and 5, the beginning of the section of the book on "what is to take place hereafter" (Rv 1:19). There we see John who was "in the Spirit on the Lord's Day" (Rev 1:10). "The Lord's Day" is the name for the first day of the week in Greek and in the Latin and Romance languages, the day called Sunday in English. It is the Lord's Day because it was the day of the resurrection. It was therefore also the day on which Christians celebrated the Eucharist.

Chapter 4 begins with John's saying, "After this I looked, and lo, in heaven an open door!" Then he describes what he saw when he went through that door. At the center point of heaven, the center point of the universe, "Lo, a throne stood..., with one seated on the throne!" The one who was seated on the throne was God the Father. He appeared as a jewel, a precious jewel, who shone out into the universe with the colors of the rainbow. We might say that he was a pure light that was refracted when it shone into our created order so that it became manifest that the whole range of the possibilities of light, of all being, were in him.

He appeared on a throne, that is, as a King, the Lord of the whole universe. This is the main way God appears to his creatures. He is their sovereign, because he has created them and therefore owns them. He is the one they should honor as Lord and no one else and nothing else.

Surrounding him are the thrones of the twenty-four elders. These elders are probably the twelve patriarchs of the old covenant people of God and the twelve apostles of the new covenant people of God,[1] now serving as ministers in the heavenly liturgy. These are the ones he has appointed to govern his people under his own authority and to preside over their worship.

The account continues, "Before the throne burn seven torches of fire, which are the seven spirits of God." This seems to be a reference to the Holy Spirit, who burns before the throne of God, likely on the heavenly altar of sacrifice, as a flame of fire. We might retranslate this as "the sevenfold Spirit of God," understanding the number seven to refer to the seven gifts he gives (Is 11:2-3).

Also surrounding the throne, likely in a circle closer to the throne than that of the elders, are four angelic beings, the "four living creatures." They sing out the song that is found in Isaiah (6:3),

Holy, holy, holy is the Lord God Almighty,
who was and is and is to come!

In doing so, they give "glory and honor and thanks to him who sits upon the throne and lives forever and ever." They chant in heaven a version of the song that we have come to know from its Latin title as the *Sanctus* and that now is used in all the Eucharistic Prayers.

The twenty-four elders then prostrate themselves before the throne of God and worship him. They throw down their crowns before him, indicating that all human rule and authority is subordinate to the majesty of God. They too sing to God, saying,

Worthy are you, our Lord and God,
to receive glory and honor and power,
for you created all things
and by your will they came into existence and have been created.

Heaven, in other words, is a throne room, the audience hall of God. It is a temple, the place of God's presence, the place where he dwells. When, in other words, God reveals himself to people on earth, they are invited into the audience hall of the King of the universe. There they find that God is surrounded by beings much more powerful than they themselves are but who nonetheless are subordinate to the Lord and honor him. He is worshiped as the Lord of the universe, King of Kings and Lord of Lords. That worship is expressed in words, but also in the way those allowed to be in his presence conduct themselves—by their position, their posture, their dress, their manner.

In heaven, then, there is liturgy. As we have seen, when the writings of Scripture speak about honoring God as God, we often find the phrase "worship and serve." "Worship" means that people express the fact that they are acknowledging God as God, usually by bowing or prostrating themselves. "Service" means that people take part in the whole ceremonial action of worshiping God. They do so according to the role that they have. When a body of people together come before him to give him honor, they "serve" him, or "perform liturgy."

The center of a "service" in the old covenant temple was sacrifice, and therefore, as we have seen, the word often refers to sacrificing. Honoring an earthly king usually involved giving him gifts. The gifts were a kind of tribute that expressed that he was someone's king and deserved to be given something because of his claim as king. When God was honored as King of his people and King of the universe, he was given a gift as well, an offering or a sacrifice.

This vision occurs to a person who has entered the new covenant. Many think that he was a priest who had taken part in temple worship, because so many details of temple worship are mentioned in his descriptions of the worship of heaven. If so, he was now part of the new covenant people who were "a kingdom and priests to our God" (Rv 5:10). His descriptions, however, indicate a correspondence between the earthly old covenant liturgy and the heavenly liturgy. We would therefore expect a sacrifice somehow to be part of the heavenly liturgy.

As Christians who acknowledge the "threefoldness" of God, we know that a description of God on the throne and the sevenfold Spirit of God before the throne is incomplete. We would therefore expect the Word of God to also appear in heaven. It is therefore no surprise to find in chapter 5, as we have already seen, the Lamb, who later turns out to be the Word of God (Rv 19:11), appearing before the throne. And we see him appearing as a sacrifice.

The Lamb stands between the elders and the living creatures and God the Father himself. He stands, in other words, in the same position as the altar, before the Holiest Place of All where God's throne is. The sevenfold Spirit is in him, still on the altar before the throne of God but now dwelling in the Lamb. The Lamb, in other words, is the sacrificial offering in the heavenly temple. As we saw at the end of chapter 3, he presents to God himself and what he has done, the sacrifice that saves us, in an act of intercession. At the same time clouds of incense are offered, which are the prayers of his people, and which, as in the temple, accompany the daily sacrifices. Then all heaven says,

> Worthy is the Lamb who was slain,
> to receive power and wealth and wisdom and might and honor and glory
> and blessing!

That worship is responded to throughout the whole universe, as in a refrain for a chanted psalm or hymn:

> To him who sits upon the throne and to the Lamb
> be blessing and honor and glory and might for ever and ever!

And the elders prostrate themselves and worship.

There is a later vision of the worship of God, this time on earth. It is found in chapter 14 of Revelation (Rv 14:1-4):

> Then I looked, and lo, on Mount Zion stood the Lamb, and with him a hundred and forty-four thousand who had his name and his Father's name written on their foreheads. And I heard a voice from heaven like the sound of many waters and like the sound of loud thunder; the voice I heard was like

the sound of harpers playing on their harps, and they sing a new song before the throne and before the four living creatures and before the elders. No one could learn that song except the hundred and forty-four thousand who had been redeemed from the earth ... [and] who follow the Lamb wherever he goes.

The 144,000 is a symbolic number for Christians, disciples of Christ who "follow him wherever he goes." He is here present on Mount Zion, on earth. His disciples are the only people on earth who can truly worship God, because they "worship him in Spirit" (Phil 3:3). They hear the worship of heaven and join in, because they have been taught the song by the Holy Spirit. "A new song" is a song sung right after a victory to celebrate something new God has done for his people (Ps 98:1-3). The new song these disciples sing is the song that celebrates the victory of Christ in his death and resurrection.

Christians, then, while still on earth, take part in the heavenly worship. Old covenant worship gives us a picture of the heavenly worship, because the ceremonial of the old covenant was modeled on the worship of heaven. God had taken Moses up to heaven and shown him how to construct the tent of meeting in the wilderness, which was in turn the model for the temple in Jerusalem (Ex 25:40; Heb 8:5). In so doing, Moses established earthly worship on a heavenly pattern.

Old covenant worship, however, is fulfilled in new covenant worship. As Jesus told the Samaritan woman, "neither [on Mount Gerizim, the mountain where the Samaritan temple was] nor in Jerusalem [the place of the Jewish temple] will you worship the Father.... True worshipers will worship the Father in spirit and truth, for such the Father seeks to worship him" (Jn 4:21, 23). In saying this, he was referring to the Holy Spirit, who produces heavenly worship in new covenant people and in so doing "spiritualizes" the old covenant pattern of worship.

Christian worship is not a matter of geographical location. There is no longer only one place on earth where certain kinds of worship can be performed and be pleasing to God. Or, better put, there is now only one place of sacrifice and only one sacrifice. Heaven itself has replaced the earthly temple. The sacrifice of Christ, now in heaven, has replaced the earthly sacrifice. The Spirit gives new covenant people access to that heavenly worship. When we take part in our earthly "liturgy," our service of God, therefore, we are sharing in the one acceptable worship, the heavenly worship before God's throne. We can do that as long as we "sing the same song," the praise of God for the salvation he has given to us through the victory of Christ, the Lamb of God, and sing it in the Holy Spirit.

The liturgy is the "summit" of the Christian life, the highest point. It is the summit because it occurs at the highest point in the universe—the throne of God in heaven. It is the summit also because the meaning of our lives as Christians is to be "priests before our God." Although our life is expressed in serving him in many ways on earth, the fullest expression of what we were made to be occurs when we stand before him and worship and serve him.

The Eucharist is the most important event in Christian worship. It is, however, no accident that the *Catechism of the Catholic Church* begins with a presentation of the liturgy as a whole and sees the Eucharist and the other sacraments in that context. Sacraments may have been instituted to give us grace, but we are given grace so that we might become true worshipers of God, worshipers in spirit and truth.[2] If we are, our worship will not be restricted to participation in the Eucharist or the other sacraments but will be "continual," throughout our lives. If we are, even the way we participate in sacraments will be worshipful, filled with the truth that all we do is an expression of love of God and that we seek to honor and glorify him as God.

In the next section of this chapter, we will look at the pattern of worship for the Christian people. We will especially look at the way it goes together into a life of prayer that allows us to continually participate in the true heavenly worship of the Lord of all. As we do so, we will look at more of the characteristics of true Christian worship.

The Consecration of Time

The phrase the *consecration of time* or, as it is often translated, the *sanctification of time* is now somewhat commonly used.[3] The understanding behind it is based on scriptural texts like Romans 12:1:

> Present your bodies as a living sacrifice, holy and acceptable to God, which is your spiritual worship.

By "bodies" Paul means ourselves, not just the physical side of us, although he is probably using the word to emphasize our everyday Christian living in all the circumstances of life: home, work, family, friends, as well as in explicitly Christian or religious activities.

We are to make all of our lives a sacrifice. But our lives are to be a living sacrifice. We do not have to become martyrs to be a sacrifice. We have to live our lives for God's glory, give ourselves and all we do to him, that in all things God may be glorified (1 Pt 4:11).

The main way we make our lives an offering to God is by living righteously in obedience to him, by living lives of faith, hope, and love. We also offer our lives to him by engaging in Christian outreach, the work of building up the new covenant temple of God, either by direct service or by financial contribution (Rom 15:16; Phil 4:8). But we also pray, and our prayers are offerings as well, as were the prayers of the Lord (Heb 5:7). The Scriptures often express this truth:

> Let my prayer be counted as incense before you, the lifting up of my hands as an evening sacrifice.
>
> PSALM 141:2

> Through [Christ] then let us continually offer up a sacrifice of praise to God, that is, the fruit of lips that acknowledge his name.
>
> HEBREWS 13:15

Our prayers are offerings to God made to acknowledge him as our God and Lord, expressions of our offering of our whole lives to him.[4]

The word *prayer* is perhaps the main word we would use to speak about setting aside some time to give our attention explicitly to God and to do something directed to strengthening our relationship with him. The English word "prayer," however, tends only to refer to something done verbally, at least internally, and so it leaves out ceremony or ritual, a central feature of scriptural "prayer." It also commonly has the connotation of something we do for personal spiritual growth, not for worship offered to God simply to honor him. It therefore does not call to mind the main scriptural orientation towards "prayer." Moreover, the English word "prayer" is used to translate a Hebrew word that refers primarily to prayers of petition and is not very often used in

Scripture to cover the whole range of our "prayer life."

But despite such considerations, "prayer" is the English word that comes closest to describing our topic. We will therefore speak here about our prayer life. We will add the words "worship," "honor," and "glorify" to indicate that when we pray we primarily turn to God to worship, honor, and glorify him and only secondarily to receive the help we need to live for him.

As we have seen, the Old Testament shows us a truth about prayer, what could be called the principle of the first fruits. When the old covenant people of God were given a harvest, they understood that that food, that means of sustenance, was a gift of God. They took the beginnings of the harvest, the first fruits, and gave it back to God as a special offering of thanksgiving for the harvest. It was only a part of the harvest, usually a small part, but it expressed their recognition that the harvest had been given them by God. It also expressed their pledge to use it, and their lives which would be sustained by it, to his glory.

Something similar is true of the meal blessing, which we have taken over from Jewish prayer. In Jewish meals, as we have seen, a blessing is said over the bread at the beginning, and in festal meals, a thanksgiving cup is at the end as well. When we say the blessing, the prayer of thanksgiving, at the beginning and end of the meal, we are offering a portion of the food and drink back to God, dedicating it to God. We are told that if we do that the whole meal is "received with thanksgiving," and "then it is consecrated [or sanctified] by the word of God and prayer" (1 Tm 4:4-5).

Our prayer is like a first-fruits offering or a meal blessing. It is a gift, a sacrifice, an offering. It is a portion of our time that is offered to God as a way of dedicating or consecrating to him all of the time God has given us. Since life is lived in time, our prayer consecrates or sanctifies our whole life to the one who gave it to us in the first place. "The consecration of time" may be a better translation of the phrase than "the sanctification of time" because "consecration" is the English word that seems to be used more commonly to refer to the actions by which we make something over to God for his glory and service.

Many would hold that the ideal is unceasing prayer or constant prayer, prayer that carries on every moment of our lives. There have been some who have claimed to be able to teach such prayer, and they have often given valuable instruction in how to pray.[5] The Scriptures, however, seem to teach something different—continual prayer. We might also translate it as regular prayer.[6] The way to consecrate time is to pray regularly. Just as the Jews would make a first-fruits offering for every harvest, not just once for the rest of their lives, just as we bless each meal and do not say a blessing once for all the meals of our lives, so do we pray day by day, week by week, year by year, and so we dedicate or consecrate our time to God as he gives it to us.

The Scripture shows us a pattern for a regular prayer life. We find it first in old covenant temple worship. There are two main texts which, when put together, give the regular pattern of temple worship: Leviticus 23 and Numbers 28–29. The Numbers passage concerns the regular offerings that are given to God, the ones that should be given according to a set pattern and not just when some need comes up, like a purification or a special vow. It presents the fuller picture of regular worship, because it includes the daily offerings.

The daily sacrifice was offered in the morning and in the evening, and it centered on the giving of a lamb, accompanied by bread and wine and oil. At the same time as the lamb was being offered on the altar before the temple building, incense was offered inside the holy place. These sacrifices were called the continual offering, because they were given every day. They were also the major daily times of prayer in the temple, and many who were in Jerusalem would come to them to worship God.

Numbers 28 continues with the sabbath, and the text in Leviticus 23 starts there and then treats the same events as the Numbers passage. The Leviticus text passes over the daily offering because it is a text on "appointed feasts" [RSV] or *solemnities*. A solemnity is a special event, as contrasted to a regular daily event. It is, therefore, a time when the people come together to worship in a special way. It either was a day of "rest" or, if it was a longer celebration, included both workdays and days of rest, that is, days off from "menial" work (certain kinds of work). During solemnities, there were offerings given in addition to the regular daily offerings to mark the day and express the importance of what was being celebrated.

The main solemnity in old covenant worship is the Sabbath, and its observance was commanded in the Ten Commandments (Ex 20:8; Dt 5:12). The Sabbath is the seventh day of the week, the regular weekly feast day. Like the other solemnities, it was set aside as a day that belonged to God, that is, a *holy day* (Ex 31:12-15). We have contracted that word to "holiday" and, as we have seen, understand it as a day off, a vacation. While the Sabbath was intended as a day off from menial work, it was also understood to be a day of special service to the Lord and therefore a day of "spiritual work." It was a day to honor

God (Rom 14:6) and celebrate his goodness, especially his goodness in his creation and his redemption of his people. It was a day with added offerings and lengthier times of prayer. It was a special day for "God's work."

The two texts go on to mention Passover, Pentecost, New Year's, the Day of Atonement, and the Feast of Tabernacles as the main solemnities that occur once each year. Three of them were also feasts on which all Israelites were to go up to Jerusalem to worship God: Passover, Pentecost, and Tabernacles. These are the solemnities most properly called *feasts* (see chapter 3, p. 82).[7]

Passover celebrated the first harvest and the redemption from Egypt. It lasted for a week, the Feast of Unleavened Bread, and began a special season, which was concluded on Pentecost. Pentecost (the Feast of Weeks) was the fiftieth day after Passover, the day after the week of weeks (seven times seven days) that followed Passover, and the conclusion of the Passover celebration. It celebrated the end of the grain harvest and also the day on which the law was given on Sinai. Tabernacles or Booths was the final harvest feast and celebrated the conclusion of the agricultural year. It also celebrated the kingdom of God as manifested in his giving of the land to his people. New Year's (*Rosh Hashanah*) and the Day of Atonement (*Yom Kippur*), the "Days of Awe," were special shorter solemnities that inaugurated the "civil" new year and atoned for the sins of the past one.[8]

The old covenant pattern, then, was daily, weekly, and yearly. It was made up of a regular pattern of daily worship with periodic solemnities. Each solemnity had a significance of its own.

Worship in the temple, of course, was not the only way Jews honored God. Those who lived in Jerusalem could go to the temple every day, or often, for the services there. Those who lived farther away, either in more remote parts of the land of Israel, like Galilee, or in foreign lands, like Rome or Babylon, could not. They, however, worshiped as well, and seem to have followed much the same pattern.

We can see how Jews who did not take part in the temple service followed the temple pattern in the example of Ezra, who prayed "at the evening sacrifice" (Ezr 9:5); of Daniel, who was praying "at the time of the evening sacrifice" when Gabriel came to him (Dn 9:21); and of Judith, who prayed "while the incense was being offered in the temple of God in Jerusalem" (Jdt 9:1). They tried to pray at the same time as the morning and evening sacrifices in the temple.

We also know that Jews would normally assemble in the synagogue for these times of daily prayer as well as for special sabbath services. They would in addition keep the solemnities with special synagogue services and festal meals, even though they were not in Jerusalem. After the destruction of the temple, they saw this prayer as a substitute for the regular temple offerings, as the following prayer from the morning service in the Jewish Prayer Book indicates:

> Lord of the universe, you have commanded us to offer up the daily sacrifice at the right times and to have priests at their service and Levites at their [music] stand. But now the temple is in ruins because of our sins, and the daily sacrifice is suspended; and we have no priest at his service and no Levite at his stand and no Israelite at his station. But you have commanded that we offer the prayers of our lips as the offering of bulls. Therefore may it be pleasing in your sight, O Lord our God and God of our ancestors, that the prayers of our lips be reckoned, accepted, and pleasing in your sight just as if we had offered up the daily sacrifice at the right time and occupied our station [in the temple].

The pattern of temple prayer has been the pattern of communal prayer and of personal prayer for Jews scattered all over the world.[9]

New Covenant Pattern of Prayer

As Christians, we are not "under the law" (Gal 5:18; Rom 6:15). That means that we do not do something simply because the Law of Moses says that we must. Because we do not belong to the old covenant people, we are not obligated to follow the old covenant law as such.[10] But the old covenant law is not simply useless for Christians. It was given for our instruction as well (2 Tm 3:16). We do not go to Jerusalem to offer lambs and bulls in the temple, but we have been "built into a spiritual house [temple], to be a holy priesthood, to offer spiritual sacrifices acceptable to God through Jesus Christ" (1 Pt 2:5). The old covenant law, properly interpreted, was intended to apply to new covenant life.

Some of what the Old Testament teaches we do because God instructed old covenant people how to live in a godly way that was in accordance with the way he made human beings. Having some pattern of prayer is in this category. If human beings are going to be godly, if they are going to give their lives to the Lord, they need some regular pattern of prayer.

Some of what we do, we do because the pattern in the old covenant has been fulfilled in Christ. We can understand how Christians should follow the Old Testament from the New Testament and patristic teaching about how old covenant realities are fulfilled in Christ. Celebrating Sunday as the day of the resurrection is one example. Christians do not keep the Sabbath (the seventh day or Saturday), unless perhaps they are Jewish Christians who believe that they should fulfil both the old and new covenant approaches to the Sabbath because they belong to both covenants. Rather, Christians observe the Sabbath commandment in a new covenant way by keeping the first day of the week, the day of the resurrection, as the "Lord's Day" (Rv 1:10).

We can see the full Christian pattern through Christian tradition, which shows us how the early Christians lived out what was taught in the Old Testament.[11] They "Christianized" what the Jews did, bringing out the significance of the coming of Christ and eliminating elements that were not helpful for new covenant people. The *Catechism of the Catholic Church* gives us a summary in section 2698 of what the tradition of the church has discerned to be the core of a pattern of Christian prayer:

> The Tradition of the Church proposes to the faithful certain rhythms of praying intended to nourish continual prayer.
> - Some are daily, such as
>   - morning and evening prayer,
>   - grace before and after meals,
>   - the Liturgy of the Hours.
> - Sundays, centered on the Eucharist, are kept holy primarily by prayer.
> - The cycle of the liturgical year and its great feasts are also basic rhythms of the Christian's life of prayer.

The focus is prayer, relationship with God regularly expressed by turning to him to honor or worship him and seek his help. Daily prayer is important for maintaining a living relationship with God. The beginning of the day and the end of the day are natural times for godly human beings to expressly honor their Creator and dedicate their day to him. They were the main daily old covenant times of prayer. Meal times are as well, because meals sustain life and our sustenance comes from God.

As the above section from the *Catechism* indicates, the "Tradition of the Church" shows that new covenant Christianity follows the same daily pattern as the Jews did.[12] As the above section of the *Catechism* also indicates, the Liturgy of the Hours gives us a Christian way of prayer that either includes morning and evening prayer or is additional, depending on our approach to using it.

The Liturgy of the Hours, sometimes called *the Divine Office* is the term the *Catechism of the Catholic Church* uses for "the prayer of the Church" and also is the name for the "prayer book" for Catholics of the Latin rite. Other rites have similar prayer books that could also be called "The Liturgy of the Hours," although they usually go by different names. The *Catechism of the Catholic Church* says in section 1174:

> The mystery of Christ, his Incarnation and Passover, which we celebrate in the Eucharist especially at the Sunday assembly, permeates and transfigures the time of each day, through the celebration of the Liturgy of the Hours, "the divine office" [see SC, ch. IV, 83-101]. This celebration, faithful to the apostolic exhortations to "pray constantly," is "so devised that the whole course of the day and night is made holy by the praise of God" [SC 84; 1 Th 5:17; Eph 6:18].

The Liturgy of the Hours is a collection of "prayer times." The two main daily ones are morning prayer and evening prayer, the same two times of prayer as in the temple service. These are scripturally based services or "offices" of praise, worship, and prayer, with Scripture readings. There are in addition shorter hours of prayer that can be used, as well as an "Office of Readings." The Office of Readings is a Christian meditation service that centers on reading the Scripture in a way that allows God to speak to us and build us up through a yearly or two-year approach to the main Scripture texts with commentaries that are mostly drawn from the Fathers.

The Liturgy of the Hours is intended to be the main prayer for Catholics. Sometimes we have the impression that Catholics are mainly supposed to pray the rosary or other devotions for their prayer life. Although many find such devotions helpful, the *Catechism of the Catholic Church* and the other Catholic instructions since the Vatican Council primarily recommend the Liturgy of the Hours (or at least the main parts of it), not the special devotions. As the *Catechism* puts it (1175):

The Liturgy of the Hours is intended to become the prayer of the whole People of God. In it Christ himself "continues his priestly work through his Church" [SC 83]. His members participate according to their own place in the Church and the circumstances of their lives: priests devoted to the pastoral ministry, because they are called to remain diligent in prayer and the service of the word; religious, by the charism of their consecrated lives; all the faithful as much as possible.

It is, in other words, intended to be the prayer for the laity as well as clergy and religious, although the circumstances of life for most of the laity mean that they will only be able to pray a limited amount of it.[13]

The main weekly time for communal prayer, the assembly of the whole community for liturgical worship, is Sunday.[14] This is the Lord's Day, the day that belongs to him and that should be set aside for his honor as a holy day. As the *Catechism of the Catholic Church* puts it (1167):

Sunday is the preeminent day for the liturgical assembly, when the faithful gather "to listen to the word of God and take part in the Eucharist, thus calling to mind the Passion, Resurrection, and glory of the Lord Jesus, and giving thanks to God who "has begotten them again, by the resurrection of Jesus Christ from the dead' unto a living hope." (SC106)

The fact that Sunday is the main time for the Eucharist tells us some important truths about the Eucharist that have not appeared clearly so far.

Many Catholics take what has been called a "devotional approach" to the Eucharist, that is, an approach that is primarily shaped by what they find helpful for personal devotion. They center on Eucharistic devotions or daily Mass to make the Eucharist a personally important part of their life. Although daily Mass and Eucharistic devotions can be helpful, the devotional approach is an incomplete approach to the Eucharist. As the *Catechism* indicates, the primary way to participate in the Eucharist is to participate in the Sunday liturgical assembly, and that fact helps us to see the Eucharist in a clearer light.

The Eucharist is first of all intended to be corporate. It is the worship of the body of Christ. As Paul put it, one bread makes one body (see 1 Cor 10:17). Paul was talking about the bread partaken together and was teaching that when a group of Christians partake of the one loaf of Eucharistic bread they are strengthened in their life as one body. The instructions he gives for the Eucharist are instructions for the assembly of the local church (1 Cor 11:17).

The local Christian assembly is not mainly a service for the more devout to attend. It is a service for all the Christians in one locality or at least some subsection of them that makes up an ordinary local community. It is intended to be the service that unites them and strengthens them as a body of Christ.[15] While the Catholic Church provides for more frequent Eucharistic services, the emphasis still is, and has always been, on the Sunday liturgy (and secondarily on special feast day liturgies) for the local community assembled together. It is no accident that one of the main traditional words for the Eucharist is *synaxis,* a Greek word meaning "gathering" or assembly (CCC 1329; see also 1348).

Second, the Eucharist is a celebration, in the sense of a special event to honor the Lord, not in the sense of a party. The Eucharist should be solemn and can even be mournful at times, for instance, during a funeral. When in ordinary society we "celebrate" something like a wedding, a graduation, the installation of a president, or the crowning of a king or queen, we do it in such a way that we express the importance and meaning of the event being celebrated. A graduation ceremony may take place in uncomfortably hot weather, be somewhat boring, and overall not be a pleasant event. It is, however, a celebration because it brings to expression the importance of something in human life so that we all together appreciate what has happened and honor it.

In the case of the Eucharist, we are celebrating the death and resurrection of Christ, the event by which we are saved. Every Eucharist does that and, according to Catholic teaching, the Eucharist is the main way to do that. If we are sick, sad, mentally distracted by the difficulties of life, we can still celebrate the death and resurrection of Christ and do so in a fitting way. We should not make the mistake of confusing how well we are celebrating with how positively we have experienced the celebration.

The Eucharist is also intended to strengthen our spiritual life, to nourish us spiritually. Again we do not have to experience its strengthening us in order for it to strengthen us. It is, in this, like regular food. We may have a meal of beans and rice that is relatively unappetizing and that may not be a high point of our day. If, however, it contains the right nutrients, it will strengthen us regardless of how much we appreciate it. We need to be in spiritual health in order to benefit from partaking of the Eucharist, just as we need to be in bodily health to benefit from our meals. But fundamentally, the strengthening we receive from physical or spiritual food is independent of our subjective appreciation.

To be sure, there are other ways of sustaining our life in Christ. Many of them we can do alone, or at least apart from liturgical events. If we look at the early Church and the whole tradition of the Catholic Church, we would have to say that the main ordinary way of strengthening the new covenant life in us has been partaking of the table of the Lord's Word, the Scripture. While we do so during the Sunday assembly, we can also do so on our own throughout the day. Personal meditation on and study of Scripture has been a central part of Christian prayer life through the centuries.

Sharing with other Christians can also be a source of strengthening. When, for instance, we have discussed how to grow in the Lord at our "review of life" meeting or our group reunion or our Bible study or our men's or women's sharing group, we have been strengthened not just by what we have done humanly to encourage and help one another but by the special presence of the Lord "where two or three are gathered in my name" (Mt 18:20). He speaks to us and strengthens us through one another.

Prayer itself, with others or individually, can also be a source of strengthening. When we come into the Lord's presence, he himself speaks to us and strengthens us directly, not necessarily using any visible means of grace. In short, there are many ways we can be strengthened in our life in Christ.

The Eucharist as sacrament, however, is not one means among many for strengthening our life in Christ. It is the chief one. We cannot understand such a truth by seeing the Eucharist as one prayer practice among many, just more important or efficacious than the others. It is a special event, the time when a local body of Christians comes together to solemnly celebrate the death and resurrection of Christ, to offer the sacrifice of his death and resurrection, and to have the benefits of that sacrifice renewed in them.

It is therefore more important for the Eucharist to be celebrated worthily than to be celebrated frequently. A "quickie Mass," so that we might get it in today, is not the kind of celebration that expresses the significance of the Eucharist. The Body and Blood of Christ should be received with interior worship and spiritual readiness, not just with frequency. Participation in the Eucharist that is in accord with the nature and importance of the Eucharist fosters   its spiritual effectiveness. It is because the Eucharist should primarily be a solemn, corporate celebration that the tradition of the Church has established the

Sunday liturgy as the main way of celebrating the Eucharist (CCC 1167), and that the modern Catholic Church has sought to renew the Sunday celebration.

Finally, "the cycle of the liturgical year and its great feasts are also basic rhythms of the Christian's life of prayer." The great feasts are Easter and Pentecost, Christmas and Epiphany. Of these the greatest is Easter, the Christian Passover, which is celebrated for a week and then for a week of weeks ending with Pentecost (the Fifty Days). Easter is the greatest feast because it is the yearly celebration of the death and resurrection of the Lord (CCC 1169).[16] Pentecost is the conclusion of the Easter season, because it celebrates the giving of the Holy Spirit, the blessing that comes to us through the death and resurrection of the Lord. These are old covenant feasts now fulfilled in Christ. We await the new covenant celebration of Tabernacles, which will only be fulfilled when Christ comes again.[17]

Christmas and Epiphany ("the twelve days of Christmas") come second. They are feasts designed to celebrate the Incarnation of Christ, his manifestation ("epiphany") in our world to save us. Even though they are now more popular feasts, they should not, in principle, be more important than the yearly celebration of the foundational Christian mystery, the death and resurrection of Christ.

There is, then, a yearly cycle for Christians, observed by Catholics and Orthodox and by most Protestants. Each year in the chief feasts we celebrate the main Christian truths and renew our appreciation of them. The greatest feasts are prepared for by "times of seeking the Lord," the "fasts" of Lent (the "Forty Days," which prepare for the Fifty Days of Easter and Pentecost) and Advent (which prepares for Christmas and Epiphany). Properly kept, the great feasts and the festal seasons connected to them mark our year by focusing us on the most central truths of what God has done for us. Observing them is a means of strengthening our life in the Lord, one based on old covenant customs but reshaped in the new covenant to express the truth that our life is made possible by the death and resurrection of the incarnate Son of God and the gift of the Holy Spirit of God that comes to us as the blessing of the new covenant.

Liturgical Renewal

We are living in a time of spiritual renewal, one that was begun or at least fostered by the Second Vatican Council. Because too often they have seen the spiritual losses that have come from the confusion caused by the changes introduced after the Vatican Council, many Catholics have sought to ignore or play down the renewal encouraged by the Council and the post-conciliar Church. As a consequence, they have often sought to restore older practices and approaches rather than renew their spirituality according to the spirit of the liturgy.

The center of liturgical renewal is a renewal in the Eucharist. But it is not primarily a devotional renewal of the Eucharist. It is a renewal of the Eucharist according to the purpose for which it was given. It is, therefore, a renewal in the Eucharist as sacrifice and sacrament. It is, however, a *liturgical* renewal of the Eucharist as sacrifice and sacrament. It is a renewal of Eucharistic practice as corporate, scriptural, and in accordance with tradition, one that puts the focus on the worship of God.

Liturgical renewal is, nonetheless, only a renewal. A renewal does not mean that we have lost something essential in doctrine or practice and now need to have it restored, although the Fathers of the Vatican Council did think a reformation was needed in the ceremonies of the liturgy (SC 1). A renewal rather means that we need to return to the core truths and in the light of those truths renew church practice as a source of life, in this case our liturgical practice.

Liturgical renewal, then, gives us an orientation to the way we approach our prayer life and sacramental participation. It first of all calls us to put the primacy on the renewal of the Church as a whole. Paul, in one of his teachings on how Christians should assemble together, gives a key principle of renewal, "Do all things for edification," that is, for the building up of the body of Christ and of our fellow Christians (1 Cor 14:26). That means that we need to put the corporate good before what we perceive to be our own individual good.

In practice, putting the emphasis on the common good often means that we need to learn to put up with the weakness and doctrinal vagueness or confusion of the contemporary Church in our parish or country. We need to accept these difficulties with some patience and ask how we can live our Christian lives so that we might be part of the solution and not part of the problem. It especially means, when we are thinking about Eucharistic and liturgical renewal, that we should ask how we can participate well in the Sunday assembly of the body of

Christians, which is our main connection with the universal Catholic Church, and help it be a source of life and a means of glorifying God.

Liturgical renewal, and with it the renewal of liturgical theology, also gives us some orientation to the question of how long to pray and how often to participate in the Eucharist. We can find this in the principle stated in the *Catechism:* "according to [our] own place in the Church and the circumstances of [our] lives" (1175). We might use a different phrase, "according to our vocation."

Our goal is to make our lives an offering to God, something that is truly his, something that is "set apart" from sin and worldliness and lived for his glory. This includes service of God by which we undertake to build the temple of God to his glory in this world. Such service includes prayer and preaching the gospel. But it also includes raising godly children; feeding and clothing the needy, especially those who belong to the body of Christ; supporting missionaries and other Christian workers by financial contribution; and many other things that cannot be carried out just by praying.

If we raise children and work forty hours or more in an occupation that is not explicitly religious or dedicated to Christian ministry or outreach, we have one "vocation." If we are a monk or nun, we have another. If we belong to a lay brotherhood or sisterhood, we have another. If we are a parish priest, we have still another. Our pattern of prayer and worship and our liturgical participation should be determined by our vocation.

It is not true that the more we pray the better. The best amount of prayer is the amount that enables us to live most fully for God's glory. Nor is it true that the more liturgical or sacramental participation the better. We know that we need to attend the Eucharist once a week at our parish (or monastery or other special community). Some of us should probably attend more often. Some of us should not because if we do we will not be able to fulfil our Christian responsibilities as well or pray as well.

Our "sacramental life," our frequency of sacramental participation, should also be shaped by a renewed understanding of the sacraments, and so should have a certain balance. There is an old principle: Our shortcomings are often the consequences of our virtues. If, for instance, we are compassionate people, we may not discipline our children or uphold public morality or call people to repentance when we should. If we are faithful people concerned to fulfil our obligations, we may not help the needy or make exceptions for the weak or encourage the discouraged the way we should. We can stress the virtues that are our strength to the neglect of others.

Catholics are sacramental people. This is one of their virtues that can lead to some of their shortcomings. It can lead them to make sacraments ends in themselves rather than means to participate in the grace of God. They may therefore take the view that sacraments cannot be emphasized enough or participated in often enough. As a result they can become externalistic or legalistic about sacramentality. Moreover they are often prone to assume that sacramental participation is a guarantee of spirituality and so neglect Scripture or even the direct personal relationship with God that sacraments are intended to foster and mediate, not substitute for. But they can maintain a sacramental emphasis without doing such things.

We are called to build a temple to the glory of God in the midst of this world. We are called to do so by making of our daily life a living sacrifice, but also by consecrating our lives through regular prayer. We are called to make our lives part of the offering that is the whole body of Christ, participating in the worship the Son offers to his Father in heaven. The more we put the worship and service of God first and the more we are communitarian in our approach to living for the Lord, the more our Christian lives will take the shape God desires for them. Liturgical renewal is not mainly ceremonial improvement, much less increasing external interactions between members of the congregation in those ceremonies, much less simply an increased participation in liturgical events or reception of sacraments. It is mainly a renewal in worship in Spirit and truth.

Meditation: Maranatha
Revelation 21–22

One of the earliest Christian prayers is "Maranatha." It is an Aramaic word and so preserves verbally a prayer that the earliest Christians used. It means, "Lord, come!" and is an invocation for the second coming of Christ.

Paul tells us, "As often as you eat this bread and drink the cup, you proclaim the Lord's death until he comes" (1 Cor 11:26). This probably means that the proclamation of the Lord's death in the Eucharist is itself intended to be praise for what he has done in this time of waiting for his coming. It also is likely an invocation for his coming. It is a proclamation to God himself to remember what his Son did and so act to bring about the fulfilment of human history. It is a proclamation to us to remind us what we are living by and for. And it is a proclamation to the whole of creation, especially to the evil angelic powers (Eph 3:10), that Christ has been victorious over sin, death, and Satan and that he will soon come to make God's creation what it should be.[18]

The life human beings live now is not life the way God intended it to be. The world around us is not the way God made his creation. It is fallen, subject to death and corruption, sinful. Only at the end of this age, after Christ comes again, will human life be fully restored so that it may fulfil God's original intention.

The Book of Revelation recounts visions of human life in the age to come. The prominence of the worship of God in those visions show us how central worship is to the relationship God intends human beings to have with himself. At the beginning of this chapter we considered the vision in Revelation 4 and 5, which portrayed the worship of the heavenly court that is going on even now and that we can participate in by following the Lamb. In the concluding vision in Revelation 21 and 22, we can see more fully the life of worship to which God is leading us.

This vision begins with one of the seven angels of the presence coming to John and saying, "Come, I will show you the Bride, the wife of the Lamb." The bride of Christ, of course, is the Church, the Christian people. John, then, is about to see the Christian people after the coming of Christ, when they will be fully united to their Lord. The description of the vision begins:

> And in the Spirit he carried me away to a great, high mountain, and showed me the holy city Jerusalem coming down out of heaven from God, having the glory of God, its radiance like a most rare jewel, like a jasper, clear as crystal. It had a great, high wall, with twelve gates, and at the gates twelve angels, and on the gates the names of the twelve tribes of the sons of Israel were inscribed.... And the wall of the city had twelve foundations, and on them the twelve names of the twelve apostles of the lamb.

John was shown the mountain of God. It will be the highest mountain on the earth, as Isaiah prophesied (Is 2:2). As the earthly Jerusalem was on Mount Zion, the mountain in the Promised Land that replaced Sinai as the main place of God's presence on earth, so the heavenly Jerusalem will also be on Mount

Zion, but Mount Zion will become the highest and most prominent place in the new earth, the Mount Everest of the new creation.

John saw the New Jerusalem coming down out of heaven. Jerusalem is a city, a city that is the center of the corporate life of God's people. To say that it comes out of heaven is to say that it is established by a relationship with God that we enter into. We do not make the city of God, neither at the beginning nor by the end. We receive it as a gift from God himself.

God established the city of God originally by giving a covenant and offering human beings, first Jews, then Jews and Gentiles alike, the chance to enter into a covenant relationship with him. At the end, we see him renewing that covenant relationship as he is transforming all of material creation. As a result, the effects of the Fall are taken away and earth is becoming something different. Heaven is coming to earth. Earth is becoming heavenly. The new city of God is also becoming heavenly.

The city is built on the twelve foundation stones which have the names of the twelve apostles on them, and its gates have the names of the patriarchs of the twelve tribes of Israel. The city has a lineage. It was begun in the old covenant for the people of Israel and established eternally for the whole human race in the new covenant. It comes from God, but it also was built up through people that God chose.

The heavenly city shines with the glory of God. God's presence so fills it that the city itself is glorified. When it is measured, it turns out to be a perfect cube, like the Holy of Holies. The foundation stones are jewels like those that adorn the high priest's garments. It is, in other words, a city in which God is worshiped, in which the worship of the old covenant law is brought to fulfilment.

After the measurement of the city, the description continues:

And I saw no temple in the city, for its temple is the Lord God the Almighty and the Lamb. And the city has no need of sun or moon to shine upon it, for the glory of God is its light, and its lamp is the Lamb. By its light shall the nations walk; and the kings of the earth shall bring their glory into it, and its gates shall never be shut by day—and there shall be no night there; they shall bring into it the glory and the honor of the nations. But nothing unclean shall enter it, nor anyone who practices abomination or falsehood, but only those who are written in the Lamb's book of life.

There is no temple in the city, because the presence of God has made the city as a whole into a Holy of Holies. There are no walls, no veil, between those who come into the city and God. The distance between God and the human race that was created by sinfulness is gone. Not only is the temple gone, but the city has no need of sun or moon, because the presence of God within it is enough not only to illumine the city but the whole earth as well. Human life on the new earth is lived in that light, and the gates are always open. Access is free to all those who belong to Christ—but only to those who belong to Christ.

The description continues:

Then he showed me the river of the water of life, bright as crystal, flowing from the throne of God and of the Lamb through the middle of the street of the city; also, on either side of the river, the tree of life with its twelve kinds of fruit, yielding its fruit each month; and the leaves of the tree were for the healing of the nations. There shall no more be anything accursed, but the throne of God and of the Lamb shall be in it, and his servants shall worship him; they shall see his face, and his name shall be on their foreheads. And night shall be no more; they need no light of lamp or sun, for the Lord God will be their light, and they shall reign for ever and ever.

As in the old Jerusalem, at the highest point in the city,[19] on top of the mountain, is the throne of God. God is reigning on the new earth from his heavenly throne. But when human beings look at the throne of God, they see the Lamb, the glorified Christ. From the Lamb streams the light of God's glory. The Lamb is a lamp in which the glory of God is manifest in a form that allows human beings to see as much as they can see of the pure uncreated light that God is, to see it without being blinded or even destroyed.

From the throne of God comes the water of life. The water of life is the Holy Spirit (Jn 7:37-39; Is 44:3). The flowing of the water of life from the throne, the water that allows the tree of life to flourish in the city, is an image of the Holy Spirit entering into those who are in the city and "healing" them. They are being given the kind of human life for which God created them. They are being constantly spiritualized, divinized, glorified—made fit and capable of being with God. Light and life come from God's presence and make all things new (21:5). Paradise has returned to earth, but an earth now transfigured by God's glory.

There are no sacraments in the New Jerusalem. There are no Scriptures in the New Jerusalem. They are not needed.[20] They were created to accompany pilgrims traveling through the fallen world, which is a valley of tears, until the God of gods is seen in the new Zion (Ps 84:6-7). The "veil that is spread over all the nations" will be destroyed when God will "swallow up death forever" (Is 25:7–8). In the New Jerusalem God's people can see, no longer in a dim mirror but "face to face" (1 Cor 13:12). The inspired words of Christ and the sacramental presence of Christ are replaced by the vision of God, the vision that itself is enough to make blessed, mediated by the glorified body of the Lord on the throne.[21]

God's servants will stand before his throne. They shall worship and serve him day and night (Rv 7:15). This is the true feast, the eternal feast, in which God's servants will rejoice in him and glorify him as King of Kings and Lord of Lords. This is what we pray to share in the Byzantine thanksgiving prayer after Communion, after we have freshly received the Body and Blood of the Lord:

Thus, when I depart from this life in the hope of life eternal, may I attain that everlasting rest where the sound of those celebrating never ceases, and where there is no end to the delight of those who behold the ineffable beauty of Your face. For You are the true object of desire and the indescribable gladness of those who love You, O Christ our God, and all creation sings Your praises for ever. Amen.

We live in an in-between time. The death and resurrection of the Messiah has come, so now the gift of the Spirit has been given, the gates of heaven are open, and the life of the age to come is in some way already here. But it is not fully here. We are like a patient in a hospital, whose life has been saved and who will soon be back to full health, but who in the meantime is covered with bandages and casts. When the "wraps are taken off" it will be apparent that health has been restored, but the wraps are not yet taken off. Like a patient who still feels weak and often in pain, we still experience our life as fallen. Yet we know that something has happened and we are on the road to full recovery.

Because we have been given the Holy Spirit, we are already participating in the life of the age to come. He is the down payment (Eph 1:14), securing what is to come. To say that he is the down payment means that we have not received all that God has for us, the full inheritance. But it also means that we have indeed begun to receive it. Through the presence of the Holy Spirit in us, we are beginning to experience what will be given fully to us after the second coming.

When we worship the Lord in the Eucharistic assembly, then, we are beginning to share in the worship before the throne of God at the end of the age. Any time, in fact, we come before the Lord in true Christian worship, we begin to share in that worship, but when we are offering the memorial of the death and resurrection of Christ in the assembly of the Church on the Lord's Day and partaking of the Bread of Life and the cup of the new covenant, we are as fully participating in the feast of the heavenly kingdom to come as is possible here.

By faith we have the substance of things hoped for, the assurance of things unseen (Heb 11:1). Yet we walk by faith and not by sight (2 Cor 5:7). The next to the last words of the Book of Revelation are the words of the Lord, speaking prophetically, "Surely I am coming soon."

The very last words of the Scriptures, the words meant to remain with us as long as the Scriptures are with us, are,

"Amen. Come, Lord Jesus."

> Dying you destroyed our death,
> Rising you restored our life,
> Lord Jesus, come in glory.

APPENDICES

Appendix 1: Introduction to the Sources

A Catholic understanding of the Eucharist is not something that theologians or teachers come up with as their own creation, but something that is passed down as part of the revelation of Christ, given to the apostles. That revelation has been lived out in a variety of ways, many of which have been preserved through texts of the Eucharistic celebration. Over the centuries that revelation has been clarified in relationship to various questions that have arisen as a result of changes in circumstances or new intellectual developments.

The following is an introduction to the sources for an orthodox Catholic understanding of the Eucharist, sources that we can use for an orthodox understanding today.

Scripture

There are only a few direct references to the Eucharistic celebration in the Scriptures, if the Eucharist is understood as the assembly of the new covenant people that contains a Liturgy of the Word and a Liturgy of the Eucharist. On the other hand, if the Old Testament background is included, there could be extensive references. At the same time there are notable conceptual questions as to which Old Testament references might be considered references to the new covenant Eucharist, that is, references to an old covenant reality that properly could be considered to be fulfilled in the new covenant Eucharist. The following will list the direct references in the New Testament and will give an orientation to the Old Testament background.

The Pattern
Broadly speaking, the early Christians followed the old covenant pattern of worship. Most fundamentally their worship was based on the pattern in the temple

liturgy. It was also based upon the synagogue service, itself in its main orientations based upon the temple liturgy. The Eucharistic meal (the Liturgy of the Eucharist) was based on old covenant festal meals. The hours of prayer seem to have been based upon the hours of prayer in the temple and synagogue worship. The final result, however, especially the Christian assembly (a service of the Word followed by a service of the Eucharist), was a special Christian development.

The following are references to the Christian pattern of worship in the New Testament:

The Christian Assembly: Acts 2:42; 2:46; 20:7-12; 1 Cor 11–14; 2 Thes 2:2; *possibly* Rv 1:10; *and indirectly* Lk 24:13-35; Rv 4–5. All the New Testament writings could be seen as background to the Christian assemblies insofar as they were likely written to have been read during them.

The Hours of Prayer: Lk 24:53; Acts 2:42, 46; 3:1; 10:9; Acts 26:7; 1 Thes 3:10; 1 Tm 5:5; 2 Tm 1:3-4; Rv 7:15; *and possibly* Mt 14:23; Eph 6:18-19; Col 4:2; Rv 12:10. New Testament references to old covenant observance of the hours of prayer: Lk 2:37; 18:7, 10; Acts 10:2; 26:7. Note that "night and day," as well as references to "continual" or "constant" prayer, likely often refer to prayer at the temple hours.

The following are the Old Testament assemblies that are often referred to by modern scholars[1] as background to the Christian assembly in its aspect of hearing the Word of God: Ex 19–24 (Dt 5); Neh 8 (9–10); Dt 27–28; Josh 24:1–28; 2 Kgs 22:3–23:3 (2 Chr 34:8-33).

The Book of Psalms is also background to Old Testament worship, both in temple and synagogue services, and therefore to New Testament worship.

The following are the main Old Testament references to the old covenant pattern of worship:

- The festal cycle: Ex 23:12-17; 34:18-24; Lv 23; Nm 28–29; Dt 16:1-17
- Particular celebrations: Ex 29:38-42 (the daily offering); 20:8-11 (the Sabbath); 31:12-17 (the Sabbath); Dt 5:12-15 (the Sabbath); Ex 12 (the Passover); Lv 16 (the Day of Atonement)
- The obligation of appearance at feasts: Ex 23:17; 34:23-24; Dt 16:16-17
- Consuming offerings: Lv 10:12-20; 21–22
- The blood of the covenant: Ex 24:8; Zec 9:11; and indirectly Ps 50:5.

The "Sacramental" Elements

The two chief "sacramental" elements in the Christian assembly are the Scriptures and the Eucharist. The following are the explicit New Testament references to scriptural texts as the inspired Word of God:

The Scriptures: Mt 1:22; 22:31; Acts 28:25; 1 Thes 2:13; 2 Tm 3:16-17; Heb 1:1-2; 4:7; 2 Pt 1:19-21; *and indirectly:* Mt 10:20; Jn 16:16; 1 Cor 2:13; 12:4-5; 14:30; 1 Pt 4:11; Rv 1:1-2, 10. Equally significant are the ways in which the New Testament texts speak about the Old Testament texts as the Word of God or the way they cite and use Old Testament texts.

The following are the direct references to the Eucharistic ceremony (the Liturgy of the Eucharist) in the Scriptures.

The Last Supper and words of institution: Mt 26:20-30; Mk 14:17-26; Lk 22:14-23; 1 Cor 11:23-26; *and possibly* Jn 6:51b. These sections need to be interpreted in the light of the accounts of the Last Supper, of which they form part.

Instructions on the Eucharist: Jn 6:51-59 (25-71); 1 Cor 10:14-22; 1 Cor 11:17-34; *and possibly* Heb 13:9-16.

The breaking of the bread as a Eucharistic ceremony: probably Acts 2:42, 46-47; 20:7-12; *and possibly* Lk 24:13-43 (see also Acts 27:35).

The references to the Eucharistic ceremony can only be understood against the Old Testament background. The primary Old Testament background is the old covenant liturgy as a whole, including the whole sacrificial system. As the previous chapters indicate, the New Testament and the Fathers saw old covenant worship as typologically fulfilled in Christ. Therefore the Eucharistic ceremony, the Eucharist as sacrifice and sacrament, can only be understood against this background. The Old Testament material on worship is extensive and could not be helpfully summarized as a limited set of references.

There are, however, Old Testament realities that are used regularly in the New Testament and still more in patristic texts to explain the Eucharist. The following are the types that seem to be most commonly used. Two of these are more properly seen as types of the sacrifice of Christ on the cross (the Tree of Life, the Paschal Lamb). The others, however, are directly typological of the Eucharistic meal.[2]

The Tree of Life: Gn 2:9; 3:22; Rv 2:7; 22:2, 14, 19.[3] Note that the Tree of Life is commonly applied to the cross.[4] The Eucharist, then, can be seen as the fruit that comes from the cross.

The sacrifice of Melchizedek: Gn 14:18-20; Ps 110:4; Heb 5:5-10; 6:20–7:28.

The Passover (Paschal) Lamb: Ex 12:1-51; Jn 1:29; 19:36; 1 Cor 5:6-8; 1 Pt 1:18-19; *and probably* Rv 5:1-14 (with subsequent references to the lamb).[5]

The manna: Ex 16:1-36; (Nm 11:1-35); Dt 8:1-20; Jos 5:10-11; Ps 78:17-31; 105:40; 106:13-15; Neh 9:9-25; Wis 16:20-21; Jn 6:25-29; 1 Cor 10:1-5; Heb 9:4; Rv 2:17. See also below on the passages about the multiplication of the loaves and fishes.

The rock at Horeb: Ex 17:1-7 (Nm 20:2-13); Dt 8:1-20; Ps 78:15-16; 105:41; Neh 9:15, 20; Wis 11:4-14; 1 Cor 10:1-5.[6]

The showbread: Lv 24:5-9; Ex 25:30; 40:23; Nm 7:7-8; 1 Sm 21:6; Mt 12:4 (Mk 2:26; Lk 4:6).[7]

Meals
Since the Eucharistic ceremony is a sacred meal and a kind of continuation of significant meals Jesus had with his disciples, meals described in the Scripture have been used particularly by modern Scripture scholars as background to the Eucharistic ceremony. These would commonly include the following:
- the ceremonial meal connected to the sacrifices, often taken in the context of a feast, most especially the meals following the thanksgiving sacrifice and the Passover meal, itself a kind of thanksgiving meal (see above).
- the ceremonial meals connected with the sealing of a covenant, most especially the meal that concluded the establishment of the old covenant in Exodus 24.
- the multiplication of the loaves and fishes as a sign of the Eucharist: Mt 14:13-33; 15:32-38; Mk 6:32-52; 8:1-21; Lk 9:10-17; Jn 6:1-15.
- Jesus' meals with his disciples.
- the festal meal or banquet as a figure of the kingdom of God: Mt 8:11-12; Lk 13:28-29; Rv 3:20.

The Fathers in their mystagogical catecheses gave Psalm 23:5 a special place in expressing the connection of the festal meal with the Eucharist.

Patristic Sources

There are many references to the Eucharist in the works of the Fathers. There are relatively few treatments devoted to the Eucharist as such. Most of the instruction on the Eucharist is to be found in commentaries on the Scriptures that refer to the Eucharist or in festal sermons.

There are, however, patristic works commonly referred to as *Mystagogical Catecheses*, instructions given to the newly baptized catechumens explaining what had happened to them in the Easter vigil. "Mystagogical" means "initiation" into "the secret things," in this case into the Christian ceremonies. Since the new Christians first received the Eucharist as part of those ceremonies, the Mystagogical Catecheses contained treatments of the Eucharistic celebration (although they rarely treated the Liturgy of the Word[8]). The main Mystagogical Catecheses which treat the Eucharist are:[9]

- Ambrose of Milan, *On the Sacraments & On the Mysteries*
- Cyril of Jerusalem, *Five Mystagogical Catecheses*
- Theodore of Mopsuestia, *Catecheses*

Beside the above, special mention should also be given to John Chrysostom, who treated the Eucharist in *On the Priesthood* and in his scriptural homilies, to Cyril of Alexandria, whose discussion of the Eucharist, especially in his *Commentary on John*, has been particularly influential, to Augustine, whose sacramental theology was formative in Western theology, and to Leo the Great, whose festal sermons have been preserved and have been very significant in Western liturgical theology.

In the Byzantine Churches, a variety of Mystagogical Catechesis developed in the form of a commentary on the divine liturgy.[10] Of these the main surviving treatments are:

- Dionysius the Pseudo-Areopagite, *The Ecclesiastical Hierarchy*
- Maximus the Confessor, *The Mystagogia*
- Germanus of Constantinople, *On the Divine Liturgy*

To this should be added two post-patristic works commonly considered to contain the best summary of the Byzantine patristic tradition on the Eucharist:

- Nicholas Cabasilas, *A Commentary on the Divine Liturgy* and *The Life in Christ.*[11]

Equally significant are the surviving liturgies from the patristic period. These can be found collected and translated into English in *Prayers of the Eucharist: Early and Reformed,* R.C.D. Jasper and G.J. Cuming, eds. (New York: Oxford University Press, 1980).[12] In addition, there is a collection of Christian prayers, including Eucharistic liturgies, by Lucien Deiss, C.S.Sp., *Springtime of the Liturgy: Liturgical Texts of the First Four Centuries* (Collegeville, Minn.: Liturgical Press, 1979).

There is a complete collection of patristic texts on the Eucharist in *Textos Eucaristicos Primitivos,* edited by Jesús Solano, S.J., 2 vols. (Madrid: Biblioteca de Autores Cristianos, 1978, 1979). The Greek and Latin originals are included, although the Syriac is not. It is unfortunately only in Spanish, although most English speakers could use it to find the references to the texts. Most of the texts referred to in Solano can be found in William A. Jurgens, S.J., *The Faith of the Early Fathers: A Sourcebook of Theological and Historical Passages from the Christian Writings of the Pre-Nicene and Nicene Eras,* 3 vols. (Collegeville, Minn.: Liturgical Press, 1970, 1979, 1979). Jurgens can also be used to find patristic references to the Scriptures and their place in the Christian life.

There is also a complete collection of Jewish and early Christian texts on the Passover and Easter in Raniero Cantalamessa, O.F.M. Cap., *Easter in the Early Church* (Collegeville, Minn.: Liturgical Press, 1993).

Later Catholic Theology

Catholic theology in the Latin West was structured in such a way that the Scripture was treated in relationship to the sources of theology and therefore usually treated before everything else. The sacraments were not defined to include the Scriptures, so that sacramental teaching did not include the Liturgy of the Word. In fact, Catholic dogmatic theology rarely treated the liturgy in a direct manner until the Second Vatican Council. Therefore, the materials for a full treatment of the Eucharistic celebration are scattered throughout the pre-Vatican II dogmatic treatises.

The doctrine of the Eucharist understood as a sacrament has been discussed extensively in Catholic theology subsequent to the patristic era. Much of that discussion has been carried on by theologians. Of these Thomas Aquinas holds a special place, both because of official Church commendation of his writings and because he was the theologian who formulated the theology of "transubstantiation" and was the author of the Feast of Corpus Christi. His mature instruction on the Eucharist can be found in:

Summa Theologiae	I, QQ101-103	(The Ceremonial Precepts)
	II-II, QQ 81-100	(The Virtue of Religion)
	III, QQ 60-65	(The Sacraments)
	III, QQ 73-83	(The Eucharist)

Aquinas' teaching on the Sacrament of the Eucharist is often read by itself, apart from its broader context, especially in the context of his understanding of the place of the sacraments in the liturgy and the Christian life as a whole. The result is that he is in effect seen to exclusively concentrate on the change of the elements, rather than present what we might call a liturgical orientation. For that reason his treatment of the ceremonial precepts of the new law and his treatment of virtue of religion are especially important for understanding his "liturgical theology."

There have also been various pronouncements of the teaching authority of the Western Church on the doctrine of the Eucharist. Of these, the most authoritative and complete are the ones made by the Council of Trent. Because Trent treated the Eucharist as a sacrament and as a sacrifice, Post-Tridentine Catholic theology of the Eucharist was structured around these two topics. The relevant decrees from Trent can be found in:

- Council of Trent, Seventh Session, Canons on the Sacraments in General
- Council of Trent, Thirteenth Session, Decree Concerning the Most Holy Sacrament of the Eucharist
- Council of Trent, Twenty-First Session, Doctrine Concerning Communion Under Both Kinds and the Communion of Little Children
- Council of Trent, Twenty-Second Session, Doctrine Concerning the Sacrifice of the Mass

An English-language collection of the sources of Catholic liturgical and sacramental doctrine from the patristic period to the present day can be found in *Sources of Christian Theology,* vol 1. *Sacraments and Worship: Liturgy and Doctrinal Development of Baptism, Confirmation, and the Eucharist,* by Paul F. Palmer, S.J. (Westminster, Md.: Newman, 1955).

The Council of Trent also was the first ecumenical or general council to define the list of books that can be considered as Scripture, as well as to treat the relation between Scripture and tradition. These can be found in:

Council of Trent, Fourth Session, Decree Concerning the Canonical Scriptures and Decree Concerning the Edition and Use of the Sacred Books

An English-language collection of the sources of Catholic doctrine concerning the Scriptures can be found in *Official Catholic Teachings: Bible Interpretation* (Wilmington, N.C.: McGrath, 1978).

Contemporary Catholic Doctrine

The Second Vatican Council instituted a major reorientation to the presentation of Catholic doctrine. In few if any places was this more significant than in the reform of the liturgy it insisted upon. Of the decrees of the Council, the following are most relevant:

The Constitution on the Church, *Lumen Gentium* (LG)
The Constitution on Divine Revelation, *Dei Verbum* (DV)
The Constitution on the Sacred Liturgy, *Sacrosanctum Concilium* (SC)[13]

There is, in addition, a set of instructions that currently provide the norm for Catholic doctrine in regard to teaching about the Eucharist. The chief of these is the *Catechism of the Catholic Church,* which now constitutes the official overall summary of basic instruction. The Eucharist is treated in "The Sacrament of the Eucharist" (1322-1419). That section, however, is an article within a larger section, "The Celebration of the Christian Mystery," which begins with an orientation to the liturgy (1066-1075) and then proceeds with a section entitled "The Sacramental Economy," treating the celebration of the paschal mystery in the liturgy (1076-1209). The Eucharist, in other words, is to be understood in the context of the liturgy as a whole.

The *Catechism of the Catholic Church* presents the instructional foundation for more practical orientations to the celebration of the liturgy. For the latter, the general instructions contain the overall orientations. The chief general instructions are:

- *General Instruction on the Roman Missal,* published as part of the Roman altar missal, March 28, 1970
- *Lectionary for Mass: Introduction,* second *editio typica* (1981)
- *The General Instruction on the Liturgy of the Hours* (February 2, 1971)

These are all instructions for the new Roman rite, which has resulted from the changes decreed by the Second Vatican Council. They are not directed to the other rites in the Catholic Church, although much in them is more broadly applicable. The *General Instruction on the Liturgy of the Hours* is perhaps the best summary of Christian prayer in the official documents of the Catholic Church.

There are various English-language collections of official documents on the liturgy since Vatican II. The most readily available is *The Liturgy Documents: A Parish Resource* (Chicago: Liturgical Training Publications, 1985).

There are also two extensive histories of the changes introduced by Vatican II. The overall development is provided by Annibale Bugnini, *The Reform of the Liturgy 1948–1975* (Collegeville, Minn.: Liturgical Press, 1990). Bugnini was personally involved in the various official bodies that worked through the changes. In addition, the changes in the Liturgy of the Hours (the Breviary) is described more fully by Stanislaus Campbell, *From Breviary to Liturgy of the Hours: The Structural Reform of the Roman Office, 1964–1971* (Collegeville, Minn.: Liturgical Press, 1995).

Ecumenical Dialogues

A new aspect of Catholic endeavor since the Vatican Council has been the ecumenical dialogues. Some of the resulting agreed statements have been definitively received by the Catholic Church. Most have not but have been positively recognized as steps in a broader process. Following the orientation of Pope John Paul II, these should be received by theologians to the degree they have been accepted by the magisterium, so that Catholic Eucharistic teaching might be ecumenically convergent. Among the most significant of those that bear upon the Eucharist are:

Eastern Orthodox—Roman Catholic

- *The Mystery of the Church and of the Eucharist in the Light of the Mystery of the Holy Trinity,* Joint International Commission, 1982
- *Faith, Sacraments and the Unity of the Church,* Joint International Commission, 1982

Oriental Orthodox—Roman Catholic

- *Agreed Statement on the Eucharist* (1983), Oriental Orthodox/Roman Catholic Dialogue in the United States

Anglican—Roman Catholic

- ARCIC I [Anglican—Roman Catholic International Commission]: *The Final Report* (1982),[14] including:
  - The Official Roman Catholic Response to the Final Report of ARCIC I (1991)
  - ARCIC II: Requested Clarifications on Eucharist and Ministry (1993)
  - Letter by Cardinal E. Cassidy (President of the Pontifical Council for the Unity of Christians) to the Cochairmen of ARCIC II (1994)

Lutheran—Roman Catholic

- *The Eucharist,* Lutheran-Roman Catholic Joint Commission, 1978
- The conclusions of the Lutheran-Roman Catholic dialogue in the United States:[15]
  - *The Eucharist as Sacrifice* (1967)
  - *Eucharist and Ministry* (1970)

United Methodist—Roman Catholic

- *Eucharistic Celebration: Converging Theology—Divergent Practice* (1981), United Methodist/Roman Catholic Dialogue in the United States

There is, in addition, the important multilateral dialogue sponsored by the World Council of Churches, in which the Roman Catholic Church participated:

- *Baptism, Eucharist and Ministry* (1982).[16]

This is the only consultation of its scope and represents a significant attempt to state a convergence on Eucharistic doctrine for all the Christian Churches, one that Catholics have found promising. The official responses of the Churches have been published, including the Catholic response.[17]

The most accessible collection of the results of the dialogues is found in *Ecumenical Documents* (Mahwah, N.J.: Paulist), of which the following contain the main statements regarding the Eucharist:

- *Growth in Agreement: Reports and Agreed Statements of Ecumenical Conversations on a World Level*, Harding Meyer and Lukas Vischer, eds., (1984)
- *Building Unity: Ecumenical Dialogues with Roman Catholic Participation in the United States*, Joseph A. Burgess and Brother Jeffrey Gros, F.S.C., eds., (1989)

This has been supplemented by:

- *Deepening Communion: International Ecumenical Documents with Roman Catholic Participation* (Mahwah, N.J.: Paulist, 1998)

The dialogues between Roman Catholics and Eastern Orthodox, including the agreed statements on the Eucharist cited above as well as other helpful material, can be found in section 1 of:

- *Quest for Unity: Orthodox and Catholics in Dialogue*, John Borelli and John H. Erickson, eds. (Crestwood, N.Y.: St Vladimir's Seminary Press, 1996; Washington, D.C.: USCC, 1996)

The later dialogues, unlike the earlier ones, contain few discussions of the Eucharist. In general, the nature of the Scriptures has not yet been a topic for the dialogues.

Appendix 2: Select Bibliography

The bibliography on the Eucharist, especially when understood as the Eucharistic celebration, is immense. The topic has been a major focus of discussion and disagreement since the early Latin Middle Ages. Even more challenging, most of theology is directly or indirectly relevant, because the Eucharist lies at the focal point of the communication of Christ's redeeming work to his people. Too often, however, the Eucharist is understood as something in itself rather than as the "source and summit" of the Christian life.

The following bibliographical note is designed to provide help for pursuing the topic further and to provide background to the approach adopted in this book. Due to limitations of space, it does not deal with all the most important publications in this area but is mainly oriented to providing an introduction to further study. It is also restricted to those works currently accessible to an English-speaking audience. The notes to the text provide references to more works.

The recommended works are restricted to twelve. In addition, some introductory readings are suggested. Two chief current standard reference works are also appended. At the end is a short introduction to modern scholarly works and therefore to the works referenced in the select bibliography and the notes in the text.

Introductory

Redeemer: Understanding the Meaning of the Life, Death, and Resurrection of Jesus Christ, by Stephen B. Clark (Ann Arbor, Mich.: Servant, 1992) contains the theological presuppositions for the importance of the Eucharist. Since the liturgy is the celebration of the Christian mystery, the Christian mystery is the foundation of the liturgy and therefore is more important than the liturgy that celebrates it. *Redeemer* gives a presentation of the foundational truths that is complementary to *Catholics and the Eucharist.*

Springtime of the Liturgy: Liturgical Texts of the First Four Centuries by Lucien Deiss, C.S.Sp. (Collegeville, Minn.: Liturgical Press, 1979) provides an introduction to early Christian liturgical prayer as well as acquaintance with the main foundational texts that are referred to in writings on the liturgy. There is no substitute for actually reading the foundational texts of Christian tradition. If this is not available, the collection in Jasper and Cuming (see below) can also serve as an introduction. The latter has the advantage of containing the original forms of most of the Eucharistic Prayers in use in the Catholic Church today, apart from those composed for the Roman rite since the Second Vatican Council. It is, however, put together and formatted in a less readable way.

The contemporary authoritative sources of Catholic teaching on this area are extensive. Of those mentioned in the essay on the sources above, the following make a good introduction to current Catholic teaching on the Eucharist:

- the relevant sections of the *Catechism of the Catholic Church* (see Appendix 1);
- the Introduction and Chapter I of *The Constitution on the Sacred Liturgy* and *The Constitution on Divine Revelation;*
- the first three chapters of *The General Instruction on the Liturgy of the Hours.*

The Scriptures

The Bible and the Liturgy by Jean Danielou, S.J. (Notre Dame: University of Notre Dame Press, 1956, reprinted Ann Arbor, Mich.: Servant, 1979) is still the best introduction to the patristic use of the Scriptures which underlies the liturgy. Without the kind of understanding provided in this book, the liturgical texts and their scriptural basis will be unintelligible.

The Temple: Its Ministries and Services, As They Were at the Time of Jesus Christ by Alfred Edersheim (Grand Rapids, Mich.: Eerdmans, 1982; Peabody, Mass.: Hendrickson, 1994) contains a description of Jewish liturgical worship at the point at which the New Testament was written. Modern scriptural scholarship on the text of the Old Testament provides only a limited and sometimes misleading perspective on the Jewish background to New Testament teaching, because the writers of the New Testament understood Old Testament worship as it was taught and lived in the first century, not necessarily as the various rites were understood at their point of origin. Although an old book, there is no other available summary that improves on Edersheim's, and it needs surprisingly little correction in the light of modern scholarship.[18] The most helpful contemporary supplement is Joachim Jeremias, *Jerusalem in the Time of Jesus* (Philadelphia: Fortress, 1969).

The Eucharist in the New Testament by Jerome Kodell, O.S.B. (Collegeville, Minn.: Liturgical Press, 1988) contains a short and readable survey of recent scriptural scholarship on the topic of the Eucharist, as well as references that allow the topic to be pursued further.

The Bible and the Mass by Peter M.J. Stravinskas (Ann Arbor, Mich.: Servant, 1989) contains scriptural comments on the details of the current Roman rite written in a popular manner. It provides a different sort of scriptural introduction to the liturgy than *Catholics and the Eucharist.*

Theology

The Mass: An Historical, Theological and Pastoral Survey by Josef A. Jungmann, S.J. (Collegeville Minn.: Liturgical Press, 1975) is the best overall treatment of the Eucharist. It is a summary presentation, not a developed explanation of the meaning of various aspects of the Eucharist, but it does give a survey of the most important matters. It also has the advantage of being written by one of the masters of liturgical theology and was written after the Second Vatican Council close to the end of Jungmann's life.

Theological Dimensions of the Liturgy by Cyprian Vagaggini, O.S.B., 2 vols. (Collegeville, Minn.: Liturgical Press, 1959) is perhaps the best overall theological summary of liturgical and sacramental theology. It was written just before the Second Vatican Council and contains a balanced synthesis of the newer liturgical theology with traditional Catholic theology. Vagaggini was the principal author of Eucharistic Prayer III as well as a participant in the commissions to revise the liturgy after the Vatican Council.

I Believe in the Holy Spirit by Yves Congar, O.P. (New York: Crossroad Herder, 1997) is a survey of the core of the Christian life which the Eucharist is intended to mediate: the life-giving presence of the Holy Spirit. It is some-thing of a summary of the theology of one of the most influential theologians at the Vatican Council and contains helpful perspectives on the liturgy. Congar's *The Mystery of the Temple* (London: Burns and Oates, 1962) fills out his understanding of these realities.

Early Christian Worship: A Basic Introduction to Ideas and Practice by Paul Bradshaw (London: SPCK, 1996) is an introductory presentation to the his-tory of liturgical practice and theology in the early patristic era.

The Holy Eucharist: From the New Testament to Pope John Paul II by Aidan Nichols, O.P. (Dublin: Veritas, 1991) is an introductory presentation of the doctrines of the real presence and the Eucharistic sacrifice in Catholic tradi-tion. It does not, however, situate those doctrines within the liturgy as a whole.

Classics of Liturgical Theology

The Church and the Catholic and *The Spirit of the Liturgy* by Romano Guardini (New York: Sheed and Ward, 1950) are two related works that express the strength of the "classical" liturgical movement[19] as a spiritual and communitarian renewal that went much beyond improvements in the exter-nal ritual of the church. These two works convey the spirit of the thrust for renewal that began about the time of World War I, which included the litur-gical movement and which resulted in the Second Vatican Council.

Catholicism: A Study of Dogma in Relation to the Corporate Destiny of Mankind by Henri de Lubac, S.J. (New York: Sheed and Ward, 1950) is another classic of the pre-Vatican renewal that provided a vision for a new Church and that was a context for the liturgical movement. It was reprinted as *Catholicism: Christ and the Common Destiny of Man* (San Francisco: Ignatius, 1988).

Liturgical Piety by Louis Bouyer (Notre Dame, Ind.: University of Notre Dame Press, 1955) is an influential presentation of the thrust of the liturgi-cal movement written at a time when it was struggling for full acceptance. It is therefore a good introduction to one of the sources of the Vatican Council by a theologian who maintained a firmly orthodox approach throughout the post-conciliar period. The British edition was entitled *Life and Liturgy* (London: Sheed and Ward, 1956).

Eucharist: The Theology and Spirituality of the Eucharistic Prayer by Louis Bouyer (Notre Dame, Ind.: University of Notre Dame Press, 1968) is a study of the foundation of the Eucharistic Prayer in Jewish and Christian tradition and lays out an influential vision of what liturgical renewal as a renewal of prayer should be. While various details would now have to be revised, the overall vision of the Eucharistic Prayer and its meaning is almost universally accepted.

Reference

The Church at Prayer, Aimé Georges Martimort, ed. (Collegeville Minn.: Liturgical Press, 1986-87) is at the moment the standard reference work to the liturgy and liturgical studies.[20] Its orientation is not primarily theological but practical, although it does not omit theology. The four volumes are:

I   *Principles of the Liturgy,* Irénée Henri Dalmais, Pierre Marie Gy, Pierre Jounel, Aimé Georges Martimort, 1986

II   *The Eucharist,* Robert Cabié, 1986. Originally *L'Eucharistie,* 1983

III *The Sacraments,* Robert Cabié, Jean Evenou, Pierre Marie Gy, Pierre Jounel, Aimé Georges Martimort, Adrien Nocent, 1987

IV   *The Liturgy and Time,* Aimé Georges Martimort, Irénée Henri Dalmais, Pierre Jounel, 1985

Prayers of the Eucharist: Early and Reformed, edited by R.C.D. Jasper and G.J. Cuming (New York: Oxford University Press, 1980) is the chief historical collection of liturgical texts readily available.

Modern Scholarship

Modern academic scholarship about the liturgy and the Eucharist has its roots in the theological faculties of Western Christendom. It is the heir to the medieval and post-Reformation problematic which developed in the context of the Roman rite and the Reformation offshoots of that rite. It is also the heir to a focus on two controversial issues: the nature of the presence of Christ in or under the Eucharistic elements, debated intensely since the early Middle Ages, and the nature of the Mass as a sacrifice, which came to the fore as an issue with the Reformation.

Only after the Reformation did the rediscovery of liturgical traditions and patristic sources other than the great "doctors of the church" begin. For instance, the *Apology* of Justin Martyr, which contains the earliest overall summary of the Eucharistic celebration, was published only in 1551, the Liturgy of St. James in 1560, and the *Apostolic Constitutions* in 1563. It was in the nineteenth century, however, with its extensive development of historical scholarship, that the main lines of the early liturgy and theology of the Eucharist and of the traditions of the various Churches before modern times was filled in, and the conclusions heavily impacted those who taught sacramental theology.

We are heirs to a movement of change in Catholic theology that began in the late nineteenth or early twentieth century and culminated in the decrees of the Second Vatican Council. It is often spoken about in reference to the liturgical movement because the changes in the external form and practice of the liturgy that resulted have received the chief attention. The movement, however, was broader than a movement for improvement of liturgical practice and was primarily theological. It included new developments in scriptural studies, patristic studies, and Scholastic and Thomistic studies.[21] It also included a serious attempt to engage in ecumenical discussion with Orthodox and Protestants.

The time leading up to the Council was a period of great theological writing among Catholics. There was little questioning of Catholic orthodoxy, but there was a serious endeavor to develop a synthesis that could incorporate the new understandings from Scripture, patristics, liturgical studies, and ecumenical discussions. In many ways the chief documents of the Second Vatican Council resulted from that synthesis.

The magnitude and suddenness of the change introduced by the Vatican Council led to a period of disorientation, both in theology and in liturgical practice. This disorientation was felt most strongly in Western Europe and North America. It went along with the cultural revolution in these countries that gave a new lease on life to "liberal" (secularizing) theology, which had been in retreat since World War I.

Perhaps the most significant, however unintended, result of the Vatican Council was the opening of the Catholic Church to a Catholic version of

Protestant liberal theology, one that preserved a Catholic facade while radically altering the content of Catholic belief. That in turn led to a greater divorce of academic scholarship from faith and theology. Even though taught in theology faculties, Scripture, patristics, and liturgical and ecumenical studies have often become primarily historical disciplines whose conclusions are either irrelevant to theological teaching or of uncertain import. Often the writings produced by Catholic academics who hold positions in these faculties do not support the Catholic theological positions that, according to Catholic doctrine, are drawn from Scripture and the consensus of the Fathers.

Contemporary scholarly writings on the liturgy and the Eucharist contain much that is valuable, but they do not provide much helpful introductory material. There is a mass of good historical discussion that is relevant to particular points of liturgical and sacramental theology, but not a great deal that contributes to an overall positive synthesis. Much of what is written comes from such a pluralism of perspective and intellectual methodology that it can be difficult even to see what theological or practical conclusions the disciplines as a whole lead to.

At the same time there is something of a resurgence of conservative Catholic scholarship. Often it is updated in the sense that it makes use of contemporary language and scholarship. It, however, most commonly renews the medieval and post-Reformation concentration on the key points of controversy in the West, so that "Catholic positions" on the real presence and the Mass as a sacrifice are treated in isolation from the liturgical and broader context that gives Catholic worship its full meaning.

In effect, conservative scholarship often ignores the work of the Vatican Council and de facto reproduces the old split between liturgy and sacrament. It also tends to ignore or give only light attention to Scripture and de facto reproduces the old split between Scripture and magisterial instruction. It is hard to see that the conservative Catholic approach will be very productive in the long run unless it integrates the concern for orthodox doctrine with the liturgical orientation the Council and post-conciliar instructions have been so emphatic on.

The *Catechism of the Catholic Church* may be the beginning of a new era. It gives an ample synthesis of Catholic doctrine with determined concern for Scripture, patristics, and liturgical and ecumenical theology. It clearly places sacramental theology within the context of liturgical celebration of the Christian mystery and shows no signs of retreating from the emphasis on the Vatican

Council's liturgical practice to a revival of the older devotions. Although Scripture is still presented almost exclusively in the context of the sources of doctrine, its centrality in the life and liturgy of the Church is upheld. The *Catechism* will perhaps inaugurate a time of putting the "post-conciliar era" behind us and working to create a synthesis of Catholic theology and practice that will sustain genuine spiritual renewal.

NOTES

PREFACE AND INTRODUCTION

1. Second Vatican Council, Constitution on the Sacred Liturgy, *Sacrosanctum Consilium* (hereafter cited as SC), 1.
2. SC 10.
3. Anglican—Roman Catholic International Commission: *The Final Report* (1982), published in Christopher Hill and Edward Yarnold, S.J., ed., *Anglicans and Roman Catholics: The Search for Unity* (London: SPCK and CTS, 1994), p. 19. The report in this edition will hereafter be cited as ARCIC I.
4. For the treatment of the Eucharist in The *Catechism of the Catholic Church* (hereafter cited as CCC), see the first appendix (pp. 234-35).
5. Second Vatican Council, The Constitution on Divine Revelation, *Dei Verbum* (hereafter cited as DV), 24; CCC 132.
6. SC 4; CCC 1200-1203.
7. John Paul II, The Encyclical Letter on Commitment to Ecumenism, *Ut Unum Sint* (hereafter cited as UUS), 80.
8. *Redeemer: Understanding the Meaning of the Life, Death, and Resurrection of Jesus Christ* (Ann Arbor, Mich.: Servant, 1992), hereafter cited as *Redeemer.*
9. John Paul II, The Apostolic Letter on Preparing for the Third Millennium, *Tertio Millennio Adveniente* (hereafter cited as TMA), 55.
10. TMA, 36.
11. For a treatment of the incarnational principle, referred to as "the law of the Incarnation," see Cyprian Vagaggini, O.S.B., *Theological Dimensions of the Liturgy* (Collegeville, Minn.: Liturgical Press, 1959), vol. 1, pp. 166-68 (hereafter cited as Vagaggini, *Dimensions*).
12. For the patristic understanding of "icon" and other terms for signs, see Vagaggini, *Dimensions*, pp. 21-26, and Paul Bradshaw, *Early Christian Worship: A Basic Introduction to Ideas and Practice* (London: SPCK, 1996), pp. 59-60, hereafter cited as Bradshaw, *Worship.*
13. For a fuller presentation of the approach taken here to the two trees, see *Redeemer*, pp. 32-36, 42-59.
14. For the definition of "sacrament" see Aquinas, *Summa Theologiae* (hereafter cited as ST), I, Q 101, a 4, ad 2.

15. For a summary of the broader and narrower uses of the word "sacrament" in Christian history, see Vagaggini, *Dimensions*, vol. 1, pp. 18-19. See also Aquinas, ST, Q 101, a 4; Q 102, a 5; III, Q 60, a 1.

ONE
The Word of God

1. For the meaning of "the breaking of bread", see 172–73, 229.
2. CCC 105-8; DV, ch. III (note footnotes).
3. For the development of the concept of revelation and its contrast with "reason," especially in response to the epistemological orientation of the Enlightenment period, see Avery Dulles, S.J., *Models of Revelation* (Garden City, N.Y.: Doubleday, 1982), pp. 4, 9-21. For the attempt to incorporate into Catholic theology an understanding of "revelation" that sees it more as the concrete God revealing himself rather than solely as a collection of truths that God has revealed, see Joseph Ratzinger, commentary on the Dogmatic Constitution on Revelation, ch. I in *Commentary on the Documents of Vatican II*, Herbert Vorgrimler, ed., Vol. 3 (New York: Herder and Herder, 1969), 170-72.
4. For "the inspiration of scripture" as referring to the result of inspiration, not the mode of inspiration, see David Carson, *Showing the Spirit: A Theological Exposition of 1 Corinthians 12–14* (Grand Rapids, Mich.: Baker, 1996), hereafter cited as *Showing*, 160-65; Dom Celestin Charlier, O.S.B., *The Christian Approach to the Bible* (Westminster, Md.: Newman, 1965), especially chap. 7; Karl Rahner, S.J., *Inspiration in the Church*, Quaestiones Disputatae Series (London: Burns & Oates, 1961), 18-24; and Alois Grillmeier, S.J., in his commentary on DV, 11 in *Commentary on the Documents of Vatican II*, vol. 3, especially p. 229. For the connection of inspiration and inerrancy in The Constitution on Revelation, see Grillmeier, above. For background, see Newman, *On the Inspiration of Scripture* (Washington, D.C.: Corpus, 1967), hereafter cited as *Inspiration* and the introductory essay to Newman's work by Robert Murray, S.J., "Newman's Place in the Development of the Catholic Doctrine of Inspiration," 48-96.
5. For Christian prophecy, see Yves J.M. Congar, O.P., *I Believe in the Holy Spirit* (hereafter cited as *I Believe*), vol. 2, p. 177-78. For the nature of New Testament prophecy and its differentiation from Old Testament prophecy, see Wayne Grudem, *The Gift of Prophecy in 1 Corinthians* (Washington, D.C.: University Press of America, 1982). For an update of the discussion and some

adjustments to Grudem's presentation, see Carson, *Showing*, 91-100. For a discussion of the contemporary practice of prophecy, see Bruce Yocum, *Prophecy: Exercising the Prophetic Gifts of the Spirit in the Church Today* (Ann Arbor, Mich.: Servant, 1976; revised edition, 1993).

6. For a list of differences between the English used by the King James Version (KJV) and that of the RSV translators, see the introduction to the Revised Standard Version of the Bible (RSV).

7. The basic presentation of the authoritative approach to this area can be found in CCC 109-14 (based largely on DV 12). For an explanation of the important statement, "Sacred Scripture must be read and interpreted in the light of the same Spirit by whom it was written," see the helpful article by Ignace de la Potterie, S.J., "Interpretation of Holy Scripture in the Spirit in Which It Was Written (*Dei Verbum* 12c)," in René Latourelle, S.J., ed., *Vatican II: Assessment and Perspectives; Twenty-Five Years After (1962-1987)*, vol. 1 (New York: Paulist, 1988).

8. The Evangelical Anglican theologian John Stott in *Understanding the Bible* (London: Scripture Union, 1972), states, "Scripture alone is God's word written, and the Holy Spirit its ultimate interpreter. The place of the individual's reason and of the Church's tradition lies in the elucidation and application of Scripture. But both are subordinate to God himself as He speaks to us through his word" (p. 217).

9. DV 8, 23; *The General Instruction on the Liturgy of the Hours* (hereafter cited as GILH), 55; Congregation for Catholic Education, *Instruction on the Study of the Fathers of the Church in the Formation of Priests* (1989), especially sections 17-29.

10. For the consensus of the Fathers, see the Council of Trent, Fourth Session, Decree Concerning the Edition and Use of the Sacred Books.

11. The authoritative approach to this area can be found in CCC 84-95, 888-92, 2032-40; LG 25; and The Code of Canon Law (1983) (hereafter cited as CJC), 747-80.

12. The recognized set of rules used by Catholic theology about which statements are certainly true and obligatory to be held and which are not is reflected in the Code of Canon Law (CJC, 749-52). Treating this area, the *Directory Concerning Ecumenical Matters*, Part Two, II, 5, says, "Students should learn to distinguish between revealed truths, which all require the same assent of faith, and theological doctrines. Hence they should be taught to distinguish between 'the deposit of faith itself, or the truths which are contained in our venerable doctrine,' and the way in which they are enunciated, between the truth to be enunciated and the various ways of perceiving and

more clearly illustrating it, between apostolic tradition and merely ecclesi-astical traditions."

13. For the possible meanings of "magisterium" and its uses throughout history, see Yves Congar, O.P., "A Semantic History of the Term 'Magisterium,'" in *Readings in Moral Theology—The Magisterium and Morality*, Charles Curran and Richard A. McCormack, eds. (New York: Paulist, 1982), 297-313. See also Congar, "A Brief History of the Forms of the Magisterium and Its Relations with Scholars," in the same collection, 314-31.

14. "The task of authentically [authoritatively] interpreting the word of God, whether written or handed on, has been entrusted exclusively to the living teaching office of the Church, whose authority is exercised in the name of Jesus Christ" (DV 10). "Authentically" here means "authoritatively," not "genuinely," the normal meaning of the English word.

15. Peter Canisius, in the course of a disputation with some Protestant Reformers, summarized the role of the Church in the interpretation of the Scripture as follows: "On one point we and the delegates of the other party are agreed, namely that we acknowledge the canonical Scriptures to be true, holy, internally consistent, and entirely divine, and of incomparable authority. Further, we hold that those Scriptures provide the best and soundest crite-rion for the adjustment of controversies in belief and religion. Whenever the Bible is clear and distinct in itself, we gladly submit to its testimony and ask for no other authority or evidence. But as soon as conflict arises about the meaning of an obscure passage and it is difficult to decide rival claims to the true meaning, then we appeal with perfect justice to the constant agreement of the Catholic Church, and go back to the unanimous interpretation of the Fathers. This is not in order that the Church may teach us without reference to the Scriptures but that the Church may show us the true and orthodox sense of the Scriptures; not that our faith may rest upon human authority without any regard to the Divine Word, but that we may learn from the explanations and instructions of holy men what the Divine Word really says. Where the sense of Scripture is clear and unambiguous we do not appeal to the Church, but, in doubtful places, we prefer the common agreement of the Church to the private exegesis of changeable men, who not seldom use diligent and pernicious endeavors to distort the sacred text." James Brodrick, S.J., *Saint Peter Canisius* (Chicago: Loyola University Press, 1962), 404-8.

16. Sacred Congregation for the Sacraments and Divine Worship, *Instruction Concerning Worship of the Eucharistic Ministry Inaestimabile Donum* (April 17, 1980), hereafter cited as *Inaestimabile*, 5.

17. See John Paul II, *Crossing the Threshold of Hope* (New York: Alfred A. Knopf, 1994), 137.

18. According to The Constitution on Revelation (DV 10), the task of authentically interpreting the word of God, whether written or handed on, has been entrusted exclusively to the living teaching office of the Church, whose authority is exercised in the name of Jesus Christ. This teaching office is not above the word of God but serves it, teaching only what has been handed on, listening to it devoutly, guarding it scrupulously, and explaining it faithfully by divine commission and with the help of the Holy Spirit; it draws from this one deposit of faith everything that it presents for belief as divinely revealed.

19. CCC 1100-1102.

TWO
Hearing God's Word

1. Newman, *Inspiration*, p. 133.

2. For a presentation of the arguments that the quoted saying refers to Jesus' words, not to "flesh" and "blood" in the previous discourse, see Raymond Brown, *The Gospel According to John* (hereafter cited as *John*), I, in the commentary on this passage.

3. "The Holy Spirit gives a spiritual understanding of the Word of God to those who read or hear it, according to the dispositions of their hearts" (CCC 1101).

4. For a traditional definition of "ceremony" in the narrow sense, see Aquinas, ST, I, Q 99, a. 3.

5. For the common patristic interpretation that it was the divine Son speaking, see Leo the Great, *Sermon* 95, 2.

6. On worship, see Aquinas, ST, Q. 84, a. 1, 2, as well as Q. 81, a. 1, 5.

7. For reverence in relation to worship, see Aquinas, ST, II-II, Q. 84, a. 1.

8. For a discussion of the loss of reverence and the damage that has come from that, see James Hitchcock, *The Recovery of the Sacred* (San Francisco: Ignatius, 1995).

9. As in the title of the Mishnaic tractate, M. Abodah Zarah.

10. For the various uses of the word "liturgy" see Aimé Georges Martimort, *The Church at Prayer* (Collegeville, Minn.: Liturgical Press, 1986-87), I, 7-10. All four volumes of this work will hereafter be cited as Martimort, *Church.*

11. For a treatment of the liturgical assembly and the role of the Word of God in it, see *God's Word and God's People* by Lucien Deiss, C.S.Sp. (Collegeville,

Minn.: Liturgical Press, 1976), hereafter cited as *Word*. For the Christian assemblies in the New Testament, see Xavier Léon-Dufour, S.J., *Sharing the Eucharistic Bread: The Witness of the New Testament* (Mahwah, N.J.: Paulist, 1987), hereafter cited as *Sharing*.

12. For the use of "Amen" see CCC 1061-65.
13. See CCC 103.
14. See CCC 1066-68 (SC 2).
15. *Inaestimabile*, 3.
16. From Joseph Cardinal Ratzinger, written interview in *Catholic World Report*, January 1994, p. 24:

   The Church takes part in the epochal crisis of the second half of the century, which for her manifests itself as a crisis of belief, of vocations, of internal unity of Church life. There is, however, an important new aspect: whereas 30 years ago, people were predicting the end of religion and a completely secular age, today we can see everywhere a new impulse toward the religious, a setting out on the path of religion. However, in general, the answer to this impulse is less likely to be sought in the great churches than in new communities, which adopt their form and content from many influences. Despite this, it would be wrong to say that the religious renaissance is passing the Catholic Church by (I am not well enough informed to be able to discuss other Christian churches). The so-called movements are just one way in which even the Church becomes a bearer of new religious awakenings.

THREE

Sacrifice and Christ

1. For further clarification of terminology in this area, see note 7 in chapter 8.
2. For the tendency to focus on the individual sacrifice, especially because of using Leviticus 1-7 as the text for exposition of the nature of sacrifice, see works like Andrew Jukes, *The Law of the Offerings* (Grand Rapids, Mich.: Kregel, 1966) and H. A. Ironsides, *The Levitical Offerings* (Neptune, N.J.: Loizeaux Bros, 1929).
3. For an overall presentation of temple worship in the time of Jesus, see, Alfred Edersheim, *The Temple: Its Ministries and Services, As They Were at the Time of Jesus Christ* (Grand Rapids, Mich.: Eerdmans, 1982), hereafter cited as *Temple;* supplemented by Joachim Jeremias, *Jerusalem in the Time of Jesus* (Philadelphia: Fortress, 1969), hereafter cited as *Jerusalem*.
4. For the understanding that the giving of the Law occurred on the Day of

Pentecost, see the current Jewish Prayer Book. See the second century B.C. *Book of Jubilees* (*Jubilees* 1:1 with 6:17) for probably the earliest Jewish reference. See Leo the Great, *Sermon 75*, for a patristic presentation. For a discussion of the interpretation of the Feast of Pentecost in relation to the giving of the Law, see Fitzmyer, *101 Questions on the Dead Sea Scrolls*, p. 87. See Jean Danielous, S.J., *The Bible and the Liturgy* (Notre Dame: University of Notre Dame Press, 1956; rpt: Ann Arbor, Mich.: Servant, 1979), hereafter cited as *Bible*, 330-32, for a summary of the Patristic approach.

5. For the way the obligation to worship was applied to men and women, see Stephen B. Clark, "Women in Mosaic Law" in *Man and Woman in Christ: An Examination of the Roles of Men and Women in Light of Scripture and the Social Sciences* (Ann Arbor, Mich.: Servant, 1980), ch. 6.

6. For the Scripture passages for the festal offering, see Deuteronomy 16:16 and Exodus 23:14. For the rabbinic interpretation of the application of those passages (i.e., giving both) see M. Hagigah 1, 2.

7. See Deuteronomy 12:5-6 and Maimonides, MT, Book 8, III, 5, 14, 11, which held that Israelites were obligated to bring all of these at the first occurring pilgrim feast, probably in that opinion reflecting first-century practice.

8. This description is taken from the sacrificial ceremony narrated in Sirach 50:5-21, about two hundred years earlier. For another description of sacrificial ceremonies in the temple see 2 Chronicles 29:20-35. The *Mishnah* and *Tosefta*, Rabbinic sources from about A.D. 200, preserve memories of the ceremonies in the last years before the destruction of the temple in A.D. 70.

9. For the two main descriptions in the Old Testament of the feasts and how they were celebrated with sacrifices, see Leviticus 23 and Numbers 28–29. See endnote 7 above for how they were combined.

10. For the peace or communion offerings (*shelamim*) see Leviticus 2 and 7:11-36.

11. See Mark 6:39-40, and behind it Numbers 2, 10:1-28, and Exodus 12:3-4.

12. The English noun "sacrifice" is drawn from the Latin noun *sacrificium*, itself derivative from the verb *sacrifico*, meaning "make sacred or holy." According to Augustine, "For even though it is made or offered by man, a sacrifice is yet a divine thing. And it is for this reason that the ancient Latins gave it the name" (*De Civ Dei*, 10, 6). According to Aquinas (ST, II-II, Q. 85, a. 3), "'Sacrifice' is derived from a man making something holy." For the various scriptural words for sacrifice and their meanings, see "sacrifice" in the ABD, V, 873. For theories of sacrifice in the Old Testament, see Roland de Vaux, *Ancient Israel*, vol. 2, 447-56. For a theological treatment, see Martin

D'Arcy, "Sacrifice and Priesthood" in George D. Smith, *The Teaching of the Catholic Church*, 478-480.

13. See the section of the Mishnah called *Qadoshim*, "Holy Things."

14. For a fuller discussion of the word "consecration" in connection to a sacrifice, see p. 95 and the note there (#95).

15. The equation of sacrifice with death seems to have been a Western Medieval notion. For this see E. L. Mascall, *Corpus Christi: Essays on the Church and the Eucharist* (London: Longmans, Green, and Co., 1965), hereafter cited as *Corpus*.

16. For a fuller presentation of fire as an indication of God's acceptance, see *Redeemer*, 251-53.

17. According to Philo of Alexandria, who lived in the first century, the food no longer belongs to the one who made the offering but to God, to whom it was given, who as "the benefactor, the bountiful ... has made the convivial company of those who carry out the sacrifices partners (*koinonoi*) of the altar whose board they share." Philo, *spec. leg.* 1.221.

18. For the atoning role of a sacrifice for sin, see *Redeemer*, ch. 5.

19. See Josef A. Jungmann, S.J. *The Mass: An Historical, Theological and Pastoral Survey* (Collegeville, Minn.: Liturgical Press, 1975), hereafter cited as Jungmann *Mass*, p. 235. As Augustine put it,

> The fact that the ancient Fathers offered animal sacrifices—which the people of God now read about but do not imitate—means only this, that those things were a sign of the things we do to draw near to God and induce our neighbor to do the same. A sacrifice, therefore, is the visible sacrament, that is a sacred sign, of an invisible sacrifice. Augustine, *De Civ Dei*, 10, 5

20. See Aquinas, II-I, Q. 102, a. 3, ad 8. For the view that, whatever the primary purpose, all sacrifices are atoning, see Hebrews 9:22-23.

21. For a complete list of the New Testament passages see *Redeemer*, pp. 301-302. For a fuller treatment of the death of Christ as a sacrifice, see *Redeemer*, ch. 5.

22. This view is expressed by Leo the Great in *Sermon 8 on the Passion of the Lord:*

> Lord, you drew all things to yourself so that the devotion of all peoples everywhere might celebrate, in a sacrament made perfect and visible, what was carried out in the one temple of Judaea under obscure fore-shadowings.... The different sacrifices of animals are no more: the one offering of your body and blood is the fulfillment of all the different sacrificial offerings, for you are the true Lamb of God: You take away the sins of the world.

See also Aquinas, ST, I-II, Q. 102, a. 3.

23. For the interpretation of this passage and its use in the New Testament, see *Redeemer*, ch. 4.

24. As Cyril of Alexandria puts it, "He here says, *I sanctify [consecrate] myself*, for, I offer Myself and present Myself as a spotless Sacrifice for an odour of a sweet smell. For that which is brought to the Divine Altar was sanctified, or called holy according to the Law" (*Commentary on the Gospel of John According to St. Cyril of Alexandria*, P. E. Pusey, trans., 1874, 410).

25. For a fuller treatment of the importance and meaning of his sufferings and painful death, see *Redeemer*, especially ch. 4 and 5.

26. For a treatment of the issues connected with the sufficiency of Jesus' death on the cross, his "finished work," and his "offering in heaven," see *Redeemer*, 249-51.

27. For this orientation, which has traditionally been described as devotion, see Aquinas, ST, II-II, Q. 82, a. 1.

FOUR
Eucharist and Covenant

1. For the Passover as the primary type of the Eucharist, see Aquinas, ST, I, Q. 73, a. 6; Council of Trent, Session XXII, ch. 1. For a summary of the different Christian understandings of the meaning of "Passover," see Raniero Cantalamessa, O.F.M. Cap., *The Mystery of Easter* (Collegeville, Minn.: Liturgical Press, 1993), 7-19, hereafter cited as *Mystery*.

2. See the Palestinian Targum on Exodus 12:42, reproduced with notes in English in Raniero Cantalamesssa, O.F.M. Cap., *Easter in the Early Church* (Collegeville, Minn.: Liturgical Press, 1993), hereafter cited as *Easter*, pp. 29-30.

3. See Genesis 15, Genesis 22, *Jubilees* 17:15 and the notes in Cantalamessa, *Easter* on pp. 123-24.

4. For a recent survey of the scholarly opinions, see Jerome Kodell, *The Eucharist in the New Testament* (Collegeville, Minn.: Liturgical Press, 1988), hereafter cited as *Eucharist*, pp. 22-37.

5. For an introductory survey of the current scholarly opinions about Paul's discussions of the Eucharist in 1 Corinthians 10 and 11, see Kodell, *Eucharist*, pp. 71-82. For a supplementary presentation from the viewpoint of Evangelical scriptural scholarship, see Gordon Fee, in *The First Epistle to the Corinthians* (Grand Rapids, Mich.: Eerdmans, 1987), hereafter cited as *First*

Epistle.

6. For the issues connected to the flow of 1 Corinthians 8–10 and the question Paul is discussing, as well as his resolution, see Peter J. Tomson, *Paul and the Jewish Law: Halakha in the Letters of the Apostle to the Gentiles* (Assen/Maastricht: Van Gorcum, 1990; Minneapolis: Fortress, 1990), hereafter cited as Tomson, *Halakha*, pp. 177-220.

7. For the altar as the place where the sacrificial gifts are made over to God, see article "Sacrifice" by Gary Anderson, *The Anchor Bible Dictionary* (ABD), V, 873.

8. For an illustration of the fact that it is not just a Catholic position that this passage shows that taking part in the Eucharist is taking part in a sacrificial meal, see Matthew Henry, the standard older Reformed exegete in the English-speaking world, whose theology of the presence of Christ in the Eucharist is Zwinglian:

    In short, the Lord's supper is a feast on the sacrificed body and blood of our Lord, *epulum ex oblatis.* And to eat of the feast is to partake of the sacrifice, and so to be his guests to whom the sacrifice was offered, and this in token of friendship with him. Thus, to partake of the Lord's table is to profess ourselves his guests and covenant people. This is the very purpose and intention of this symbolical eating and drinking; it is holding communion with God and partaking of those privileges, and professing ourselves under those obligations, which result from the death and sacrifice of Christ.

9. For a continuation of Paul's usage of the terms "bread" and "wine" for referring to the Eucharistic elements after the consecration, see Eucharistic Prayer IV (see the ICEL translation: "By your Holy Spirit, gather all who share this bread and wine..."); as well as Eucharistic Prayer I (the Roman canon) and Eucharistic Prayer II (referring to the elements after the words of institution as "the [holy] bread of eternal life and the cup of [perpetual] salvation").

10. See ARCIC I, *Final Report*, 6; ARCIC II, *Church as Communion*, 24; Lutheran-Roman Catholic Joint Commission, *Church and Justification*, 3.3.

11. For the interpretation of "participation" (*koinonía*) here as "eating" and "drinking" and its significance, see Edward J. Kilmartin, S.J., *The Eucharist in the Primitive Church* (Englewood Cliffs, N.J.: Prentice-Hall, 1965), pp. 80-81; hereafter cited as *Eucharist.* See also Jerome Murphy-O'Connor, "Eucharist and Community in First Corinthians," *Worship* 51 (1977), reprinted in R. Kevin Seasoltz, O.S.B., ed., *Living Bread, Saving Cup: Readings on the Eucharist* (Collegeville, Minn.: Liturgical Press, 1982, 1987), 18-20; hereafter cited as *Living Bread.*

12. *On the Psalms,* Ps 64:14-15.

13. See Henri de Lubac, S.J., *Catholicism: A Study of Dogma in Relation to the Corporate Destiny of Mankind* (New York: Sheed and Ward, 1950), hereafter cited as *Catholicism*, 51-63 for a summary of the patristic evidence; see also Aquinas, ST, Q. 73, A. 3 for the *res* of the sacrament as "the unity of the mystical body."

14. For whether all of the Eucharistic Prayers of the early church made use of the actual words of institution, see the introductory summaries for the Anaphora of Addai and Mari and for the prayers in *The Didache Apostolorum*, 9-10 in *Prayers of the Eucharist: Early and Reformed*, R.C.D. Jasper and Cuming and G.J. Cuming, eds. (New York: Oxford University Press, 1980), hereafter cited as *Prayers*. See also Bradshaw, *Worship*, 49.

15. Tomson, *Halakha*, 141.

16. For examples of Jewish meal blessings, including Sabbath blessings, see Lucien Deiss, C.S.Sp., *Springtime of the Liturgy: Liturgical Texts of the First Four Centuries* (Collegeville, Minn.: Liturgical Press, 1979), hereafter cited as *Springtime*, 5-9, or Jasper and Cuming, *Prayers*, 9-10, or any Jewish prayer book today. The blessings as used in the second century and almost certainly in the first century can be found in M. Berakoth 6, 1-3.

17. For the understanding in rabbinic and later Jewish tradition of a similarity between meals and temple worship, see Ganzfried-Goldin, *Code of Jewish Law*, I, 41, 6; II, 50, 1 and A.Z. Idelsohn, *Jewish Liturgy and Its Development* (New York: Schocken, 1932), 122. For raising of the bread and cup as an act of offering, see Jungmann, *Mass*, 11-13, and Robert J. Ledogar, "The Eucharistic Prayer and the Gifts over Which It Is Spoken, in Seasoltz, *Living Bread*, 70-72. For the connection between thanksgiving and offering in the early Christian Eucharistic Prayers, see Jungmann, *Mass*, 118-19, and Gregory Dix, *The Shape of the Liturgy* (London: Adam & Charles Black, 1945), hereafter cited as Dix, *Shape*, 272.

18. See Joachim Jeremias, *The Eucharistic Words of Jesus* (Philadelphia: Fortress, 1966), hereafter cited as *Eucharistic Words*, 232-33.

19. For the relationship of the Passover to the Last Supper, see note 5 for this chapter. See also the important presentation of David Daube, *He That Cometh* (lecture given October 1966 at St. Paul's Cathedral, privately printed), not noted over by Kodell. For the methodology for understanding the relationship between the two events, see Joseph Cardinal Ratzinger, "Form and Content in the Eucharistic Celebration" in *The Feast of Faith: Approaches to a Theology of the Liturgy* (San Francisco: Ignatius, 1986).

20. For the meaning of the words in the Last Supper (and multiplication) accounts "having blessed" and "having given thanks," see Jeremias,

Eucharistic Words, 175.

21. For descriptions of how the blessing would have happened, see Jeremias, *Eucharistic Words,* 108-11.

22. See Yves Congar, O.P., *I Believe in the Holy Spirit* (New York: Crossroad Herder, 1997), hereafter cited as *I Believe III,* 233.

23. M. Pesachim, 5.

24. For a fuller presentation of the connection of Christ's death with Isaiah 53, see *Redeemer,* 97-102.

25. For the separation of the Body and the Blood as indicating the sacrificial death of Christ, see Jeremias *Eucharistic Words,* 221-22; Jungmann, *Mass,* 11; and Bertil E. Gartner, "The Eucharist as Sacrifice in the New Testament" in *Lutherans and Catholics in Dialogue III,* 28.

26. For the view that the bread already represented the Passover lamb and that the Passover lamb may have been absent in the ceremony Jesus celebrated, even if it was a Passover celebration, see Daube, *He Who Cometh,* 9-10. Cf. also Thomas Corbishley, S.J., *One Body, One Spirit* (Leighton Buzzard: Faith Press, 1973), 22.

27. Jeremias, *Eucharistic Words,* 178-79.

28. Jeremias, *Eucharistic Words,* 233. In regard to the difference between the Last Supper and the Eucharist, see Ratzinger, "Form and Content": "As such, the Christian Eucharist is not a repetition of the Last Supper (which was in fact unique)," and, "The day of the resurrection is the matrix of the Eucharist." See also *Church and Justification: Understanding the Church in the Light of the Doctrine of Justification,* Lutheran/Roman Catholic Joint Commission (Lutheran World Federation, 1994), 27: "Thus with effective signs Jesus gave his disciples an anticipatory share in the saving event of his atoning death as a once-for-all sacrifice, through which all who believe in him have been redeemed from sin (cf. Mt 26:28) and freed for life in the Spirit." See also Edward Kilmartin, S.J., *Church, Eucharist, and Priesthood: A Theological Commentary on* The Mystery and Worship of the Most Holy Eucharist (New York: Paulist, 1981), 6-7.

29. For the cultic meaning of "do" in a context like this, see Léon-Dufour, *Sharing,* 109.

30. Ratzinger, "Form and Content," 40, 42-44; Dix, *Shape,* 55-56.

31. For "remember," "memorial" and "remembrance" as words used to designate calling something to God's attention in a liturgical ceremony, see Max Thurian, *The Eucharistic Memorial,* two vols. (Richmond, Va.: John Knox, 1960, 1961), hereafter cited as *Memorial.*

FIVE
The Eucharistic Offering

1. Against Heresies 4, 17, 5: *novi Testamenti novam docuit oblationem; quam Ecclesia ab Apostolis accipiens, in universo mundo offert Deo.* In quoting Malachi 1:11 right afterwards, the Latin version of *Adversus Haereses* (the only version we have for this passage) uses the translation *sacrificium purum* rather than *oblatio munda*, the phrase used in the Vulgate translation and in the Eucharistic prayers.

2. For the terminology of the Eucharist as a relative, not an absolute, sacrifice, see Jungmann, *Mass*, 88.

3. As the Church of England Bishop of Westminster, Mark Santer, put it in the introduction to Kenneth W. Stevenson, *Eucharist and Offering* (New York: Pueblo, 1986), "During the first 1,500 years of the Church's history nobody doubted that the Eucharist was a sacrifice."

4. The Sixty-Seven Articles of Ulrich Zwingli (1523), 18: "Christ who has once offered himself as a sacrifice, is for eternity a perpetually enduring and efficacious sacrifice for the sins of all believers. Therefore we conclude that the Mass is not a sacrifice but a memorial of the one sacrifice and a seal of redemption that Christ made good for us." For some important early statements, see The Augsburg Confession (1530), 24; The Heidelberg Catechism (1563), QQ. 75, 80; The Second Helvetic Confession (1566); The Thirty-Nine Articles of the Church of England (1571), 31.

5. See the Council of Trent, Chapter I and Canon 1 on "The Sacrifice of the Mass," for the Eucharist as a "true and proper" sacrifice. For the lack of a commonly accepted definition of sacrifice as applied to the mass, see B. V. Miller in "The Eucharistic Sacrifice" in George Smith, ed., *The Teaching of the Catholic Church*, vol. II (New York: MacMillan, 1949). For a discussion of the nature of the Eucharist as a sacrifice, see the same essay of Smith, and E. L. Mascall, *Corpus*, chapters V and VI. For an example of the difficulties caused to ecumenical dialogue by the lack of a consensus definition in Catholic theology, see Gartner's "The Eucharist as Sacrifice in the New Testament," in *Lutherans and Catholics in Dialogue III: The Eucharist as a Sacrifice* (Washington, D.C.: USCC, 1967), hereafter cited as Lutheran-Catholic Dialogue, 32 and 33, where the position is close to the Catholic position but he decides it is not a sacrifice on the basis of a definition most Catholic theologians would not use. For a post-Vatican II summary of the Catholic teaching on the Eucharist as a sacrifice, see CCC 1356-81 and Jungmann, *Mass*, 111-20. For Aquinas' explanation, see ST, III, Q. 83, a. 1.

260 / Catholics and the Eucharist

6. For the convergence, see the dialogues cited in Appendix 1. For this question as lacking full consensus, see John Paul II, UUS 79.

7. For the origins of our Eucharistic Prayer from the blessing over the cup at a festal meal (the Birkat Ha-Mazon), see Thomas J. Talley, "From Berakah to Eucharistia" in René Latourelle, S.J., ed., *Vatican II: Assessment and Perspectives; Twenty-Five Years After* (1962-1987), vol. 1 (New York: Paulist, 1988) and Enrico Mazza, *The Eucharistic Prayers of the Roman Rite* (New York: Pueblo, 1986), hereafter cited as *Prayers*, 250-55.

8. Dix, *Shape*, 48-50.

9. For the principle of Catholic liturgical theology, *lex orandi, lex credendi* (apparently originally *legem credendi lex statuat supplicandi* from Prosper of Aquitaine, Ep. 8), what the Church prays indicates what the Church believes or should believe, see Martimort, *Church*, I, 277, and Alexander Schmemann, *Introduction to Liturgical Theology* (Leighton Buzzard, Beds: Faith Press, 1966), 13-16.

10. See Basil of Caesarea, *On the Holy Spirit*, 66.

11. Cf. Justin Martyr, First Apology, 66. For Old Testament background, see Exodus 12:3-4, 43-50; M. Pesachim 8).

12. Cf. *The Didache Apostolorum*, 14.

13. Dix, *Shape*, 121-25, and Jungmann, *Mass*, 185-191.

14. Nicholas Cabasilas, *A Commentary on the Divine* Liturgy (London: SPCK, 1960), 2-4.

15. For the relationship of the Father and the Son in the death and resurrection of Christ, see *Redeemer*, ch. 6-7.

16. Cf. CCC, 1357-58. For a discussion of prayer directed to the Father, see Josef A. Jungmann, S.J., *The Place of Christ in Liturgical Prayer* (New York: 1965).

17. For the use of Eucharistic Prayer III for presenting Catholic theology of the Eucharistic sacrifice, see John Paul II, *Dominicae Coenae*, 9. For a summary of the four main Eucharistic Prayers of the Roman rite and their distinctive features, as well as the reasons for adding three more to the Roman canon, see Alan F. Detscher, "The Eucharistic Prayers of the Roman Catholic Church" in Frank C. Senn, ed., *Eucharistic Prayers: An Ecumenical Study of Their Development and Structure* (Mahwah, N.J.: Paulist, 1987).

18. See M. Berakoth, 7, 3.

19. CCC, 1359-61.

20. For the atoning or propitiatory nature of the Eucharist, see The Council of Trent, Session XXII, Ch. 2 and Canon 3; and Jungmann, *Mass*, 142-152. For a patristic treatment, see Cyril of Jerusalem, Cat Lect XXIII(V), 8, 10. For

the meaning of the words, see *Redeemer,* 125-30.

21. For the fact that peace offerings, which included thanksgiving offerings but excluded sin offerings, were the only ones with festal meals like the Eucharist, see Leviticus 4:8-11, 19-21; 6:26, 30; 7:3-7.

22. Cf. Dix, *Shape,* 238: "'Consecration' is in fact only the description of the offering and acceptance of the sacrifice."

23. Cyril of Jerusalem, Catecheses, XXIII (V), 7.

24. Cf. the recommended prayer after communion in the Byzantine liturgy, "I thank you, O Lord my God, that you have not rejected me a sinner, but have deemed me worthy to be a partaker of your Holy Things."

25. For these words as the "form of the sacrament" see the Council of Florence (DS 1321). For the view that "by the power of these words" the change in the elements is effected see of the Council of Florence (DS 1321) and the Council of Trent (DS 1640).

26. Justin Martyr, First Apology I, 67.

27. For the institution narrative, the role of the priest, and the place of the epiclesis, see Yves Congar, O.P., "The Eucharistic Epiclesis" in *I Believe,* 228-249. See also the Oriental Orthodox/Roman Catholic Dialogue, Agreed Statement on the Eucharist.

28. Cf. Mazza, *Prayers,* 131.

29. For a discussion of the word *hostiam,* the actual word in the prayer, and *victima,* the word normally translated "victim," and their use in the prayer, see Mazza, *Prayers,* 136-37.

30. Aquinas, ST, III, 72, 6 (*"tamquam continens Christum passum"*). For the view that we are offering an action, Christ's offering of himself, not just the victim, Christ himself, see Anscar Vonier, O.S.B., *A Key to the Doctrine of the Eucharist* (Westminster, Md.: Newman, 1946); and Odo Casel, O.S.B., *The Mystery of Christian Worship and Other Writings,* Burkhard Neunheuser, O.S.B., ed. (Westminster, Md.: Newman, 1962). For effective critiques of this view, see Vagaggini, *Dimensions,* I, 57-61 and James T. O'Connor, *The Hidden Manna: A Theology of the Eucharist* (San Francisco, Ignatius, 1988), 240-45, hereafter cited as *Manna.*

   For sympathetic presentations of this view, see Louis Bouyer, *Liturgical Piety,* (Notre Dame, Ind.: University of Notre Dame Press, 1955), chap. 7., hereafter cited as *Piety;* Jungmann, *Mass,* 104-106, Mascall, *Corpus,* and Robert Sokolowski, *Eucharistic Presence: A Study in the Theology of Disclosure* (Washington: CUA Press, 1994), 97, hereafter cited as *Presence.* For examples of the pervasiveness of the view, see William Barden, O.P., "The Presences of Christ in the Eucharist," Appendix 2 in St. Thomas Aquinas, *Summa theolog-*

icae, Blackfriars edition and translation, vol. 58, *The Eucharistic Presence* (New York: McGraw-Hill, 1965), 207-14, who seemingly presents a Caselian view while commenting on Aquinas' view, which shows no trace of Casel's view; or Kilmartin, who in *Church, Eucharist, and Priesthood,* his commentary on John Paul II's *Dominicae Coenae,* critiques the Pope's presentation as not being in accord with modern Eucharistic theology and presents an "action view" as simply the accepted theology.

31. For "represent" as "presenting again," see CCC 1366; Jungmann, *Mass,* 112 bis, and North American Lutheran–Catholic Dialogue, p. 13. For "represent" as "show" or "make manifest," see the Council of Trent, Session XXII, ch. 1; DS 1740 (cf. O'Connor, *Manna,* 243).

32. Council of Trent, Session XXII, Ch. I (DS 1740) and Ch. II (DS 1743), CCC 1367, John Chrysostom in *Hom. In Heb.* 17.6 (PNF, 14, p. 449).

33. CCC 1368.

34. For Christ's heavenly intercession, see *Redeemer,* 253-56.

35. "Acting in the person of Christ, [the ministerial priest] brings about the Eucharistic sacrifice and offers it to God in the name of all the people [*nomine totius populi Deo offert*]. For their part, the faithful join in the [act of] offering [oblationem] of the Eucharist by virtue of their royal priesthood," Second Vatican Council, Constitution on the Church, *Lumen Gentium,* 10, hereafter cited as *LG.*

36. Cf. Sokolowski, *Presence,* 82-95.

37. For the elevation as in origin an act of presenting or offering to God, not an action of showing to the people, see Jungmann, *Mass,* 120.

38. Cf. the statement of "growing convergence" of the Final Report (1978) on the Eucharist (the Lord's Supper) of the Joint Roman Catholic - Lutheran Commission, 61: "According to Catholic doctrine the sacrifice of the Mass is the making present of the sacrifice of the cross. It is not a repetition of this sacrifice and adds nothing to its saving significance. When thus understood, the sacrifice of the Mass is an affirmation and not a questioning of the uniqueness and full value of Christ's sacrifice on the cross."

SIX

The Eucharist as Life-giving

1. For a summary of the patristic approach to the story of Melchizedek, see Danielou, *Bible,* 142-47. For the possibility that a ritual meal is being described, see Bruce Vawter, *On Genesis* (Garden City, N.Y.: Doubleday, 1977), 199.

2. For such meals in the Dead Sea Scrolls see Fitzmyer, *Response to 101 Questions on the Dead Sea Scrolls*, 73-74.
3. For this understanding, see the endnote to p. 90.
4. For the meaning of "mysteries," see Casimir Kucharek, *The Sacramental Mysteries: A Byzantine Approach* (Allendale N.J.: Alleluia Press, 1976), 56-64, 325-334; hereafter cited as *Mysteries*; Timothy Ware, *The Orthodox Church* (Harmondsworth: Penguin, 1972), 281-83; Vagaggini, *Dimensions*, 18-19.
5. *Didache Apostolorum*, 14. In 1 Corinthians 10, the manna and the water are "spiritual," probably in the sense of being typological, but that means that they are physical old covenant realities that point to something that will be brought about by the Holy Spirit, in this case, food and drink that he uses to sustain us in the wilderness of this life by strengthening our sharing in Christ.
6. Irenaeus, AH, IV, 18.
7. M. Pesachim, 10, 1.
8. Sermon 63, 7. See also the Septuagint translation of Psalm 23 (22):5 ["your inebriating chalice"] and Danielou, *Bible*, 183-186 for a summary of patristic usage.
9. Fulgentius of Ruspe, *A Treatise Against Fabianus* 28: "That is why all the faithful who love God and their neighbor truly drink the cup of the Lord's love, even though they may not drink the cup of his bodily suffering. And becoming inebriated from it, they put to death whatever in their nature is rooted in earth."
10. *"Laeti bibamus sobriam ebrietatem Spiritus."*
11. For "The Bread of Life Discourse" and the Eucharistic reference in it, see Raymond E. Brown, *The Gospel According to John*, The Anchor Bible, vol. 29 (hereafter cited as Brown, *AB*), 260-304.
12. Brown, *AB*, 277-80.
13. Cyril of Jerusalem, *Cat. Lect.* XXII (*On the Mysteries* IV) 4, speaking of this passage says, "They, not receiving His saying spiritually, were offended, and went backward, supposing that He was inviting them to eat flesh."
14. Brown, *AB*, 285.
15. For an exposition of the view that this verse contains a version of the Eucharistic words of institution, see Jeremias, *Eucharistic Words*, 107-8, and Brown, *AB*, 285.
16. For an explanation of Cyril's theology of the gift of the Spirit and the Eucharist, see Daniel A. Keating, *The Appropriation of Divine Life in Cyril of Alexandria* (Oxford: unpublished dissertation, 2000), ch. 2.
17. Kodell, *Eucharist*, 126-28. Cf. Gaudentius of Brescia, *Tract.* 2 (CSEL 68, 26), "It is significant, too, that his blood should be given to us in the form of

wine, for his own words in the gospel, *I am the true vine*, imply clearly enough that whenever wine is offered as a representation of Christ's passion, it is his blood."

18. Deiss, *Springtime*, 163.
19. For "forgiveness of sins," see *Redeemer*, 81-84.
20. Congar, *I Believe*, III, 229.
21. For the use of the term "breaking of the bread," see Jungmann, *Mass*, 18-19. For this passage, see Léon-Dufour, *Sharing*, 21-29.
22. For the meaning of Pentecost in patristic teaching see Danielou, *Bible*, ch. 19.
23. For the patristic understanding of Tabernacles, see Danielou, *Bible*, ch. 20.

SEVEN
The Eucharistic Presence

1. Kodell, *Eucharist*, 110-11.
2. Cf. the distinction in John Henry Cardinal Newman, *Grammar of Assent* (Garden City, N.Y.: Doubleday, 1955) between "real" and "notional" assent in Part I to indicate the effective realization of some reality.
3. See Aidan Nichols, O.P., *The Holy Eucharist* (Dublin: Veritas, 1991) ch. 3 for a summary; hereafter cited as *Eucharist*.
4. Léon-Dufour, *Sharing*, 6-7; Thurian, *Memorial*, 6.
5. See "The Manifold Presence of Christ in the Liturgy" by Michael G. Witczak [*Theological Studies* 59 (1998), 680-690] for a survey of contemporary magisterial instruction on the various presences of Christ. See also ARCIC I, Final Report, "Eucharistic Doctrine," 7, for a use of this theme in the ecumenical dialogues.
6. Kodell, *Eucharist*, 72.
7. Murphy-O'Connor, see note 11 for chapter 4; and Kilmartin, *Eucharist*, 79-82.
8. Nichols, *Eucharist*, 32; Fee, *First Epistle*, 559-561.
9. Cf. M. Kerithoth.
10. The Council of Trent, Thirteenth Session, Ch. III. See also ARCIC II, *Requested Clarifications on Eucharist and Ministry (1993)*, "Eucharist"; hereafter cited as *Clarifications*, "Eucharist."
11. Cyril of Alexandria, *John*, I, 419.
12. For the more precise terminology, which speaks of Christ as truly, really, and substantially present in the Eucharistic elements, see the Council of Trent,

Decree Concerning the Most Holy Sacrament of the Eucharist, Ch. I and III (DS 1636, 1640). For a modern restatement, see John Hardon, S.J., *Modern Catholic Dictionary*, (Garden City, N.Y.: Doubleday, 1980), 487.

13. CCC 1373-76. Council of Trent, Thirteenth Session, Canons 1 and 2. For the ecumenical convergence in the understanding of the presence of Christ in the Eucharist, see ARCIC I, *Final Report*, Eucharistic Doctrine, The Statement (1971), 6-11, Elucidation (1979), 6; and ARCIC II, *Clarifications;* Joint Roman Catholic–Lutheran Commission, *The Eucharist*, 15-16, 48-51.

14. For a modern presentation of the meaning of "substantially" and of the related term "transubstantiation," see O'Connor, *Manna*, 268-87. For a discussion of the historical background to "transubstantiation," its theological status, and the freedom to use other ways of speaking, see Kilian McDonnell, O.S.B., *John Calvin, the Church, and the Eucharist* (Princeton: Princeton University Press, 1967), 295-319; hereafter cited as *Calvin*. For a summary of Aquinas' approach, see William Barden, O.P., "The Metaphysics of the Eucharist," Appendix 3 in St. Thomas Aquinas, *Summa theologicae*, Blackfriars edition and translation, vol. 58, *The Eucharistic Presence* (New York: McGraw-Hill, 1965), 207-14.

15. For the view of St Thomas Aquinas that Christ is not "locally present" in the Eucharistic elements, see Q. 76, a. 5, and a. 6 ["In no way is Christ's body locally in this sacrament."]. For the truth that his glorified body is at the right hand of the Father, see Council of Trent, Session XIII, Ch. 1 (DS 1636); Clement IV (DS 849); and Paul VI in *Mysterium Fidei* and *The Credo of the People of God*.

16. For difficulties connected with Eucharistic devotions, see Bouyer, *Piety*, 243-56.

17. See the Council of Trent, Ch. V: "The sacrament ... [was] instituted by Christ the Lord in order to be received" (DS 1643). See also Kilian McDonnell, *Calvin*, 308, and Karl Rahner, "Christ in the Sacrament of the Lord's Supper," *Theological Investigations*, IV, 309.

18. CCC 1378-80. For Eucharistic devotions and their history, see Martimort, *Church*, II, 233-53; Nathan Mitchell, O.S.B., *Cult and Controversy: The Worship of the Eucharist Outside Mass* (New York: Pueblo, 1982); and Benedict J. Groeschel, C.F.R., and James Monti, *In the Presence of the Our Lord: The History, Theology and Psychology of Eucharistic Devotion* (Huntington Ind.: Our Sunday Visitor, 1996). For the absence of Eucharistic devotions in the Eastern churches, see Casimir Kucharek, *Mysteries*, 335-41.

For a discussion of the current situation, see "Eucharistic Exposition: An Obsolete Relic?" by Kilian McDonnell, O.S.B., *America*, vol. 160, no. 7; February 25, 1989.

19. See Karl Rahner, "On the Duration of the Presence of Christ After Communion" in *Theological Investigations*, IV.

20. Cf. David N. Power, O.M.I., *The Sacrifice We Offer: The Tridentine Doctrine and Its Reinterpretation* (New York: Crossroad, 1987) on "Doctrine Concerning the Sacrifice of the Mass" issued in the Twenty-Second Session.

21. For a treatment of the priest's role as the president of the assembly, see Jungmann, *Mass*, 121-27.

22. For the Byzantine use of the term and for the view that in regard to approach to the sacraments or mysteries "the gap between Latin Catholics and Byzantine Catholics is far greater than that between Byzantine Catholics and Orthodox," see Kucharek, *Mysteries*, 6.

23. For a defense of the Eucharistic prayer as a prayer of petition, see Cabasilas, *Commentary*, 29. See also Jungmann, *Mass*, 145-46.

24. For the role of the Holy Spirit and faith in personal renewal through the Eucharist, see Congar, *I Believe*, 258-66.

25. According to the statement of "growing convergence" of the Final Report (1978) on the Eucharist (the Lord's Supper) of the Joint Roman Catholic—Lutheran Commission, 61, "According to Catholic doctrine the *ex opere operato* should witness in the context of the sacramentology to the priority of God's action. To stress this priority is likewise the concern of Lutherans."

26. For a fuller presentation, see *Redeemer*, ch. 12.

EIGHT
Worship the Lord

1. For the alternate but not incompatible view that the twenty-four elders are the heads of the (heavenly) courses of priests who go to the temple to take turns in being responsible for the temple worship, see Edersheim, *Temple*, 49.

2. See Aquinas, ST, III, Q. 63, a. 1 ("The sacraments of the New Law are ordained for ... the perfecting of the soul in things pertaining to the Divine worship"). See also Vagaggini, *Dimensions*, 68-70.

3. GILH, 10-11; CCC 1163-78.

4. For a helpful discussion of the meaning of calling our prayer an offering, see A. M. Roguet, O.P., *The Liturgy of the Hours: The General Instruction on the Liturgy of the Hours* (London: Geoffrey Chapman, 1971), 98-101.

5. For a description of the patristic roots of this approach and its development in the early ascetic movement, see Bradshaw, *Worship*, 73-74.

6. See Menachem Haran, *Temples and Temple Service in Ancient Israel* (Winona Lake, Ind.: Eisenbrauns, 1985), hereafter cited as *Temples*, 207.

7. For "solemnity" or "appointed feast" (RSV), the Hebrew *mo'ed*, see Leviticus 23:1 and M. Mo'edim. For "feast" proper, the "pilgrimage feasts," the Hebrew *chag*, see Exodus 23:14-17.

8. For the various "New Year's" in the Jewish calendar, see M. Rosh Hashanah, 1.

9. For a treatment of the early rabbinic approach, see George Foote Moore, *Judaism*, 3 vols. reprint (Peabody, Mass.: Hendrickson, 1997) II, 218-19. For an introduction to the Jewish Prayer Book, including a history of its origins, and a treatment of the relationship of Jewish prayer (and the contents of the Jewish Prayer Book) to Christian prayer, see Carmine Di Sante, *Jewish Prayer: The Origins of the Christian Liturgy* (New York: Paulist, 1991).

10. Aquinas, ST, I-II, Q. 98-104.

11. The *Catechism of the Catholic Church* (CCC), *the General Instruction on the Liturgy of the Hours* (GILH), and behind them both, the Constitution on the Liturgy (SC), seem clearly to presuppose that the basic pattern of prayer as summarized in the quote in the text is a datum of Christian tradition. For the discussion on the historical development of the pattern, see Martimort on "The Liturgy of the Hours" in *The Church at Prayer*, IV. See also Bradshaw, *Worship*, 70-74; Robert Taft, S.J., *The Liturgy of the Hours in East and West: The Origins of the Divine Office and Its Meaning for Today* (Collegeville, Minn.: Liturgical Press, 1986); and, for the Byzantine Church, Alexander Schmemann *Introduction to Liturgical Theology* (Leighton Buzzard, Beds: Faith Press, 1966). For the distinction between the "cathedral office" and the "monastic office" for the pattern of daily prayer, see Anton Baumstark, *Comparative Liturgy* (Westminster, Md.: Newman, 1958). For the view of morning and evening prayer as the "hinges" or "chief prayers," see the GILH, 37.

12. See also GILH 37, 42.

13. For additional encouragements for the laity to use the Liturgy of the Hours beyond those in the text, see GILH, 27, 32; CJC 1173-75; SC 100.

14. For a summary of the present state of the theological understanding of the place of Sunday and the current Catholic practice, see Joseph Cardinal Ratzinger, "The Resurrection as the Foundation of Christian Liturgy: On the Meaning of Sunday for Christian Prayer and Christian Life," in *A New Song for the Lord: Faith in Christ and Liturgy Today* (New York: Crossroad, 1996). See also John Paul II, *Dies Domini*.

15. For the tradition of special communities in the church, see Stephen B. Clark, *Unordained Elders and Renewal Communities* (New York: Paulist, 1976).
16. For Easter, see Danielou, *Bible*, ch. 17; Cantalamessa, *Mystery*.
17. For a summary of the scriptural understanding of the Feast of Tabernacles and the Christian interpretation of it as presented in patristic writings, see Danielou, *Bible*, ch. 20.
18. For the evangelistic consequences, see Gregory the Great in *Moral Reflections on Job*, 13, 23.
19. For the interpretation of the name "Zion" in the first century and for the significance of the location of the upper room as the beginning of the establishment of the new covenant temple and people in the upper room on this Mount Zion, see Bellarmino Bagatti, O.F.M., *The Church from the Circumcision: History and Archaeology of the Judaeo-Christians* (Jerusalem: Franciscan Printing Press, 1971) and Jean Brian, *Sion* (Jerusalem: Franciscan Printing Press, 1973).
20. For the ceasing of our need for Scripture, see Augustine, *A Treatise on John*, 35, 8. For the ceasing of the Eucharist, see Theodore of Mopsuestia, *Catecheses*, IV, 4.
21. For the sense in which the Eucharist can be said to be abiding, see Aquinas, ST, III, 80, 2 and Cabasilas, *Commentary*, 43.

APPENDICES

1. For a presentation of the Old Testament assemblies understood as background to the Christian assemblies in the way that became classical in the liturgical movement, see Bouyer, *Piety*, ch. 4, and Deiss, *Word*.
2. See Danielou, *Bible*, 143, for a discussion of this distinction.
3. Other references to "a tree of life" are Prv 3:18; 11:30; 13:12; 15:4.
4. See *Redeemer*, 299.
5. For New Testament references to the Passover lamb in connection with the redeeming blood of Christ, see *Redeemer*, appendix 1.
6. For the water from the rock at Horeb, see Danielou, *Bible*, 150-52. For patristic examples, see Ambrose, *Sacraments*, V, 4, and John Chrysostom, *Catecheses*, 3, 27.
7. For examples, see Cyril of Jerusalem, *Mystagogical Catecheses*, IV, 5 and John Damascene, *The Fount of Knowledge*, IV, 13.

8. For the reason, see Danielou, *Bible*, 127, and E.J. Yarnold, S.J., *The Awe-Inspiring Rites of Initiation* (London, St. Paul, 1972; Edinburgh: T&T Clark, 1994) hereafter called *Rites*, 41.

9. A collection and introduction can be found in Yarnold, *Rites*. A study can be found in Enrico Mazza, *Mystagogy: A Theology of Liturgy in the Patristic Age* (New York: Pueblo, 1989).

10. For an introduction to these see Robert F. Taft, S.J., "The Liturgy of the Great Church: An Initial Synthesis of Structure and Interpretation on the Eve of Iconoclasm" in *Liturgy in Byzantium and Beyond* (Collected Studies Series 493).

11. Cabasilas, *Commentary* and *The Life in Christ* (Crestwood, N.Y.: St Vladimir's Seminary Press, 1974).

12. Another older collection in English is F. E. Brightman and C. E. Hammond, eds., *Liturgies Eastern and Western, Vol. I, Eastern Liturgies* (Oxford: Clarendon, 1896, reprinted 1965). For historical background to the Western liturgies, see Josef A. Jungmann, S.J., *Mass*, or more fully, *The Mass of the Roman Rite: Its Origins and Development*, 2 vols (New York: 1951-55), originally titled *Missarum Sollemnia*. For historical background to the Byzantine liturgy, see Robert F. Taft, S.J., *The Byzantine Rite: A Short History* (Collegeville, Minn.: Liturgical Press, 1992.

13. The official edition of the documents of the Second Vatican Council can be found in Second Vatican Ecumenical Council, *Constitutiones, Decreta, Declarationes* (Vatican City: The General Secretariat of the Second Vatican Ecumenical Council, 1966). The two main English editions are Second Vatican Council, Austin Flannery, O.P., ed., *Vatican Council II, The Conciliar and Post Conciliar Documents* (Northport, N.Y.: Costello, 1981); and Second Vatican Council, Walter M. Abbott, S.J., ed., *The Documents of Vatican II* (New York: Guild, 1966).

14. Christopher Hill and Edward Yarnold, S.J., ed., *Anglicans and Roman Catholics: The Search for Unity* (London: SPCK and CTS, 1994).

15. *Lutherans and Catholics in Dialogue*, 6 vols. (reprinted Minneapolis: Augsburg, vol. 1-3, n.d.; vol. 4, 1979).

16. *Baptism, Eucharist and Ministry*, [BEM, The Lima Statement, Faith and Order Paper No. 111], (Geneva: The World Council of Churches, 1982).

17. *Churches Respond to BEM: Official responses to the "Baptism, Eucharist and Ministry" Text*, Max Thurian, ed. [Faith and Order Paper No. 144] (Geneva: World Council of Churches, 1988). The Roman Catholic response is in vol. VI.

18. For a survey of Old Testament liturgical texts and practice in the light of modern scholarship see Haran, *Temples,* and *The Anchor Bible Dictionary* (ABD) article on "Sacrifice" by Gary Anderson.
19. For the term "classical" to designate the liturgical movement before the Second Vatican Council, see Hitchcock, *The Recovery of the Sacred* (San Francisco: Ignatius, 1995), 19-23.
20. A reference work in the process of appearing in English is the *Handbook for Liturgical Studies* edited by Anscar J. Chupungco, O.S.B. (Collegeville, Minn.: Liturgical Press, 1997).
21. For a short introduction to the theology of the liturgical movement, see Charles Davis, *Liturgy and Doctrine: The Doctrinal Basis of the Liturgical Movement* (New York: Sheed and Ward, 1960).

ABBREVIATIONS

ABD - *Anchor Bible Dictionary*

ARCIC - Anglican-Roman Catholic International Commission

CCC - *Catechism of the Catholic Church*

CJC - *Code of Canon Law*, 1983

DS - Denzinger-Schönmetzer, *Enchiridion Symbolorum, Definitionem, et Declarationum de Rebus Fidei et Morum*, 1965.

DV - Dogmatic Constitution on Divine Revelation *Dei Verbum*

LG - Dogmatic Constitution on the Church *Lumen Gentium*

M. - *Mishnah* (followed by the name of the Tractate)

NAB - *New American Bible*

NIV - *New International Version* (of the Bible)

RSV - *Revised Standard Version* (of the Bible)

SC - Constitution on the Sacred Liturgy *Sacrosanctum Concilium*

TMA - Apostolic letter on Preparing for the Third Millennium *Tertio Millennio Adveniente*

UR - Decree on Ecumenism *Unitatis Redintegratio*

UUS - Encyclical Letter on Commitment to Ecumenism *Ut Unum Sint*

INDEX OF TERMS

*The following are terms cited according to the location
in which their meaning or use is explained.*